Researching Language Learning Motivation

Also available from Bloomsbury

Researching Language Learning Motivation

A Concise Guide

EDITED BY ALI H. AL-HOORIE AND FRUZSINA SZABÓ

BLOOMSBURY ACADEMIC
LONDON · NEW YORK · OXFORD · NEW DELHI · SYDNEY

BLOOMSBURY ACADEMIC
Bloomsbury Publishing Plc
50 Bedford Square, London, WC1B 3DP, UK
1385 Broadway, New York, NY 10018, USA
29 Earlsfort Terrace, Dublin 2, Ireland

BLOOMSBURY, BLOOMSBURY ACADEMIC and the Diana logo
are trademarks of Bloomsbury Publishing Plc

First published in Great Britain 2022

Cover design: Charlotte James
Cover Images © iStock (santypan, FatCamera, monkeybusinessimages, vgajic, sturti,
olesiabilkei) and Shuttestock (Olesia Bilkei).

A catalogue record for this book is available from the British Library.

A catalog record for this book is available from the Library of Congress.

ISBN: HB: 978-1-3501-6688-2
       PB: 978-1-3501-6687-5
       ePDF: 978-1-3501-6690-5
       eBook: 978-1-3501-6689-9

Typeset by Integra Software Services Pvt. Ltd.
Printed and bound in Great Britain

To find out more about our authors and books visit www.bloomsbury.com
and sign up for our newsletters.

This book is dedicated to Zoltán Dörnyei
for his 60th birthday (belatedly)

CONTENTS

FIGURES

TABLES

THE EDITORS

Ali H. Al-Hoorie works at the Jubail English Language and Preparatory Year Institute, Royal Commission for Jubail and Yanbu, Saudi Arabia. He completed his PhD in applied linguistics at the University of Nottingham, UK, under the supervision of Professors Zoltán Dörnyei and Norbert Schmitt. His research interests include motivation theory, research methodology, and complexity. His publications have appeared in various journals, including *Language Learning, Modern Language Journal, Studies in Second Language Acquisition, ELT Journal, Language Teaching Research*, and *Learning and Individual Differences*. His books include, with Phil Hiver, *Research Methods for Complexity in Applied Linguistics* (2020) and, co-edited with Peter McIntyre, *Contemporary Language Motivation Theory: 60 Years Since Gardner and Lambert (1959)* (2020). The latter book is the winner of The Jake Harwood Outstanding Book Award.

Fruzsina Szabó is Lecturer at the Institute of English and American Studies at the University of Debrecen, Hungary, where she also completed her PhD. She teaches methodology, SLA courses, and is involved in teacher training. Her research interest includes classroom implications of motivation, language aptitude, translanguaging in low socioeconomic environment, teacher identity, and teacher well-being. She was a member of the Hungarian National Academy MTA-DE Research Group on Foreign Language Teaching that developed digital course material for pupils from disadvantaged backgrounds (2016–2021). She is the author of various Hungarian and English articles, and co-editor of *Innovatív Oktatás*, a book on innovative education in Hungary.

CONTRIBUTORS

Ahmed Al Khateeb is Associate Professor and Chair of English Language Department, King Faisal University, Saudi Arabia. He is a PhD holder in applied linguistics from Southampton University, UK. He is a Fulbright scholarship winner and Visiting Scholar at the University of Massachusetts, Amherst, USA. His research interests are technology-enhanced language learning, telecollaboration and language learning, and psychology of language learners.

Vera Busse holds a PhD from the University of Oxford and is Professor of Multilingualism and Education at the University of Münster, Germany. She has published widely in both the general field of education and in language education. She and her team work on a range of educational issues pertaining to teaching and learning in linguistically and culturally diverse classrooms and are interested in finding ways to better prepare teachers for diversity.

Jean-Marc Dewaele is Professor of Applied Linguistics and Multilingualism. He has published widely on individual differences in Second Language Acquisition and Multilingualism. He is former president of the *International Association of Multilingualism* and the *European Second Language Association*. He is also General Editor of the *Journal of Multilingual and Multicultural Development*. He received awards from the *International Association of Language and Social Psychology* and the *British Association for Counselling and Psychotherapy*.

Joseph Falout is Associate Professor at Nihon University, Japan. He has published over sixty papers and chapters, primarily on language learning and teaching: demotivation, remotivation, past selves, future selves, ideal classmates, group dynamics, present communities of imagining, belonging, voice, hope, and critical participatory looping. He received an award from the Japan Association for Language Teaching for his publications and presentations.

Yoshifumi Fukada is Professor in the Department of International Studies at Meisei University, Tokyo, Japan. His research interests involve L2 learners' situated learning, dynamic identities, and agency and motivation in language learning and TL-mediated socialization. He recently published *L2 Learning during Study Abroad: The Creation of Affinity Spaces* (2019).

Tetsuya Fukuda teaches English in the English for Liberal Arts Program at the International Christian University in Japan, coordinating courses and analysing test scores. His research interests include psychological factors involved in language learning such as L2 motivation, belonging, engagement and group dynamics as well as program evaluation.

Ofelia García is Professor Emerita of Urban Education and Latin American, Iberian, and Latino Cultures at the Graduate Center of the City University of New York, USA. The American Educational Research Association has awarded her three Lifetime Research Achievement Awards – Social Contexts in Education, Bilingual Education, and Second Language Acquisition. She is a member of the US National Academy of Education.

Flor-de-lis González-Mujico holds a PhD and MA in applied linguistics and a BA (Hons) in modern languages. She has imparted language modules at the Universitat Oberta de Catalunya, Spain; University of St Andrews, UK; King's College London, UK; University of Northampton, UK; Royal Holloway, University of London, UK; and Laureate International Universities. Her fields of research include L2 motivation, self-regulation, and digital learning environments.

Tammy Gregersen is Professor of TESOL at the American University of Sharjah in the United Arab Emirates. She received her MA in education and PhD in linguistics in Chile. Her research passions include language teacher well-being, positive psychology, nonverbal communication in the language classroom, and language learning and teaching psychology.

Alastair Henry is Professor of Language Education at University West, Sweden. With Zoltán Dörnyei and Peter MacIntyre, he co-edited *Motivational Dynamics in Language Learning* (2015), and with Martin Lamb, Kata Csizér, and Stephen Ryan, he co-edited the *Palgrave Handbook of Motivation for Language Learning* (2019). He is the co-author, with Zoltán Dörnyei and Christine Muir, of *Motivational Currents in Language Learning: Frameworks for Focused Interventions* (2016).

Phil Hiver is Assistant Professor of Foreign and Second Language Education at Florida State University, USA. His research explores the complex and dynamic interface between individual differences and instructed language development and pedagogy. He is co-author, with Ali Al-Hoorie, of *Research Methods for Complexity Theory in Applied Linguistics* (2019).

Emiko Hirosawa is a private elementary school teacher in Tokyo, Japan, while also doing her doctorate at Waseda University, Japan. She researches elementary school English education and motivation and is a co-editor of the textbook series Smile, specifically for private elementary schools in Japan.

Jim King is Director of Research and Enterprise (joint) in the School of Education, University of Leicester, UK. His books include *Silence in the Second Language Classroom* (2013), *The Dynamic Interplay between Context and the Language Learner* (2015), and *East Asian Perspectives on Silence in English Language Education* (2020).

Zana Ibrahim is the chair of the English Department at the University of Kurdistan Hewlêr. He holds a PhD in English from the University of Nottingham in the UK under the supervision of Zoltán Dörnyei, and an M.A. in TESOL from Indiana University of Pennsylvania in the USA. His research interests lie mainly in the area of second language acquisition and pedagogy, second language motivation, positive affect, and sustained flow. He is the co-theorist of the directed motivational currents concept, and along with Zoltán Dörnyei and Christine Muir co-authored the first publication on the construct in 2014.

Martin Lamb is Director of International Education and a lecturer in TESOL in the School of Education, University of Leeds, UK. He is interested in the personal and social factors conducive to learning at all life stages. He also enjoys teaching undergraduate and postgraduate courses related to TESOL.

Kate Maher is Assistant Professor in the Department of British and American Studies at the Kyoto University of Foreign Studies, Japan. She is a PhD candidate at the University of Leicester, UK. Her main research interests are student silence, speaking-related language anxiety, and psychological aspects of language learning.

Sarah Mercer is Professor of Foreign Language Teaching and Head of ELT at the University of Graz, Austria. She is the author, co-author, and co-editor of several books in the field of language learning psychology. In 2018, she was awarded the Robert C Gardner Award for excellence in second language research.

Christine Muir is Assistant Professor in Second Language Acquisition at the University of Nottingham, UK. Her research interests include the psychology of language learning and teaching, particularly the area of motivation, and her publications include *Directed Motivational Currents and Language Education: Exploring Implications for Pedagogy* (2020).

Tim Murphey is series editor for TESOL's *Professional Development in Language Education*, co-author, with Dörnyei, of *Group Dynamics in the Language Classroom* (2003), author of *Music and Song* (1991), and co-editor of *Meaningful Action* (2013). He has also been a plenary speaker twenty-one times in fifteen countries since 2010.

Robert Murphy received his PhD in applied linguistics from the University of Nottingham, UK, and MA TESOL from the University of Birmingham, UK. He researches teacher education and authors neuroELT-based textbooks. He is co-founder of FAB neuroELT conferences, stemming from studies in Mind, Brain, and Education at the Harvard Graduate School of Education, USA.

W. L. Quint Oga-Baldwin trains teachers and researchers at Waseda University, Japan. He has authored papers using self-determination theory in journals such as *Contemporary Educational Psychology*, *Motivation and Emotion*, and *Learning and Individual Differences*. He is co-editor of a 2019 special issue in *System* on New Directions for Individual Differences Research in Language Learning.

Lourdes Ortega is Professor at Georgetown University, USA. She investigates second language acquisition, particularly usage-based, bilingual, and educational dimensions in adult classroom settings. Her books include *Understanding Second Language Acquisition* (2009) and, co-edited with Annick De Houwer, the *Handbook of Bilingualism* (2019). She is the general editor of *Language Learning*.

Rebecca L. Oxford is Professor Emerita and Distinguished Scholar-Teacher at the University of Maryland, USA. She has published fifteen books, including *Peacebuilding in Language Education* (2021). She is also series co-editor for *Spirituality, Religion, and Education* and *Transforming Education for the Future*.

Mostafa Papi is Assistant Professor of Foreign and Second Language Education at Florida State University, USA, where he teaches graduate classes on second language acquisition, research methods, and teaching methodology. He has published extensively on the role of motivation, personality, and emotions in language learning.

Matthew E. Poehner is Professor of World Languages Education and Applied Linguistics at the Pennsylvania State University, USA. He is associate editor of the journal *Language and Sociocultural Theory* and is co-editor, with J. P. Lantolf, of the *Handbook of Sociocultural Theory and Second Language Development*.

Amy S. Thompson is Professor of Applied Linguistics, Department Chair of World Languages, Literatures, & Linguistics, and the Director of International Relations and Strategic Planning of Eberly College of Arts and Sciences at West Virginia University, USA. Her research interests involve individual differences in SLA and the relationship to bi-/multilingualism. Examples of her research can be found in journals such as the *Modern Language Journal*, *TESOL Quarterly*, *Foreign Language Annals*, and *IJBEB*.

Ema Ushioda is Professor and Head of Applied Linguistics, University of Warwick, UK. She has research interests in L2 motivation and autonomy, and has collaborated on various publications with Zoltán Dörnyei. Her most recent book is *Language Learning Motivation: An Ethical Agenda for Research* (2020).

FOREWORD

In this Foreword I honor Zoltán Dörnyei for his incalculable, worldwide contributions to second language acquisition (SLA), and I congratulate him for being so prolific in writing during his sixty years, with many more to come. He has published twenty-five books, and his river of articles, chapters, questionnaires, and translated works is vast. To get a sense of the abundance and quality of his writings, readers need only go to his meticulously ordered website at https://www.ZoltánDörnyei.co.uk/. The fact that he does not list his many awards on his website signals modesty amid immense productivity.

The first time I ever conversed deeply with Zoltán Dörnyei was approximately a quarter century ago in Budapest, years before he and his family left Hungary for the UK in 1998. He had invited me to Budapest to give talks about my research. At that time, he was teaching in the School of English and American Studies at Eötvös Loránd University. Zoltán was sandy-haired, young-looking, and full of energy, not so different from how he looks today. His slightly formal demeanor was leavened with personal warmth. I observed his dedication to and ambition for his students and the esteem in which they held him. I was happy to have the opportunity to chat with his brilliant wife, Sarah Thurrell, and I could imagine the fascinating discussions they must have at home.

I recognized the nature of Zoltán's intellect: constantly questing and questioning; loving the process of theory creation but with an urgency to apply theory to real problems and situations; willing to collaborate in order to push theory and practice to new levels; and using his capacious memory and his native abilities in synthesizing and analyzing. His cognitive faculties have a scope so wide and so deep that the best scholars in any field might have cause for envy. He also empathizes with L2 teachers and students, having intensively experienced both roles.

I recall Zoltán showing me around Budapest and pointing out the Chain Bridge (officially known as the Széchenyi Chain Bridge), which spans the broad Danube River and unifies the two parts of the city, Buda and Pest. The image of the bridge has been in my mind's eye ever since that brief visit to Budapest. The Chain Bridge is long and graceful, suspended by strong chains in an astounding feat of hope and engineering. Despite a terrible attack by the Wehrmacht at the end of the Second World War, the bridge was successfully rebuilt. It reopened in 1949, a century after its original opening in 1849. It is fair to say that the Chain Bridge is resilient, upright, and purposeful, that it assists many people on their way, and that it richly deserves the worldwide attention it receives. The same could be said about Zoltán. I learned more about the Chain Bridge recently. It was the product of efforts by a Hungarian social reformer, Count István Széchenyi, and two specialists from the UK: Adam Clark, the onsite supervising engineer for the ten years of construction, 1839–49, who stayed in Hungary for the rest of his life, and the designer William Tierney Clark. The bridge's nineteenth-century Hungary–UK links reminded me of Zoltán's Hungary–UK ties in the twentieth and twenty-first centuries.

In a deeper sense, Zoltán has long been a scholarly "bridge." Here are a few examples.

- Zoltán was *a bridge from other fields to SLA*, introducing ideas about "possible selves" from psychologists Markus and Nurius (1986, 1987). He built on concepts from Markus and Nurius as he created the "L2 Motivational Self-System," which includes ideal and ought-to future self-guides and the L2 learning environment (Dörnyei, 2005, 2009a, 2009b). The clarity and practical applicability of this self-system theory have sparked a remarkable amount of research and has encouraged classroom use.

- Zoltán was again a *bridge from other fields to SLA* as he employed neurobiological and cognitive neuropsychological findings to explain that humans have two sensory systems (physiological and mental) and that both systems have implications for L2 teaching and learning. The first sensory system involves the obvious senses of sight, hearing, touch, smell, and others. In the first system, the word "vision" refers only to sight. In the second sensory system, "vision" refers broadly to mental imagery of any kind (e.g., visual, auditory, tactile, and olfactory[1]), and this information was a partial basis for research on L2 learners' future self-images, sensory styles, and mental imagery capacity (Dörnyei & Chan, 2013). According to cognitive neurological research, mental imagery relies largely on the same neural pathways and regions that are used by the actual physiological senses (Dörnyei & Chan). A deepening understanding of mental imagery led to the theory of Directed Motivational Currents, or DMCs, defined by Muir and Dörnyei (2013) as motivational drives that involve vision and goals and that stimulate long-term, focused behavior.

- As a *bridge from other fields to SLA* and as a *bridge from theory to practice within SLA*, Zoltán worked with Magdelena Kubanyiova to draw on theories and practices of imagery enhancement from education, psychology, and sports. The two researchers brilliantly

designed and tested methods of imagery enhancement useful for L2
learners and teachers (Dörnyei & Kubanyiova, 2014).

- Zoltán *bridged two fields—theology and psycholinguistics*—when
  he earned an MA and a PhD in theology after earning a PhD in
  psycholinguistics and a DSc in linguistics. He integrated tenets and
  findings from many more fields in his book *Vision, Mental Imagery
  and the Christian Life: Insights from Science and Scripture* (Dörnyei,
  2019c), in which he explained why humans' dual sensory system is
  so important for receiving communication from God. He posited
  that Divine vision draws on familiar imagery from the earthly,
  material world and then shifts attention to an alternate, spiritual
  reality. For me, this book offered Zoltán's most detailed and most
  personally moving discussions of vision.

- An excellent intellectual historian, Zoltán has served as a *bridge
  within* SLA to help explain the historical-theoretical evolution of
  L2 motivation (Dörnyei, 2019a; Dörnyei & Ryan, 2015). Though
  not shy about his own theories, he respectfully elaborated on other
  important and influential theories, such as the socio-educational
  model, which was developed and extensively researched by Robert
  C. Gardner (1985, 2010) and his colleagues. A recent journal article,
  "Psychology and Language Learning: The Past, the Present and the
  Future" (Dörnyei, 2019b), underscored to me Zoltán's sharp insight
  and foresight, as well as his accurate hindsight on many topics.

I could explore more examples from the areas of interest and activity that
Zoltán and I share, such as self-regulation, complexity theory, principled L2
teaching, and (in the distant past) coursebook-writing, but I will stop here. I
have done what I intended to do: to shed light on Zoltán as a person and as
a scholarly "bridge." In many expected or unexpected ways, he will continue
to be a bridge, and SLA and the world will be better for it.

Rebecca L. Oxford, PhD
Professor Emerita and Distinguished Scholar-Teacher
University of Maryland (USA)

Introduction

Ali H. Al-Hoorie and Fruzsina Szabó

This book deals with one of the most crucial concepts in second language learning: motivation. In recognition of the fact that motivation plays a pivotal role in understanding the processes of second language acquisition, there has been a rapid expansion of research, journal articles, books, and conference presentations attempting to better understand what motivation is and how to best apply its principles to the classroom (Al-Hoorie, 2017, 2018; Boo, Dörnyei, & Ryan, 2015).

This rapid expansion has come at a cost, however. It has become increasingly challenging to keep up with all the latest findings and developments in this burgeoning field. Even edited volumes, which are typically intended to provide a less technical account than journal articles, are growing in number by the day. At the time of writing this Introduction, two major edited volumes on motivation have just appeared (Al-Hoorie & MacIntyre, 2020; Lamb, Csizér, Henry, & Ryan, 2019) and two others are in the works (Hiver, Al-Hoorie, & Mercer, 2021; Li, Hiver, & Papi, 2021). Some readers, especially newcomers to the field, would probably find these rapid developments overwhelming. This book attempts to address this situation by providing accessible, "bite-size" chapters that are less formidable to read and that address key research directions.

In order to achieve this aim, we approached a number of active language motivation researchers and invited them to contribute in their areas of expertise. We received positive responses from scholars at leading universities all over the world, ranging from the Americas through Europe and the Middle East to Japan. This international group of scholars is a further testimony of the popularity of language motivation research in recent years.

The topics these scholars address fall under five primary parts. Part 1 deals with **General Reflections** on the field. Ushioda reflects on the ethical question of the extent to which the teacher can influence/control students' choices and behavior. Poehner uses the sociocultural notion of mediation to reexamine how the field understands motivation from a dialectical view. García ends this part with a yet alternative perspective, questioning the dominance of the psychological paradigm and showing what a sociological paradigm could offer to language motivation.

Part 2 addresses the critical issues of **Language Engagement.** Mercer starts by exploring the rationale for researchers and teachers to understand the role of engagement and outlines a research agenda for research on this area. Hiver argues for the need to view engagement from a complex dynamic perspective and to draw from advances from the learning sciences and from the psychology of language learning. Henry discusses the role of goal-setting and how the type of goals can have considerable implications for goal pursuit and for successful goal achievement. Oga-Baldwin and Hirosawa introduce self-determination theory and how it offers an explanatory mechanism for the dialogic interaction that teachers use to draw students into learning activities.

Part 3 focuses on **Selves Approaches.** MacIntyre critically reviews the L2 Motivational Self System, assessing how well this model has taken advantage of the conceptual affordances of self theory and avoided its pitfalls. Papi highlights several ways in which future selves can be employed to enhance language teaching practice, including developing a motivational vision, reducing negative emotions, and increasing positive emotions. Thompson considers learning a language other than English, concentrating on the feasibility of creating a vivid ideal L2 self with limited contact with or resources regarding the target language. González-Mujico examines the impact of technology on L2 selves and how mental visualization of an L2 possible self using digital tools can enhance learning engagement and L2 language acquisition.

Part 4 is concerned with **Emotions and Affect,** a relatively new subfield of language motivation. Dewaele provides a personal-historical reflection on the development of emotion research in the field of language learning. Maher and King examine the anxiety of silent learners using cognitive-behavioral theory and suggest activities to promote both positive emotional and social engagement. Gregersen and Al Khateeb explore the phenomenon of emotional contagion and how teachers and learners can capitalize on it. Muir turns to group-level affect and how it applies in the context of understanding and supporting directed motivational currents and long-term motivation.

The last part, Part 5, expands the discussion to more **Emerging Topics** that are only recently appearing in the research arena. Al-Hoorie and Hiver review the recent move of complexity theory from offering metaphors guiding thinking to highlighting empirical methods to investigate motivation phenomena. Lamb presents a critical discourse analysis perspective on language motivation and applies it to the Indonesian context. Busse ventures into extending the research landscape beyond the monolingual bias in motivational research, adding research from a multiethnic school setting. Ibrahim draws on the notion of English as a lingua franca and how it can be utilized in motivating English learners through offering a realistic goal: to successfully communicate while using accurate grammar. Murphy reviews seven key neuroELT maxims that have been shown to directly relate to success in raising classroom motivation. Finally, Fukada and colleagues examine how group dynamics contribute to psychological and physical well-being and to motivation in learning foreign languages from anthropological, affective, and social perspectives.

We hope that the format of this book—with its brief and accessible chapters, and with its focus on both established topics and emerging trends—would appeal both to those who feel discouraged by the bewildering research output on language motivation and to those who come from sister sub-disciplines and are thus reluctant to invest much time and effort into reading on the topic of motivation.

This book is a celebration of Zoltán Dörnyei's sixtieth birthday. Quite unexpectedly, the COVID-19 outbreak struck, disrupting pretty much everyone's career, activities, and everyday plans worldwide. Just as it affected most people on a global scale, this pandemic has also affected the contributors to this volume. Most of them had to struggle with lockdowns, isolation, preparation for online classes, and homeschooling their children—in addition to diligently writing their contribution to this book and trying to submit it on time. One contributor, Ofelia García, actually contracted COVID-19 while writing her chapter. She subsequently self-isolated until she fortunately recovered. She asked us to emphasize that she feels fortunate that she was able to see a doctor and get a test when many other people were not able to and "when so many in [her] city are suffering the injustices of the virus and of racism." Other contributors had to deal with the illness and loss of family members and friends due to the virus. One contributor had several family members infected, and their city became an epicenter of the virus. Another contributor had two family members dying during this pandemic. One died directly as a result of the virus and the other indirectly through not being able to obtain critical medical treatment. We were eventually able to finish the book and submit it to the publisher, though we did miss Zoltán's birthday. We hope that Zoltán, who was unaware that this project was taking place, will understand.

PART ONE

General Reflections

CHAPTER 1

Motivating in the Language Classroom: A Discourse of "Social Control"?

Ema Ushioda

Introduction

In this chapter, I focus on what Dörnyei (2001) has characterized as "motivational teaching practice" and consider the recommendations for classroom management and pedagogy that we develop for teachers based on our research. I examine how we portray the role of teachers as motivators who seek to shape students' behaviors by using certain motivational strategies. Taking a critical perspective, I discuss some moral and ethical complexities in the motivational language teaching practices that we proffer, drawing partly on arguments I have developed at greater length in Ushioda (2020a).

I will begin by discussing the significant role that Dörnyei has played in making our research relevant to language teachers.

From "Motivation" to "Motivating": Making Research Relevant to Teachers

Among Zoltán Dörnyei's many contributions to the field of L2 motivation research, I think one of the most important has been to bridge the divide between research and practice, in an effort to make motivation theory and associated empirical insights relevant to language teachers. As those familiar with the sixty-year history of L2 motivation research will know, addressing the practical needs and concerns of language teachers was not traditionally a focus of our academic field of inquiry. In fact, this relative lack of emphasis on language teachers' perspectives characterized the origins of the wider field of SLA (second language acquisition) research in the late 1960s and early 1970s. Essentially, SLA research sought to establish itself as the scientific study of second language *learning* from the perspective of the learners' internal mental and psychological processes and linguistic development, rather than as the study of second language *instruction* and its impact on learning. Thus, in SLA research on motivation, as Dörnyei (1994a) neatly encapsulated it, the focus was on "motivation"—that is, on understanding this theoretical construct and its role in successful language learning—rather than on "motivating"—that is, understanding how to motivate language learners. Through the 1990s, growing debate across the L2 motivation field eventually brought about a greater concern with the latter more practitioner-oriented perspective, some thirty years into the field's long history (for an overview, see Dörnyei & Ushioda, 2011).

While this concern helped to stimulate more classroom-based forms of research inquiry, such research did not perhaps really speak to teachers directly until the publication in 2001 of Dörnyei's now classic text on *Motivational Strategies in the Language Classroom*. Following a concise and accessible summary of approaches to theorizing motivation in language education and educational psychology, the book discussed what "motivational teaching practice" should look like and provided a detailed account of the strategies that language teachers might use to implement such practices to motivate their students. The taxonomy of strategies illustrated in the book was based on the findings of empirical research conducted with teachers of English in Hungary (Dörnyei & Csizér, 1998). In other words, this was a landmark text that translated theory and research into comprehensive practical guidance for language teachers.

In more recent years, we have seen a growing number of such books aimed at the professional language teaching community (e.g., Dörnyei, Henry & Muir, 2016; Dörnyei & Kubanyiova, 2014; Hadfield & Dörnyei, 2013). Moreover, as evident from Lamb's (2017) extensive review of the literature, the motivational dimension of language teaching has now grown to become a major area of empirical inquiry, thus strengthening the links between research and practice that Dörnyei sought to establish. Furthermore, we are seeing a small, but growing, body of research on motivation that is being conducted by teachers themselves in their own classrooms, through various forms of practitioner inquiry such as action research or exploratory practice (e.g., Banegas, 2013; Pinner, 2019; Sampson, 2016). In short, a focus on motivating language learners from the teacher's perspective is now firmly established as a significant domain of inquiry in our field, and there is now a flourishing empirical literature on language teachers' use of various strategies, practices, and interventions to motivate their learners (for a review, see Lamb, 2017).

The Role of Teachers in Motivating Students

Yet, a basic question I wish to pose in this chapter is whether we should indeed portray the role of teachers as motivators who seek to shape their students' behaviors, as implicit in the pedagogical strategies for managing and enhancing classroom motivation that we advocate based on our research. The idea that teachers can resourcefully use various techniques, strategies, or a "bag of tricks" to motivate their students is certainly long established in the wider field of educational psychology. As Danziger (1997) highlighted in his historical overview of psychology as an emergent discipline, research interest in motivation evolved through recognition of the practical value of understanding how to influence people's behavior. As he notes, this was particularly the case in relation to managing and influencing children's behavior in the classroom following the widespread reforms and expansions of educational systems in the early twentieth century. Within mainstream educational psychology, this applied focus on how to motivate students has sustained the research agenda for many decades and continues to be a major area of inquiry (for an overview, see Schunk, Meece, & Pintrich, 2014).

However, if we return to Danziger's (1997) historical account of psychology as an emergent discipline, we find that this applied interest in understanding how to influence people's behavior (whether in the classroom, the workplace, or the consumer market) meant that motivation research in the early twentieth century became situated in a discourse of "social control" and of understanding "how to play upon what individuals wanted" (p. 113) in order to influence and manipulate their behavior. This discourse was reflected, for example, in the use of rewards and incentives to motivate students, or to increase the productivity of a workforce; or in the use of clever advertising strategies aimed at the creation of desirable new "wants" (p. 112) or, in today's vernacular, new "must-haves," in order to increase consumer spending. It is this uncomfortable association between motivation and social control that gives me pause for thought and leads me to pose the question about how we portray the role of teachers in motivating their students and how we advocate the use of motivational strategies. In essence, the principle of applying strategies to motivate students raises some complex ethical issues about control, power, and manipulation in the classroom. It is to a critical consideration of these issues that I now turn. I will begin by examining the important distinction between internal and external control of motivation.

Internal versus External Control of Motivation

Across the major theoretical frameworks that have been influential in the L2 motivation field, we find a common distinction between internal and external motivational factors, or between internalized and less internalized forms of motivation. For example, in Gardner's Lambert's (1972) Social Psychological Model of L2 motivation, there is the distinction between *instrumental orientation* and *integrative orientation*. The former is defined by pragmatic extrinsic goals, such as learning a language in order to improve one's employment prospects, while the latter is defined by a deep-rooted personal interest in the target language culture and people, and, in its strong form, an internal desire to be part of their community. In Deci and Ryan's (1985) Self-Determination Theory (SDT) that has been influential in our field, particularly through the work of Kim Noels and her colleagues (e.g., Noels, Clément, & Pelletier, 1999; Noels et al., 2008; see also Oga-Baldwin & Hirosawa, this volume), there is a similar distinction between *intrinsic motivation* and *extrinsic motivation.* When people are intrinsically motivated in an activity, their motivation comes from internal rewards such as feelings of enjoyment or a satisfying sense of challenge deriving from the process of activity engagement itself. When people are extrinsically motivated to do something, they engage in the activity as the means to some separable or external outcome, such as financial reward or career progression. Within SDT, there is also the distinction between *internal* and *external regulation* of motivation, which depends on the extent to which motivation originates within the person and is self-determined, or the extent to which motivation is controlled by external social forces such as teachers, parents, curriculum demands, or exam pressures. Finally, in Dörnyei's (2009a) L2 Motivational Self System, a distinction between internalized and less internalized forms of motivation is what separates an *ideal L2 self* from an *ought-to L2 self.* The former represents how we want to see ourselves in the future as someone with proficient L2 skills, while the latter represents how others want or expect us to be, even if we may not fully identify with this future representation of ourselves. (For an overview of these theoretical frameworks, see Dörnyei and Ushioda, 2011.)

More recently, of course, there is now a growing focus on the interactions between internal and external or social-environmental influences on motivation, reflected in the application of complexity thinking to understanding the dynamics of L2 motivation (e.g., Dörnyei, MacIntyre, & Henry, 2015). Fundamentally, nevertheless, the distinction between internal and external motivation remains conceptually important in defining sources of influence and the locus of control from a pedagogical perspective. After all, in their relationship with their students, teachers are necessarily part of the external social environment, and hence the strategies they use to shape students' motivation may serve either to strengthen their external control over this motivation or to foster its internal growth and self-regulation. For example, strategies such as using rewards, incentives, grades, or sanctions to motivate students to apply effort and work hard may achieve observable short-term effects. However, such external "carrot-and-stick" strategies keep motivation and student behavior firmly in the teacher's control and power. This means that students may become dependent on the teacher to do the motivating for them, and they may struggle to develop any sense of personal control and agency in relation to their motivation and their learning. Controlling motivational strategies of this kind may thus lead to student behaviors such as obedience, compliance, fear, resistance, or even defiance, rather than to healthy forms of motivation. In contrast, strategies such as supporting students' sense of autonomy and encouraging them to make personal choices and decisions about their learning may help to foster more internalized and self-determined forms of motivation (Ushioda, 2003). Within mainstream motivational psychology, there is substantial research evidence to show that fostering the internal growth and self-regulation of motivation are vitally important for promoting lasting behavioral change and psychological well-being (e.g., Ryan & Deci, 2017).

In this respect, this is certainly the message that we tend to highlight when we translate our theoretical and research insights into implications for practice for language teachers. By and large, in other words, we argue against the use of controlling strategies by teachers, and we highlight instead the importance of nurturing students' own motivation to learn. In Dörnyei's (2001) framework for motivational teaching practice, for example, the essential starting point is to create "basic motivational conditions" in the classroom through establishing a positive and cohesive learning environment that will facilitate the healthy internal growth and development of motivation. In my own writing about motivation too, I have consistently emphasized the importance of promoting positive interpersonal relations, supporting students' sense of autonomy, and fostering internally driven forms of motivation (e.g., Ushioda, 2003, 2012). The basic principle here is that, instead of looking for ways of motivating students through various external regulatory strategies, we should look for ways of orchestrating the conditions within which students will motivate themselves. Other researchers have similarly highlighted the value of autonomy-supportive teaching approaches in enhancing language learners' intrinsic motivation (e.g., Noels, Clément, & Pelletier, 1999). In the contemporary era, this emphasis on promoting internally driven motivation is often associated with encouraging students to develop personally valued self-and-identity goals linked to language skills and supporting them in their motivational pathways toward achieving these desired future selves (e.g., Dörnyei & Kubanyiova, 2014; Hadfield & Dörnyei, 2013).

A Discourse of "Social Control"?

Yet, however much we motivation researchers may want to advocate pedagogical approaches that promote internal rather than external forms of motivation, we are clearly doing language teachers a disservice if we ignore the challenging and complex realities they may face in their classrooms. After all, in many language classrooms around the world, students are there not out of personal choice or interest but because of curriculum requirements, as is almost invariably the case with the learning of English in compulsory education and university settings in non-Anglophone countries. Where foreign language skills and particularly English language skills are concerned, the primary emphasis in educational policies across the world is on their economic and social value in facilitating advantage and mobility in today's competitive global marketplace. Thus, even while language teachers may strive to nurture students' personal goals and interests and to foster internally driven forms of motivation, they may struggle to do so against a wider public policy and discourse of "social control" emphasizing the instrumentalist value of language skills for economic and social advancement.

This raises a critical question about the pedagogical complexities of managing these tensions between internal and external control of motivation. After all, however much they may want to encourage students to develop enjoyment in language learning and pursue their own goals and interests, teachers are all too aware of their professional responsibilities in guiding their students to meet externally imposed educational goals and curriculum requirements and to achieve the necessary learning outcomes for successful academic and social progression. How should teachers manage these motivational tensions?

Autonomy-Supportive Approaches as a Solution?

One approach that we commonly advocate in this regard is to support students' sense of autonomy in making informed choices and decisions about their learning, within the necessary constraints of the curriculum framework (e.g., Dörnyei, 2001; Ushioda, 2003, 2012). As research evidence shows (Ryan & Deci, 2018), people's readiness to align their behaviors with social regulations and constraints depends on the degree to which the social environment supports their sense of autonomy in making personal choices and decisions within this context. This is explained in relation to self-determination theory, according to which people have an innate psychological *need for autonomy*—that is, the sense that our actions and behaviors are self-determined, reflecting an authentic expression of our agentic self and our internal values. Importantly, this authentic expression of our agentic self and our internal values will entail aligning with behaviors and values in our surrounding sociocultural environment, since our need for autonomy is also linked to our psychological *need for social relatedness* and belonging (Deci & Ryan, 1985). In other words, people are more likely to be willing to do what they know they should do in society if they feel that they are exercising autonomy and personal choice. By the same token, they are less likely to feel willing if they experience no personal control or choice in the matter.

From a pedagogical perspective, therefore, autonomy-supportive approaches that promote students' opportunities for choice and decision-making within a given framework are generally advocated as a constructive way for teachers to manage the tensions between internal and social control of motivation. The idea is that teachers can thus support students' sense of autonomy in making choices and decisions that are true to their own values and that also align with what is socially valued and desirable and that are perceived (by the wider society) to be in their best interests. As Bronson (2000) has commented in relation to the socialization of children in this regard, their internal motivation to engage with culturally valued goals and activities is socially acquired in this way, or, as she succinctly puts it, "the child learns what to want" (p. 33).

Some Critical Perspectives from Nudge Theory

However, it seems to me that there is a delicate fine line between supporting students' autonomy and internal motivation in this way, and essentially influencing and exercising "social control" over their motivation. Again in the context of wider public policy and discourses of "social control" around the instrumentalist value of language skills, I think it is especially pertinent here to refer to the concept of *nudge theory* from the field of behavioral economics, as elaborated and popularized by Thaler and Sunstein (2008), and as widely adopted in public policy in many countries across the world. In essence, nudge theory is described as a form of "libertarian paternalism" (Thaler & Sunstein, 2008, pp. 7–10) in that it promotes the *libertarian* view that people should be free to exercise autonomy and make their own choices, and yet it also promotes the *paternalistic* view that people should be steered—that is, *nudged*—to make the optimal choices that will be good for them and good for society. Nudging people in this way is achieved by strategically arranging the *choice architecture* in such a manner that people are more likely to make the "right" choices, such as selecting healthy food options, reducing their carbon footprint, or (at the time of writing this chapter manuscript) practicing social distancing responsibly during a global pandemic. In relation to selecting healthy food options, for example, arranging the choice architecture may involve physical designs and displays, such as making plentiful fresh fruit and salads visible at eye-level in self-service cafeterias; or it may entail strategic social messaging such as showing influential celebrities with glowing skin and toned bodies talking about the benefits of healthy eating. A basic principle in nudge theory is that people remain essentially free to make their own choices and decisions, yet they will almost invariably respond to the subliminal nudging practices used in public policy and choose well.

Despite the popular applications of nudge theory, its use in social and public policy to influence and subtly control people's behavior inevitably raises some ethical and moral issues, since it seems to entail a degree of psychological manipulation and undermining of authentic free choice. This is a critical issue acknowledged by Sunstein himself (one of the co-authors of the original best-selling volume on nudge theory cited earlier) in a book significantly entitled *The Ethics of Influence: Government in the Age of Behavioral Science* (Sunstein, 2016). This ethical concern connects with the earlier historical discussion of psychology as an emergent discipline, where we noted Danziger's (1997) commentary on how motivation research in the early decades of the twentieth century became situated in a discourse of "social control" and of understanding how "to play upon what individuals wanted" (p. 113) in order to manipulate their behaviors.

Although nudge theory has not featured explicitly in the recommendations for practice that stem from L2 motivation research, its core principle of ostensibly promoting autonomy while subtly controlling people's behavioral choices seems to cast something of a shadow on the motivational teaching practices that we do advocate, at least from an ethical perspective. As teachers try to manage the tensions between promoting students' internal motivation to learn (through engaging their personal interests, goals, and choices), and steering them toward externally regulated syllabus goals and educational pathways, are we effectively advocating the use of *nudging practices* to "control" students' motivation and maneuver it in the "right" direction? When we say that teachers should create a supportive social learning environment and orchestrate the classroom conditions so that students will feel motivated and autonomous (e.g., Dörnyei, 2001; Ushioda, 2003, 2012), are we effectively advocating a subtler approach to "controlling" (manipulating?) students' motivation and learning behaviors than more obvious controlling strategies such as applying incentives, deadlines, and sanctions?

Clearly, I am putting a rather negative critical spin here on the motivational teaching practices that we advocate. At a fundamental level I do not believe that those of us in the L2 motivation research community who engage with language teachers through our writing or through professional development forums would conceive of these motivational teaching practices in this way—that is, as a means of subtly "controlling" students' motivation and behavior. Instead, we will want to counter any such negative critical spin by emphasizing the fact that teachers have an educational and moral responsibility to steer students toward making optimal choices and pursuing the best pathways, and that therefore they are entirely justified in arranging the *choice architecture* strategically to *nudge* students' motivation in the right direction. Examples of such nudging practices (i.e., motivational strategies) might include bringing into the classroom former students or people from different professions who can demonstrate how language skills proved invaluable in shaping their career success; or inviting students themselves to identify their own role models in language learning and to share their accounts of these role models with the rest of the class. At a basic level, these examples take the same approach as the nudging practices illustrated earlier for promoting healthy eating. Yet, from an educational and pedagogical perspective, such practices seem entirely principled and appropriate in this context.

However, as a research community that engages with teachers, I think it is important for us to be reflexive and aware of the moral and ethical complexities inherent in the discourse of motivation as "social control," and it is also important that we enable teachers to navigate these complexities in a principled and reflective way. Where there are uneven power relationships, such as in the classroom, managing motivation becomes inevitably bound up with managing these relationships of power and control, and as I commented earlier, there is a rather fine line between socializing students' motivation (i.e., fostering its healthy growth in alignment with educational goals) and controlling their motivation (i.e., shaping it to meet these educational goals). As noted earlier too, this situation is potentially exacerbated when the larger educational and societal context imposes external pressures on teachers and students through public and institutional discourses of "social control" that emphasize the instrumentalist value of language skills.

Concluding Remarks

As I highlighted at the beginning of this chapter, a significant legacy of Zoltán Dörnyei's work in the L2 motivation field has been the much greater prominence we now give to the practical dimensions of motivation in relation to teaching, classroom management, and teacher–student relations. This greater prominence is realized both in terms of our increased research focus on classrooms and in terms of our increased engagement with teachers through various channels such as publications and seminars that have a practical professional development orientation.

However, when it comes to the principles we discuss and advocate for motivating students in the language classroom, we need to make sure that we give careful consideration to the ethical values and complexities underpinning these principles and how they might be put into practice. This means guarding against simply translating theory and research into generalizable and decontextualized principles for motivational language teaching practice. Instead, we must take into account the local classroom realities and wider institutional and societal discourses that impact on students' motivation to engage with language learning and that impact on teachers' efforts to navigate tensions between promotion of internal motivation and alignment with external requirements and expectations. This necessitates careful critical reflection on our part, and it necessitates engagement of teachers in similar critical reflection on their part.

CHAPTER 2

Motivation, Mediation, and the Individual: A Sociocultural Theory Perspective

Matthew E. Poehner

Introduction

Given the theoretical and practical need to account for the variability of "outcomes" or "end states" in L2 acquisition, it is perhaps not surprising that motivation emerged as a topic of such importance in the field. In their book on individual differences and L2 learning, for instance, Dörnyei and Ryan (2015) distinguish motivation as the topic that has generated the most interest among researchers, an observation further supported by Boo, Dörnyei, and Ryan's (2015) identification of more than 400 conceptual and empirical papers published on the topic during the period 2005–14. Dörnyei and colleagues also note the considerable development in how the construct of motivation has been operationalized by researchers over the past quarter century. Specifically, they point to the adoption of related constructs from cognitive and educational psychology during the 1990s (e.g., self-determination, self-efficacy) that subsequently informed Dörnyei's (2006) influential L2 Motivational Self System model as well as more recent efforts to connect learner motivation with complex dynamic systems approaches to L2 acquisition. In this work we see a continued commitment to motivation as a psychological trait, a feature of one's personality, while simultaneously attempting to take account of how manifestations of this trait can be understood in relation to a broader array of factors, including environmental ones. Dörnyei, Ibrahim, and Muir's (2015) proposal of "directed motivational currents" offers a helpful example of this work. The authors propose these "currents" as a metaphor for representing changes ("surges") in motivation that may endure for short periods as learners regulate various systemic factors that interact with and influence their language development. These include a *vision*, or specified goal, and corresponding *action structure* in pursuit of that goal as *behavioral routines* are established and maintained and short-term *proximal subgoals* are identified and achieved. In keeping with tenets of complex dynamic systems theory, Dörnyei and colleagues acknowledge that a directed motivational currents approach cannot be used to accurately predict with certainty changes in learner motivation, but they propose that the metaphor may be helpful in understanding *how* such changes may occur and *how long* they might last, that is, the dynamic relation between motivation as internal to learners and those factors external to them.

Recognition of the importance of interpreting learner beliefs, behaviors, and values in relation to the environments, or social worlds, they inhabit has been a central theme of research framed according to learner investment (Norton Peirce, 1995). Grounded in post-structuralism, research into investment and its relation to learner identity construes the environment not as a set of factors that might trigger or activate learner traits (e.g., motivation) but rather as constituted by discourses in which learners participate and that serve as sites to construct, reconstruct, contest, and explore identities (see Fukada, Murphey, Fukuda, and Fallout, this volume). Investment concerns learners' emergent commitments to languages, to learning, and to communities that languages might allow them to access. Darvin and Norton (2015, p. 37) characterize investment as "a sociological complement to the psychological construct of motivation," adding that it brings particular attention to "the socially and historically constructed relationship between language learner identity and learning commitment." They continue,

> While constructs of motivation frequently view the individual as having a unitary and coherent identity with specific character traits, investment regards the learner as a social being with a complex identity that changes across time and space and is reproduced in social interaction.
>
> (ibid.)

As they argue elsewhere, defining motivation as a fixed trait of personality fails to fully explain, for instance, how a learner otherwise regarded as highly motived might "resist opportunities to speak in contexts where he or she is positioned in unequal ways" (Darvin & Norton, 2016, p. 20). Understanding this, they maintain, requires focusing our attention on learners' social worlds.

The present chapter adopts a sociocultural theory (henceforth, SCT) perspective. As will be clear, SCT refutes neither a cognitive/psychological focus, as proposed by researchers in the individual differences tradition, nor a focus on social contexts and learner beliefs and perceptions, as maintained by identity researchers. However, SCT proceeds from a fundamentally different vantage point for understanding individuals and environments than either of these traditions. In particular, SCT does not require us to choose between the cognitive/psychological and the social but regards them in dialectical relation to one another (Vygotsky, 1987). The task becomes one of understanding the processes through which the social forms our psychological abilities, which in turn transform our engagement with the social world. Particularly relevant to the topic of motivation is Vygotsky's (1998) discovery of *perezhivanie* as a coherent unit for understanding the dynamic person–environment dialectic. Perezhivanie enabled Vygotsky to recognize the formative but not deterministic role of the environment in psychological development. It also brought to light the intellectual-emotive processes through which individuals experience the world and become motivated to act.

Dialectics as the Foundation of a Scientific Psychology

While Vygotsky's work may be most familiar to readers of this book through efforts to bring his ideas to bear on questions of instructed L2 development (e.g., Lantolf, Poehner, & Swain, 2018), Vygotsky himself was primarily concerned with building the foundation for a general science of psychology that could provide a full account of human consciousness in all its manifestations (Vygotsky, 1997). Vygotsky insisted upon the inadequacy of building his new science by simply adopting methods from the natural sciences, turning instead to the writings of Marx for a meta-theoretical orientation. Detailed consideration of Marx's influence on Vygotsky's thinking is beyond the scope of this chapter (for discussion, see Lantolf & Poehner, 2014; Ratner & Silva, 2017). For the present discussion, what is most relevant is that he (a) arrived at a dialectical rather than deterministic view of individuals and their environments in which we determine the conditions in which we live through our purposeful activity of shaping material nature, which in turn has an effect on our consciousness and understanding of reality and our relationship to it; and (b) adopted an historical method by which he sought to understand consciousness by studying the process of its development, a process he regarded as centrally concerned with mediation.

For Vygotsky (1987), engagement in activities in which others interpret the world for us, draw our attention to particular aspects of reality in particular ways, and model for us ways of thinking and acting opens what he described as the cultural lines of development. Here our naturally endowed abilities are organized and transformed through the introduction of practices and meanings that are available in our social and cultural environment. As we *internalize* these mediational means through our social relations, we come to use them to regulate our own psychological activity in a manner parallel to how others used them to regulate our engagement in social activity. Cognitive actions such as memory and perception, for instance, are no longer simply a direct response to stimuli in the immediate field of perception but come to be mediated by signs. Thus, entering a room comes to be perceived according to the (cultural) meanings we have for how rooms are organized, what functions particular kinds of rooms serve, the objects we may expect to find in rooms, and so forth. Similarly, remembering may occur as a process of reconstructing past events in thought, especially verbal thinking, and we may even create a mnemonic to enhance memory (see Murphy, this volume). It is in this regard that Vygotsky conceived of culture as holding the potential to perfect what is given by nature and that led him to characterize development as the "path along which the social becomes the individual" (Vygotsky, 1998, p. 198).

It is also important to note that Vygotsky shared Marx's moral and ethical commitment to determining how processes of change can be directed for the better. Indeed, Valsiner (2001) argues that a "present-to-future" or future-in-the-making orientation to development guided Vygotsky's efforts in both general and special education to determine forms of mediation (e.g., environments, activities, materials, types of interactions) that might be introduced to transform individuals' *actual* psychological functioning to a *potential future* development. Of course, as a dialectical thinker, Vygotsky was careful to avoid assigning a fully deterministic role to mediation. Practical experience, too, reinforces the point that children in the same family or learners in the same classroom do not develop in precisely the same ways. Understanding the dynamics that explain how the social world comes to mediate and give rise to higher forms of consciousness became a major concern in Vygotsky's work. It is against this backdrop that he elaborated the concept of perezhivanie.

Perezhivanie as a Unit for Understanding the Social Situation of Development

Mok (2015) notes that the Russian term Vygotsky employed in this work, *perezhivanie*, had also gained currency in the approach to acting pioneered by Stanislavsky as a forerunner to "method" acting. As Mok explains, Stanislavsky emphasized that actors inhabit the roles they perform by drawing upon their own life to "experience" something of the life of their character, including his/her emotions, passions, and motivations to act (e.g., reliving one's own experience of loss in order to authentically portray a character suffering personal loss and whose actions must be understood in relation to that experience). In such contexts, perezhivanie has been rendered in English as a full, lived experience. Vygotsky's elaboration of perezhivanie in psychology, however, might be more appropriately understood as a kind of experience of experience. For Vygotsky, the *social situation of development*, as he termed it, is not a backdrop or context in which humans live but rather constitutes a relation of the environment to the individual. This relation is not deterministic in its influence on individuals but is, rather, a coming together of the individual and his/her personal history *with* an environment; the relation is between the person's psychology and the objective environment s/he encounters. In this regard, it is possible to distinguish an "objective" event that may be identified and described through objective means (e.g., the delivery of a lesson in a language classroom) from a "subjective" or "individual" experience of that event (e.g., how that lesson was experienced by particular individuals). Crucially, this subjective individual experience can be apprehended only by taking account of the person's psychology. Furthermore, because individuals' behaviors in any given situation are motivated by their construal of the present and their previous experiences, perezhivanie also compels us to examine the ways in which environments are sustained, negotiated, and transformed by the actions of those involved. In short, this person–environment dialectic means that the influence of the environment on individuals serves to motivate individuals' actions, and these actions contribute to the environment itself, forging the social situation that leads to further development. As Vygotsky (1998, p. 294) put it in a discussion focused specifically on the social situation of development for children, "the child is a part of the social situation, and the relation of the child to the environment and the environment to the child occurs through experience and activity of the child himself."

As a simple illustration of Vygotsky's point that the environment must be conceived in relation to the individual's psychology, we might consider the everyday phenomenon of two friends going to the cinema and "experiencing" a movie in such different ways that they are afterward left asking whether they had in fact seen the same film. Similarly, many of us have found that rereading a novel after many years amounts to a very different "experience" of it. In both situations, it is clearly not the film or novel that has changed but rather the psychology of the individual that comes into contact with it—whether two individuals watching the same movie or the same person reading a novel at different points in his/her life—and this results in different experiences. Those features of the film/novel that are appearing especially meaningful are in fact imbued with meaning by the individual according to his/her history. When considered developmentally, this framing enabled Vygotsky to interpret the formative influence of the social situation of development on individuals. As he explained, "perezhivanie ... determines *what kind of influence* this situation or this environment will have" with regard to an individual's development (Vygotsky, 1994, pp. 339–40, emphasis added). He elaborated that it is not any specific environmental factor per se that will exert an influence on the individual but rather how those factors are "refracted through the prism" of the individual's perezhivanie that must be understood (ibid.).

Vygotsky's use of the metaphor of "refraction" merits some consideration. Veresov and Fleer (2016) maintain that refraction rather than reflection denotes an essential difference in how the environment functions with regard to psychological development. They explain that reflection involves light waves following a direct linear path between the eyes of a viewer, a reflective surface such as glass, and returning to the viewer's eyes. It is in this way that images are reflected, mirrored, and not distorted. Refraction, in contrast, occurs as light passes through a medium and is distorted according to its refractive index; light waves are bent, and images are not reflected but undergo change. For Veresov and Fleer (2016), this is the key to understanding Vygotsky's position that the environment is the source of psychological development but that it does not determine it: reflection would indeed connote a deterministic role of the environment, but Vygotsky contended instead that the environment is *refracted*—imbued with meaning, assigned relevance—by individuals according to their psychology (see also Veresov, 2017). They argue that to understand this relation requires taking account of "what I am experiencing" (the ontological) and "how I am experiencing" it, that is, my experience of the experience (Veresov & Fleer, 2016, p. 2).

Mok (2015) draws our attention to Vygotsky's (1994) illustration of perezhivanie and the social situation of development through the tragic case of a single, alcoholic mother and her three children. In brief, Vygotsky relates that the social environment of the three children was ostensibly the same: a mother who was at times caring but whose dependence on alcohol led her to frequently become violent and abusive. The social situation of development created by the children's psychology and this set of circumstances was unique to each of the three boys, and this was manifest in the way they were affected by the situation (for further analysis of the relative position of the child, see Bozhovich, 2009). The youngest son was reticent to speak, and, when he attempted to do so, he suffered from a stammer. The middle son evidenced an attachment-avoidance relation to his mother, alternating between feelings of love for her and fear of her. The oldest son, around ten years of age, was unusually serious and mature, having served as a protector of his siblings and even caring for his mother, but he was also developmentally behind his age peers with regard to various intellectual abilities. As Mok (2015) explains, perezhivanie enabled Vygotsky not simply to *observe* that the three children each had difficulties that likely resulted from an abusive mother but rather to *explain* the differential effects of the environment through what in fact constituted different experiences of living through that situation for each according to his psychology. Following Vygotsky, our history as individuals orients us to the world, enables us to perceive it and to make sense of it in particular ways. Furthermore, it is through this process that we form our experiences and take action, actions that in turn contribute to our environment.

A final point that is in fact central to Vygotsky's enterprise concerns the outcome of analysis framed according to perezhivanie. While Vygotsky's (1994) discussion of the children and their abusive mother does not include details of any effort to remediate the psychological consequences of the children's experiences, his commitment to psychological science as a Marxian enterprise meant that he did not accept the conventional schism between "basic" and "applied" research or indeed between research and practice. He argued passionately that the future of all psychology is applied psychology (Vygotsky, 1997), positioning his own work in response to the pressing social needs of his time, such as the creation of a centralized public education system and recognition of the importance of helping individuals with special needs. In this regard, Vygotsky maintained that while some developmental difficulties may be biological or congenital, others result from the social situation of development. Vygotsky (1993) offered examples of children who had a *primary disability* (e.g., visual or hearing difficulty) and who, as a result of that special need, were denied access to schooling or other typical opportunities for socialization. He explained that the children therefore experienced a kind of "distorted development" leading to various *secondary disabilities* (i.e., learning difficulties). In his view, the latter may be addressed through efforts to organize a social situation of development that takes account of the individual's primary special needs and establishes appropriate access to the mediational means of development. As he put it, "the path of cultural development is unlimited" (Vygotsky, 1993, p. 169).

Perezhivanie and L2 Research and Practice

As discussed at the outset of this chapter, approaching learner motivation from a vantage of individual differences suggests particular methods and research designs for documenting manifestations of motivation and interpreting it in relation to other factors, individual or environmental, while the tradition of identity research emphasizes personal meanings and experiences of L2 learners. As the reader will hopefully appreciate, SCT offers yet another orientation, a dialectical approach in which objective, material circumstances must be fully accounted for but that interprets their developmental significance through the prism of individuals' psychology. Vygotsky's discussions of perezhivanie do not offer a specific method for investigation, but one possible source is found in the subsequent work of his close colleague, A. R. Luria.

Unlike Vygotsky, whose life was cut tragically short, Luria continued to work for decades, emerging as a founding figure in neuropsychology. In his intellectual autobiography, Luria (Cole, Levitin, & Luria, 2014) describes his approach to research and his particular form of case studies that became celebrated even beyond his professional research community, as *romantic science*. Without going into a detailed discussion of Luria's work, his view of romantic science was a break from the classic science that accepted the Cartesian dualism between the domain of the physical world, that could be perceived through the senses, objectively defined, and measured, and the spiritual world that could not be studied through scientific means. Like Vygotsky, Luria regarded this delimiting of the scope of science as reductive, and he expressed concern that an exclusive focus on what could be objectively measured as counter to efforts to understand the full lives of human beings. Luria's romantic science was intended to counter this by infusing more conventional reporting of the neurological condition of his patients, which included individuals with various brain injuries, pathologies, and disorders, with detailed accounting of their *experience* of their condition. This focus on individuals' experiences of their afflictions also included his efforts working alongside them to reorganize their lives in order to regain or maintain their functionality. To my knowledge, Luria did not overtly reference perezhivanie in this context, but it is clear that he regarded the appropriate focus of his work to include both the neurological (i.e., the functioning of the central nervous system) and the psychological (which he understood to be social and cultural) in diagnosing human beings and in helping them to live full lives.

Early in his career, the celebrated neurologist and popular author Oliver Sacks drew inspiration from Luria's work and maintained a correspondence with him until his death, consulting with him on especially perplexing cases. With a career extending from the 1970s through the early twenty-first century, Sacks even more acutely than Luria may have felt pressure to conform to the tendency toward "data-driven" medicine and randomized clinical trials in medical research. Nonetheless, Sacks integrated conventional methods in neurology such as clinical observation, blood work, physiological measures, and brain scans, with extensive interviewing of patients and careful construction with them of narratives of their experiences. These narratives were central to Sacks's efforts to understand how individuals' neurological conditions shaped their engagement with the world and in particular their social relations. Like Vygotsky and Luria, Sacks understood social relations as central to psychology and therefore as offering possibilities for individuals to continue to function even when neurological afflictions altered the workings of the brain. For this reason, Sacks insisted on engagement with patients not only in hospitals and care facilities but in the real contexts— neighborhoods, shops, and even homes—in which they lived their lives. Howarth (1990, p. 119 emphasis added) writes of Sacks's commitment to a nonreductive approach to understanding and helping individuals that "patients have always represented to him the opportunity to establish a *full ecology of healing*." He continues,

> in his literary response to the classical and romantic paradigms for science, he [Sacks] has looked for ways to express past and future, logic and emotion, series and flow, within narrative forms. His more successful works have recounted the process of discovery that rises from relations with patients, through intense Socratic dialogues.
>
> (pp. 118–19)

Sacks himself, referencing the influence and legacy of Vygotsky and Luria, described this orientation as an effort of "creating, if it were possible, a *biological biography*, in which all the determinants of human development and personality would be exhibited as coexistent, coacting, and interacting with one another in continuous interplay" (Sacks, 2014, p. 524). Like Vygotsky then, Sacks seems not to have perceived an unbridgeable divide between scientific and humanistic ways of understanding reality but adopted an ontological position that regarded them as necessarily interrelated and as together comprising a more complex unity. Moreover, Sacks clearly shared Vygotsky's commitment to not only arriving at a full, nonreductive understanding of people and their worlds but to also actively engaging with them to improve their lives.

Turning to the matter of L2 motivation, we might ask how the field can work to arrive at a "full ecology" of L2 learner development and how this could contribute to research and practice. Perezhivanie has come to the attention of L2 SCT researchers only relatively recently (e.g., Lantolf & Swain, 2020; Mahn & John-Steiner, 2002). Studies to date have primarily sought to understand the concept itself, and empirical investigations of its implications in L2 contexts are only beginning. An important contribution of this work at present has been to raise awareness among L2 SCT researchers of their own tendency to examine cognitive dimensions of psychological development with little attention to the emotive. It has also opened a new way of approaching L2 learners and their relation to their instructional environments, expanding the previous focus on the *provision of mediation* to investigate this mediation *in relation to* learner psychological history. The emphasis in SCT research on, for instance, particular forms of dialogic and symbolic mediation and learner development of L2 conceptual knowledge is likely continue, and research practices such as examination of learner L2 production and assessment performance as well as analysis of learner–learner and teacher–learner interactions remain indispensable. Future work informed by perezhivanie may need to more fully integrate accounts of learner histories (e.g., previous formal and informal language-learning experiences) as well as their perceptions of the classroom environment (their peers, the teacher, and instructional materials, technologies, and tasks). Interviewing, journaling, and composition of narratives each constitute interpretive acts

through which learners can formulate connections and assign meanings—
"experience" their experience—and construct an object for continued
individual and cooperative contemplation. In keeping with Vygotsky's
commitment to praxis, research that understands learner motivations,
actions, and developmental processes at the nexus of their social situation
of development and their psychology also demands consideration for how
that social situation may be reconfigured to better promote the development
of all learners.

CHAPTER 3

Too Much Psychology? The Role of the Social in Language Learning Motivation

Ofelia García

Introduction

Motivation research in language learning has leaned heavily on psychology. Although psychology has played a major role in shaping our understandings of motivation in the learning of additional languages, I argue here that social theories, and in particular, the contributions of sociology of language in all its forms and extensions, have much to offer the study of motivation in language learning.

Zoltán Dörnyei has reminded us that research on learners' motivations to become bilingual made a big leap forward when Robert Gardner and Wallace Lambert (1959) added a social dimension to motivational psychology and introduced the concept of "integrative motivation" (Dörnyei, 2019a). Much research on motivation in the learning of a second language has been based on Gardner's (1985, 1988) socio-educational model of second language acquisition, characterized as "the combination of *effort plus desire* to achieve the goal of learning the language plus *favourable attitudes* toward learning the language" (1985, my emphasis, p. 10). Gardner eventually expanded understandings of motivation in language learning to other factors beyond instrumental and integrative purposes, such as persistence and attention (Tremblay & Gardner, 1995). However, motivational research on language learning has been deeply influenced by the socio-psychological work of Gardner, most often focused on individual effort, desire, and positive attitudes to integrate into another language group. Wallace Lambert (1969) referred to this positive attitude in motivation as the "adoption of aspects of behavior which characterize *another linguistic-cultural group*" (p. 95). More recently Noels and her colleagues (Noels et al., 2001, 2008) have advanced a motivational orientation framework in terms of the degree to which it is perceived as freely chosen and self-determined.

Motivational research in *language learning* is deeply tied to *language teaching*, since teachers' pedagogical practices are expected to engage students' motivation. In studying the role of motivation in task completion, Dörnyei (2019b) has gone *beyond* motivation as simply socio-educational or cognitive-situated. He has proposed that there is an interaction of learner-specific factors, learning situational factors, task-related factors, and external factors such as distractions, disruptions, and time-related. An adequate language learning task promotes what Dörnyei, Henry and Muir (2016) call directed motivational currents. This includes having a vision or goal, a sense of ownership, the skills required, behavioral routines, concrete subgoals, regular progress checks, and affirmative feedback. It is not that the social has not been included in psychological motivation research; it is that the social continues to be defined as the context of the learner, their "social milieu" without taking into account past histories of colonization and conquest, socioeconomic structures, and ideologies of racism, linguicism, and sexism.

Taking up Dörnyei's (2016) call for an explicit/implicit *cooperation* in studying motivation, I try here to highlight the importance of the social in language learning. I focus on how bilingual learners think, feel, and behave, and its relationship to not just internal psychological motivation, but also to external socioeconomic and sociopolitical structures that interact and cooperate with internal psychological processes (see also Poehner, this volume). I show how the personality/identity of the language learners has to do not only with aptitude and internal motivation, or even with vision and goals, but with how the learner as a subject is positioned in society. I claim that without attention to how sociopolitical structures and ideologies obstruct the desire and positive attitudes of learners, their self-determination, and their vision of a process, this work positions learners as if they were passive individual agents without histories or circumstances.

I address in this chapter why it is that the psychological study of motivation in language learning leaves out what the Portuguese philosopher Boaventura de Sousa Santos has referred to as knowledge systems from "the other side of the line" (Santos, 2007, 2009, 2014). I first describe here how the study of language and society took up bilingualism and in so doing made us aware of language learners on that other side of the line, first relegated to a separate colonial territory, and today found in the metropolis itself. Yet, by continuing to impose systems of knowledge that emerged from the metropolis to produce colonial conditions, schools and language educators continued to view racialized bilingual learners through *absences*, through what they are said *not to have*—standard language, bilingual ability, and motivation to meet educational standards and to become what is established as being bilingual. I argue here that it is not just the social that we have to bring into the study of motivation, but it is *another view of the social*, one that sheds the hegemonic eye with which language scholars have viewed these learners, and *re-views* them through the copresence of an ecology of knowledges working in cooperation toward *emergence* of new meanings and possibilities (Santos, 2007).

Contributions of Sociology of Language

The study of language and society does not start or end with Joshua A. Fishman, but his foundational work on sociology of language in the 1960s ensured that bilingual speakers and bilingual learners were always positioned socially within groups, communities, and nation-states. The study of bilinguals' beliefs and attitudes toward ethnolinguistic groups and language learning was then always related to the beliefs and attitudes of those with whom they interacted, where they interacted, when, and how (Fishman, 1965, 1968, 1972).

Like Gardner, Lambert, and Dörnyei, Joshua A. Fishman was a social psychologist, and he taught until his retirement on the faculty of a graduate school of psychology. But his scholarship on language and bilingualism never reduced language learners or language activists—two of his most studied groups of people—to purely psychological beings. Instead, he studied how their language learning and language activism was marked by their social affiliations—linguistic, ethnic, historical, economic, national. The individual language user and learner was never seen as divorced from its community and group—a community laden with differential political and economic power, numerical size, degree of bias, and sociohistorical considerations. The language users' and learners' sense of selves, their emotions and affect, their self-regulation could not be understood, Fishman argued, unless these individuals were positioned within a social structure, with its historical and present conditions. Language was seen by Fishman (1968) as structuring the social context in ways that make it possible to identify the origins of inequality among speakers. Fishman argued that learning or not learning an additional language has more to do with how language functions to structure hierarchies of social groups within society, than with psychological motivation.

Before the 1960s, the research on language education was dominated by the learning of European languages by speakers of other European prestigious languages, especially French, English, German, Italian, and sometimes Spanish. The invisibility of any power dimension in learning language meant that researchers were able to study motivation as a mostly psychological phenomenon. This, however, started to change as different groups came into view.

Sociolinguistics was developed in the 1960s as language scholars could no longer ignore the multilingual realities and the colonial conditions of the many African and Asian people in countries that were achieving independence, as well as the many autochthonous and indigenous peoples who clamored for their language rights. Joshua Fishman's sociolinguistic work emphasized bilingual groups that had been minoritized. For example, he titled his collection of essays from a lifetime of work, *Language and Ethnicity in Minority Sociolinguistic Perspective* (1989). This renewed emphasis on the study of minoritized bilingual and multilingual users and how they languaged bilingually meant that traditional language teaching and language learning, as in "foreign" language classrooms, were no longer appropriate.

In the colonies throughout the nineteenth and early twentieth centuries, only selected few colonized multilingual speakers had been taught European languages, always with traditional pedagogical practices used in the empire to teach "foreign languages." After independence, these same ways of teaching and learning were adopted, now to teach people for whom the language used as medium of instruction was not "foreign," but constructed as "national" or "official" *for all*. In what was accepted as an important part of the field of language planning and policy that was emerging as part of the sociolinguistics of the time (Rubin & Jernudd, 1971), "acquisition planning" (Cooper, 1989), that is, planning for the acquisition of a chosen national language, became important. In order for all to learn the language selected as "national" or "official," often a colonial language or the language of the dominant majority, that language had to be used as medium of instruction. The adoption of mostly transitional bilingual education programs in some localities disrupted some of the policies and practices of "foreign" language programs, but, traditional theories of language learning and teaching continued uninterrupted. This was so, even though these theories were based on experience with monolinguals, now being imposed on minoritized bilingual and multilingual subjects.

When Gardner and Lambert (1959) recognized motivation to learn an additional language not just as instrumental, but also as integrationist, they were responding not just to shifts in psychological understandings, but rather to how the social movements of the time—those of independence of new countries in Africa and Asia, but also, the ethnic revival and civil rights movements affecting the globe—were shaping those who were language learners. Most language learners now needed a "second language" not just for individual instrumental purposes as was the case in the learning of "foreign languages," but because it was the dominant language in a society that had colonized them. Yet, the burden for language learning continued to be placed on speakers, on their motivation and their choice to integrate, without considering how the colonizers constrained the language choices and self-determination of subaltern subjects. The learning of the "new" language was now to be subtractive (Lambert, 1974), always accompanied by having to forget their own language practices, as well as the history of conquest, suffering, and genocide that accompanied these efforts.

In time, people with colonial status started to move to the metropolis in great numbers, establishing communities that often lived side-by-side with other racialized autochthonous and indigenous people of the region. There were now more people that needed to be taught a dominant language, although just as a "second" language. On the other hand, a neoliberal economy that facilitated movement and migration, but not equity in living conditions and job and educational opportunities, made visible the inequities in the teaching of those languages. We address next how these sociopolitical changes have also expanded our views of the study of language in society. In so doing, we reflect on how critical post-structuralist sociolinguistic positions today can cooperate with motivational studies on language learning and teaching in this neoliberal era.

Language and Society in the Twenty-first Century

As people started to cross the colonial line that had rendered them invisible "on the other side," it became more difficult to ignore and not "see" these bilingual and multilingual learners. These were not sequential learners motivated by instrumental or even integrative needs. Many were simultaneous bilinguals, born into communities with other language practices, where their only way of being and doing language was bi-/multilingual, despite a school system that insisted on teaching them a second language at the expense of their home language practices.

The physical and material exploitation of subaltern subjects in colonial contexts was substituted by the discursive production of colonial subjects as inferior, and their knowledge systems, including their language, as being flawed and corrupted. The Peruvian sociologist Aníbal Quijano (2000) has called this process *coloniality*, arguing that race and racism became the organizing principle that structured all the hierarchies of people into superior and inferior. Sociolinguists started contesting the production of inferior subjectivities and knowledge through language. In interaction with social theories of postcolonial and decolonial thinkers, sociolinguists began identifying what Foucault (1980) called "technologies of power." These were used in *normalization processes* that led people to accept what society and its institutions, and in particular schools, defined as language, bilingualism, language learning, and language teaching, in ways that benefitted monolingual dominant language users. A most important technology of power has been ideologies. Ideologies explain why it has been so easy for people to have naturalized understandings of language and bilingualism in ways that benefit monolingual white speakers and that leaves racialized bilinguals without motivation to learn the language of the dominant majority. The study of ideologies in language learning has helped shift the focus from how bilingual *speakers* do language to how white monolingual *listening subjects* construct these marginalized bilingual users, ushering in the study of raciolinguistic ideologies (Flores & Rosa, 2015; Rosa & Flores, 2017). We address below first the changing understandings of language, bilingualism, and language learning and teaching, and the consequences of these new insights for studies of motivation. We then explore language ideologies and the shift in focus from motivating language learners to motivating other listeners.

Language, Bilingualism, and Language Learning

The fields of language learning and of motivational studies of language learning have always relied on the concept of language as a named autonomous structure. Students are said to learn named entities—English, Spanish, Chinese, Arabic, and so on. But the question for critical poststructuralist sociolinguists in this neoliberal era (García, Flores & Spotti, 2017) has been: *What is language and whose vision of language does the language learning profession uphold, and why?* We attempt here to answer this question and propose another view of language, bilingualism, and language learning and teaching that has much relevance for psychological studies of motivation.

Bauman and Briggs (2003) have documented how language was invented by European elites as "reductionist, atomistic, and individualistic" and how this "then became a model not just of communication but of thought, rationality, and sociability" (p. 299). That is, those who were said to have these discrete European languages were then said to be rational, intelligent, and socially valuable. Sinfree Makoni's and Alistair Pennycook's *Disinventing and Reconstituting Languages* (2007) also reminded us how "named languages" in colonial contexts were invented by missionaries and linguists and had little to do with the language practices of people themselves, with their *languaging* (Becker, 1995; Maturana & Varela, 1984).

The bilingualism of racialized speakers is different from the notions of bilingualism that have been constructed with sequential white dominant bilingual learners when students were similar in terms of social, economic, historical, and geographic position. The acquisition of bilingualism by minoritized speakers could not be simply additive, with one named entity being added separately to another named language (Lambert, 1974). Instead, their bilingualism has been said to be dynamic (García, 2009). That is, these bilinguals engage in what many sociolinguists and applied linguists have called *translanguaging* (García & Li Wei, 2014). Translanguaging theory poses that bilinguals do not "have" two separate languages with their own grammatical systems and psycholinguistic reality; bilinguals "do" language with a unitary repertoire from which they select features to make meaning and communicate (Otheguy, García & Reid, 2015, 2019). This unitary repertoire goes beyond the purely linguistic, integrating other modes, all interacting to engage and motivate learners (Hua, Li, & Jankowicz-Pytel, 2020; Lin, 2019; Li, 2011, 2017; Li & Lin, 2019). Bilingual learners leverage their entire meaning-making repertoire as they learn, and effective language teachers must enable them to be active agents assembling their full repertoire in the process of learning (Pennycook, 2017). Even if the product or task is said to be in a "named language" or a mode that has been selected by the teacher, the *process of learning* must engage bilingual students' translanguaging (García, Johnson & Seltzer, 2017). García, Johnson, and Seltzer (2017) call this the translanguaging corriente, which is always present with bilingual learners. For example, if reading, bilingual learners must be encouraged to bring all of themselves into the text to make meaning of the text. This means motivating students to leverage their translanguaging, and freeing up other knowledge and language systems, other than that of the text (García, 2020; García & Kleifgen, 2019). Dörnyei's motivational current has to engage with the translanguaging corriente.

But this bilingual languaging, this translanguaging, is often not part of what teachers are encouraged to leverage in teaching languages or in motivating learners of languages. Instead, teachers insist that only one language, constructed as the "standard" by dominant monolingual and bilingual speakers, is used. These minoritized learners are often told to "forget" their language, to think only in the "school" language, to "leave their language behind." In the rare instances in which these racialized bilingual learners are engaged in bilingual education, they are taught as if they were two monolinguals in one (Grosjean, 1982), insisting on developing parallel bilingualisms (Heller, 1999) in ways that do not in any way fit their bilingual lives and their language practices as people.

The notion of language and bilingualism that is upheld in education strictly benefits dominant white majority speakers, leaving little room for bilingual learners' practices. As we think about how sociolinguists and psychologists can cooperate in motivational research, it is important to understand that translanguaging pedagogical practices do little to transform learners if they remain apolitical, as Flores (2014) has warned. It is not enough to just transform our understandings of language, bilingualism, and language learning to motivate language learning; we also need to motivate and transform *listeners* and their *ideologies*.

Listeners and Ideologies

Racialized bilingual learners, especially those who have been deprived of rich educational opportunities, rarely do language in the same ways as monolinguals. But these differences are not recognized as sociopolitically and socio-educationally produced, but are used to manufacture their enregisterment (Agha, 2005) as inadequate invalid people. Their language is said to be "non-standard," full of "interferences," exhibiting bilingual deviant phenomena such as "code-switching." When these racialized bilingual learners are taught what has been constructed by dominant majorities to be the "standard," their language practices are then produced as non-standard. Why would they be motivated to learn a language that is not theirs when that is precisely what produces their marginalization?

Scholars working on language ideologies (Silverstein, 1979) have shown how certain linguistic forms become associated with certain types of people through semiotic processes that construct social and linguistic categories (Irvine & Gal, 2000). Language is used to racialize, that is, to ascribe and prescribe a racial category to a group of people (Urciuoli, 2011). It is, after all, listening subjects that are authorized to legitimate or not the representations of speakers. The joint work of sociolinguists and anthropological linguists has advanced the concept of raciolinguistic ideologies (Flores & Rosa, 2015; Rosa & Flores, 2017), focusing on how white monolingual listening subjects construct racialized bilinguals as having inappropriate language, even when they are producing what in the lips of others might be considered appropriate.

To break out of the coloniality of listening with dominant monolingual "ears," Mignolo (2000, 2002) recommends adopting an ideology of "otherwise than" in order to rethink, reread and rewrite a world organized otherwise, conceptualized from the borderlands (Anzaldúa, 1987, 2015). To do so would require adopting what Santos (2009, 2014) has called an "epistemology of the South." For Santos, the South is not geographical, but stands as a metaphor of systemic and unjust human suffering caused by colonialism and global capitalism. Santos calls for going beyond what he calls abyssal thinking, an epistemological perspective from the side of the line of those who command and have a monopoly on knowledge. He encourages us to situate our epistemological perspective on the social experience of those on the other side of the line, enabling us to view and listen to the two sides of the line simultaneously, in the copresence of what he calls *post-abyssal thinking* (Santos, 2009). Ensuring the copresence of knowledge systems from both sides of the line would then also transform the ways in which we all listen, as we start to develop thinking and listening that is post-abyssal. It is in this post-abyssal space where motivational research on bilingualism must be situated in the future, as dominant listeners engage with minoritized bilingual learners. The question then would be: *How can we motivate listeners to overcome listening with white dominant monolingual knowledge? How can they listen in a space of copresence of people, knowledges, and languaging?* To attempt this would mean going beyond the psychological aspects of motivation to encompass how political and economic structures hinder or assist listeners in hearing, viewing, and thinking post-abyssally.

Conclusion

The psychological study of motivation in language learning has viewed and listened to learners only from the side of the line of those who command and have a monopoly on the nature of knowledge and language. This renders other knowledge and linguistic practices as popular, not academic, not scientific, and these other learners as deficient, lazy, lacking, absent of potential. Incorporating social theory can open up the study of motivation so it does not view learners solely through a hegemonic eye, but from an ecology of presences, and not of absences.

Despite motivational studies being directed toward a future, its strong reliance on psychological factors has rendered many learners as not displaying the effort, desire, and attitudes that make good language learners. Motivational research on language learning has often focused on absences, of what learners do not have. We argue here for a type of motivational research in which psychology and social theory would cooperate in amplifying conceptions of language and bilingualism. In this way, motivational research might be able to uncover new constellations of meanings that include all speakers and all listeners as equals and copresent.

Social justice has been at the core of sociolinguistics since its emergence as a field in the 1960s, and as it has evolved in connection to anthropological linguistics. If motivational research in language learning is going to reclaim the important place it must have, it needs to nurture itself from the work of critical post-structuralist sociolinguists in order to counteract the social inequalities that have been produced by language ideologies that naturalize how power operates. I have argued here for language motivation research to center the role of language in producing social inequalities, and its interrelationship with other forms of social inequality such as race, social class, gender, and sexual orientation.

PART TWO

Language Engagement

CHAPTER 4

Engagement: The Active Ingredient in Language Learning

Sarah Mercer

Introduction

In this chapter, I examine the construct of engagement, which is something of a relative "new kid on the block" in language learning psychology (Reschly & Christenson, 2012, p. 14). Concise definitions of engagement are difficult given its multidimensionality and the different theoretical frames and timescales under which it has been examined. In this chapter, my focus is on learner engagement in the context of classroom tasks and activities. I define engagement as the learner's volitional active involvement in the learning task. This comprises involvement on an emotional, cognitive, and behavioral level situated within a nested system of multiple social contexts. The defining characteristic of engagement is that learners are actively involved in their learning, not just complying or conforming to social expectations, but volitionally engaged in authentic, meaningful learning.

In this chapter, I wish to reflect on the position of the construct of engagement within the field of SLA (second language acquisition) and motivational studies specifically. I begin the chapter by charting developments in the field that have led toward the growing prominence of the construct. Then, I consider how it can be conceptualized in SLA and suggest a specific model for understanding it in the language classroom. The chapter concludes with reflections on future directions for research in this area.

From Motivation to Engagement

As with the emergence of all supposed "new" lines of thinking or constructs, engagement is not really new and all current work and thinking stand on the shoulders of previous giants from within and beyond SLA, in particular in this case the work of Zoltán Dörnyei. There are perhaps three main lines of development in L2 motivation research that have laid down the foundations for the current interest in learner engagement: focus on the teaching/ learning context, focus on process and temporality, and focus on task-level motivation. These overlap but are marked by specific developments in thinking that have contributed toward the current climate in which engagement has emerged as a construct of interest.

Focus on the Teaching/Learning Context

Perhaps a turning point in the development of L2 motivation research was Crookes and Schmidt's (1991) seminal article which challenged the dominant views of the time which focused on attitudes and the social-psychological by calling for more research in actual L2 classrooms in line with the discourse and perceptions of practitioners. Their contribution was important in connecting the field with developments in educational psychology and also opening up notions of diverse empirical designs. They conclude their paper calling for research that is "congruent with the conception of motivation that teachers are convinced is critical for SL success" (Crookes & Schmidt, 1991, p. 502). Indeed, some thirty years later, the impetus for the turn to engagement is driven by several of the same concerns such as a need to connect with mainstream educational research and a need to reflect the practical concerns of educators in contemporary classrooms. In a recent overview of the field, Ushioda (2016, p. 574) comments that the focus of L2 motivation research "has tended to remain on general principles (such as types of learner motivation or motivational strategies), and much less on motivational phenomena in particular classrooms in relation to particular teachers and learners." It would seem that the need for more classroom-based understandings of motivational processes has not yet been fully met, although there are increasing steps in that direction, including a turn to engagement.

The focus on classroom contexts was further emphasized by Dörnyei (1994b) who drew attention to what he referred to as "learning situations." He divided motivation in this framework into three components: course-specific, teacher-specific (including some elements of task presentation), and group-specific. His appeal to practitioners in this article is explicit including a heading: "how to motivate L2 learners." His publication in 2001 developed this further by focusing on "motivational strategies" that teachers could use in the classroom and highlighted the practical dimension ensuring a transition from theoretical and empirical work to the practical domain.

However, an overview of L2 motivational research between 2005 and 2014 showed that research papers on the theory of motivation still outnumbered practice-oriented papers in a ratio of 2:1 (Boo et al., 2015). Indeed, the transfer of theory to practice remains an ongoing challenge for work on motivational processes.

Another notable publication from around this time by Williams and Burden (1997) was their book *Psychology for Language Teachers*, which has been influential for the emergence of the whole field of psychology of language learning but also for the engagement of language teachers with a broader range of psychological constructs beyond merely motivation that has dominated SLA. Notably, they took a social-constructivist view of motivation that was not yet a mainstream perspective at least within SLA. They defined motivation as being:

- a state of cognitive and emotional arousal,
- which leads to a conscious decision to act, and
- which gives rise to a period of sustained intellectual and/or physical effort
- in order to attain a previously set goal (or goals).

(Williams & Burden, 1997, p. 120)

This is especially interesting in light of current conceptualizations of motivation as it conceived of motivation following three sequential stages: "Reasons for doing something—Deciding to do something—Sustaining the effort, or persisting" (p. 121). It is one of the first models to highlight the notion of action on the part of the learner as well as the need to sustain that action over time highlighting the dynamism of motivational processes and the qualitative differences between the processes at different stages such as having a reason to do something but then actually deciding to do it.

Focus on Temporality and Process

The notion of temporality and process in L2 motivation has been another key development that has set the stage for the arrival of engagement. Although Williams and Burden (1997) clearly point at these features, the seminal paper is perhaps Dörnyei and Ottó (1998), who presented a process model of motivation which they referred to as "motivation in action." One main contribution of the paper is to seek to understand the transition from *intention* to *action*. They divide motivational processes into three main phases: The "preactional phase," which they describe as choice motivation emerging from wishes and hopes, goals, and intention. The second phase is termed the "actional phase" and refers to executive motivation, which drives the action as it is being carried out. It is driven by appraisal processes and action control (or self-regulatory processes) during the task. Depending on the outcomes of the task (goals either achieved or not), the third and final phase is referred to as the "postactional phase," which involves critical reflection on evaluating the process. Interestingly, they describe the model as being accompanied by "motivational influences," which can impact on the actional phases of the model acting as "energy sources" which can enhance or inhibit the processes on a higher level across the whole model (p. 51).

This model is especially pertinent as a precursor for contemporary notions of engagement for two main reasons. Firstly, the key definitional distinction between motivation and engagement is that motivation reflects an intention to act and engagement reflects the action itself (e.g., Reschly & Christenson, 2012). From an engagement perspective, the actional phase of the model could be seen as reflecting engagement and the preactional phase could be understood as reflecting conceptualizations of motivation in which the intention to act is developed. The second point is the focus again on different stages in motivational processes looking at pre- and during action, implying a qualitative difference to the factors and processes at play at each stage. The key lessons from this model are there is a distinction between processes which lead to the intention to act and those which lead to actual action and these processes interact and are dynamic across time.

The role of dynamism and temporality has also been foregrounded in dynamic systems theory, which has become a major theoretical frame in motivational research (see, e.g., Al-Hoorie & Hiver, this volume; Dörnyei, MacIntyre, & Henry, 2015). Such a lens often considers actions as taking place within nested systems that can be distinguished according to their primary level of context (i.e., at task level, institutional level, or societal level) and their typical timescale of change (i.e., across minutes, months, or years) (Mercer, 2015). These differing levels of granularity enable a focus on different constructs—what motivational processes look like on one timescale and at one level of granularity is not the same as on another. In other words the motivation to begin studying a language is qualitatively and conceptually not the same as the motivation to engage in a specific classroom task. As such, scholars need to specify the level of context and timescales of dynamism under investigation.

Focus on Task-Level Motivation and Behaviors

This increasing focus on the context and the tighter levels of granularity being used in research has become apparent through the growing body of work examining motivation on the level of a learning task in class. Indeed, Dörnyei (2002, p. 137) noted that "taking tasks as the basic level of analysis is also a logical step in the study of motivation to learn a foreign/second language (L2)." In general, SLA has a strong history of research studies focusing on the context of tasks (e.g., Ellis, 2009; Robinson, 2007, 2011) and a strong pedagogical interest in task-based learning (e.g., Ellis, 2003; Nunan,

2004; Willis & Willis, 2007). In respect to motivation, Dörnyei (2002) noted the trend of moving from studies examining overarching dispositional motivational traits toward more situated designs examining "how student motivation is reflected in concrete classroom events and processes" (p. 138). He goes on to explain how a focus on task-level motivation is in many ways the natural culmination of an "educational approach whereby the significance of motivation is seen in its explanatory power of why learners behave as they do in specific learning situations" (p. 138).

This has led to an increasing interest in what has been termed "task motivation" (Kormos & Wilby, 2020) which refers to a learner's motivation to participate in and complete tasks. An early paper using this terminology was Julkunen (2001), who drew on work by Boekaerts (1987) to suggest a model of situation-specific motivation which incorporates trait-like motivation and state-like motivation, which leads to the emergence of "situation-specific-action-tendency" (p. 30). Julkunen's study is notable for its distinction between motivation on different timescales—the more stable, long-term, trait-like motivation and the more dynamic, closely situated, state-like motivation. The model also distinguishes between the intention to participate (state/trait motivations) and the subsequent action.

The importance of research examining motivational processes at the task level has been reiterated in a recent contribution by Ushioda (2016), who argues that motivation researchers need to look at motivation "through a small lens." Her concern is that more general global approaches to motivation do not make it possible to connect motivation with specific aspects of SLA and linguistic development. Instead, she calls for motivation research in respect to specific classroom events such as at the level of tasks that reflect "the basic unit of instructed SLA" (Dörnyei, 2020, p. 52). However, if the focus of a study is on the action of the learners and the indicators used to measure task motivation are things such as the effort expended, degree and amount of participation, and attention, these are factors typically used as indicators of engagement (e.g., Lambert et al., 2017). Thus, if we are interested in aspects of learner behavior known to be critical to learning success such as attention and noticing (Ushioda, 2016), then it is most likely that engagement is the relevant construct. Indeed, a number of scholars looking at the task level have already begun to make that switch in focus such as Svalberg (2009) who has examined how learners engage with language and Philp and Duchesne (2016) who argue in favor of examining engagement on language learning tasks from a multidimensional perspective.

Engagement

As has been seen, the field has been gradually moving closer to the study of engagement. It has taken a stronger focus on situated approaches to motivation (see also Ushioda's [2009] "person-in-context" view) and increasingly recognizes the need for pedagogically grounded models that reflect the actual teaching context and aspects a teacher can more readily influence in class such as task design, classroom climate, and interactional formats. The focus on process, dynamism, and an awareness of different levels of granularity and timescales has also highlighted the need to distinguish between constructs. However, societal changes are also drawing increased attention to engagement in education. Barkley (2010, p. xii) notes the "profound and ongoing challenge" for teachers having to compete for learners' attention and keep them engaged in classes. As such, teachers are constantly seeking to find ways to ensure their students stay focused, on task and engaged in meaningful learning without becoming distracted by any number of possible diversions. Thus, scholarship is moving toward more nuanced, dynamic, and contextually defined forms of motivation and teachers are voicing practical concerns looking for concrete suggestions for actual classroom practice. In this instance, all roads lead to engagement.

Defining the Construct

Engagement is best understood as comprising three main components: behavioral, cognitive, and affective (Fredricks et al., 2004). Most scholars tend to agree on the multidimensionality of engagement (Appleton et al., 2008), although there are divergent views on which components to include. For example, additional components have been proposed, for example, by Reeve (2012) who added agentic engagement or Svalberg (2009) who added social engagement to reflect the specific interactional nature of language classrooms. In this chapter, I view all components of engagement as being socially situated and behavior as inherently social and thus interactional. For these reasons, I will maintain the definition of language learning engagement as having three interrelated subcomponents including cognitive, affective and behavioral elements, all of which are socially embedded.

An important aspect when discussing the multicomponentiality of the construct is the notion of authentic engagement (see Mercer et al., 2021). Nystrand and Gameron (1991) distinguish between *procedural engagement* (going through the motions of school) and *substantive engagement* (a sustained commitment to and involvement with academic work). In other words, not all engagement is qualitatively the same. Mercer et al. (2021) show how learners may "fake" their engagement by going through the behavioral motions but not being genuinely engaged on a cognitive or affective level. Therefore, researchers and practitioners need to consider that in defining engagement, the multidimensionality is an important facet if we wish to understand authentic, deep engagement; remaining mindful that it is possible to be differently engaged along each dimension (Trowler, 2010). In other words, a learner might be strongly cognitively invested and thinking hard about a task but not necessarily displaying a high level of action or feeling deeply emotionally invested in the thinking processes.

One of the biggest definitional challenges facing scholars in this area is teasing apart the relationship between motivation and engagement. A number of scholars use the terms interchangeably (Reschly & Christenson, 2012) depending on the theoretical lens used; however, the prevailing view is that the two are distinct phenomena. The predominant view reflects that of Reschly and Christenson (2012, p. 14), who note that "motivation represents intention and engagement is action." The critical qualitative and functional difference of the two is further foregrounded by Reschly and Christenson (2012, p. 14) who state, "engagement and motivation are separate, but related constructs, wherein motivation is necessary but not sufficient for engagement." Dörnyei (2020, p. 57) reinforces this distinction in SLA by referring to engagement as "the behavioural outworking of motivation."

Engagement in SLA

Engagement has been gaining increasing attention within SLA in recent years (e.g., Mercer, 2019; Oga-Baldwin, 2019; Philp & Duchesne, 2016; Svalberg, 2009). Two recent book-length publications have further drawn the attention of practitioners (Mercer & Dörnyei, 2020) and scholars (Hiver, Al-Hoorie, & Mercer, 2021) to the construct. Mercer and Dörnyei (2020, p. 5) explain that the predominance of five decades of research on motivation in SLA has meant that motivation has "stolen the show" and taken attention away from engagement. It means that sometimes scholars may have chosen to describe new forms and levels of motivation, when perhaps the more appropriate construct at times would have been engagement. It is not one construct or the other; both are relevant and related, but they serve different functions.

Precision in the use of constructs would ensure that scholars within SLA are able to connect with the large, relevant body of scholarship in educational psychology, which is admittedly also plagued by "jingle, jangle, and conceptual haziness" (Reschly & Christenson, 2012). However, if constructs are clearly defined and used consistently, it could potentially help create clarity between different psychological processes that are aimed at achieving different purposes—creating motivation or creating engagement. Especially with recent calls for more nuanced work at higher levels of granularity and precision, a focus on tasks could be an appropriate context in which to utilize engagement.

A Tripartite Model of Classroom Engagement

In a recent publication aimed at educators, Mercer and Dörnyei (2020) structured their book round an underlying implicit model of engagement. The model has three overlapping and interconnected components: willingness to engage, triggering engagement, and maintaining engagement (see Figure 4.1).

The tripartite structure resembles several models that distinguish between different motivational processes—those that foster intent and willingness to engage as well as those that foster action and actual engagement (e.g., Dörnyei, 2001; Dörnyei & Ottó, 1998). The model is focused on the level

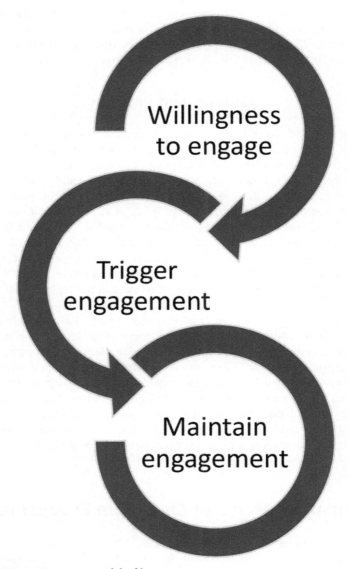

FIGURE 4.1 *Tripartite model of learner engagement.*

of the classroom and the intention is to support teachers as designers of learning experiences to maximize student engagement.

The process begins when a learner has a *Willingness to Engage (WTE)* (Wang & Mercer, 2021). This refers to an emergent psychological state in which the intention to engage (motivation) comes together with other determinants such as feeling psychologically safe, having a sense of efficacy, facilitative beliefs, social support, and a knowledge of behavioral strategies for the tasks at hand, and so on. The teacher can focus on designing learning environments that foster positive learner mindsets, teacher–student rapport, and group dynamics. If a learner feels confident, secure, and motivated, then they are more likely to be willing to engage in the tasks presented in class. However, as with motivation, WTE is no guarantee that this will translate into actual engagement, although it is a facilitative state. Interestingly, highly engaging task designs could potentially overcome a lower level of WTE as the three stages of the model are not viewed as being separate and distinct. Rather, they overlap and can influence each other.

Triggering engagement is where the task design and task set up play a role in capturing learners' situational interest, attention, and curiosity. It is the point at which learners become involved in a task. This stage recognizes that having the intention and willingness to act still needs something additional to take the learner over the threshold and become actively engaged in a task. Naturally, in compulsory education, initial engagement in behavioral terms at least may stem from compliance with expectations to work on a task but that alone will not lead to lasting, deeper, or authentic engagement (Nystrand & Gameron, 1991). Yet, if a task design can successfully capture learners' attention, imagination, and curiosity, then they may become engaged on emotional, cognitive, and behavioral levels (Sulis, 2020).

Once learners have taken the step to become initially engaged, the task has to be designed in such a way as to *maintain that engagement* or indeed further enhance it over the duration of the task—however long that may be. Naturally, the quality of their experience during the task as well as the dynamic ongoing sense of WTE will dictate whether they stay engaged or disengage. Also aspects that are relevant for triggering engagement may remain pertinent in maintaining engagement. Here teachers can attend to task design in terms of how interactive a task is, how much autonomy learners have, the nature of goals and ability to see progress, the relevance of the task for learners, and the overall emotional tone of the task.

The model is one way of making visible the distinct characteristics of different processes in the language learning classroom. WTE is built up over days, weeks, months, and possibly years of interaction to create a climate in which a learner feels confident and safe to participate. This is conceptualized as comprising motivation (the intention and drive to act) but recognizes that other components play a notable role too and can combine to lead to an emergent state termed WTE to reflect the willingness and intention (including motivation) to engage in a task. The model then moves into the actional stages of learning and distinguishes between two processes that have different functions, qualities, and timescales. The first reflects how learners can initially become engaged in a task and the second stage reflects how learners' engagement can be maintained or heightened throughout the duration of the task.

Engagement in Research

The question scholars are inevitably posed to ask is whether engagement is merely motivation under another guise—old wine in new bottles. I would argue that this is not the case and, in fact, I would suggest perhaps engagement has been here all along but under the misnomer and hidden identity of various forms of motivation. The addition of engagement as a construct to the field can add some clarity to the multitude of terms and perspectives that have mushroomed around the notion of motivation. It enables scholars in SLA to tease apart processes and constructs but also to connect with the broad body of relevant research in educational psychology. It also appeals to educators given its close ties to classroom practice.

For future empirical work, it would be important to clarify whether a study is referring to motivation or engagement. The two constructs are undoubtedly closely interconnected and, as Dörnyei (2020, p. 57) reminds us, "when students are 'engaged', they are inevitably fuelled by some motivation that has given direction to their action." However, they are distinct. They take place on different timescales typically and are thus differently connected to social contexts. They serve different functions and purposes. They are reflected in different indices or proxy. They are qualitatively and phenomenologically different. To ensure the field moves forward with some degree of clarity and consistency, when investigating engagement, there are at least four core questions to ask:

- *Action or intention*: Does the proxy being used for engagement have a focus on action?

- *Multiple components of engagement*: To what extent are learners engaged in cognitive, affective, and behavioral terms?

- *Level of granularity*: What is the context of engagement and on what timescale does it function?

- *Stage of the engagement process*: Is the study concerned with how engagement is triggered, how it is maintained, or both?

To gain better conceptual clarity, we now need research to show specifically how motivational processes and engagement processes can be distinguished and how they interconnect (e.g., Sulis, 2020). We need empirical work to investigate and add nuance to the model such as examining the processes at the different stages and their interconnected dynamics.

Future Directions

There is much work to be done. The construct of engagement is in its infancy in our field, but there is a notable body of work in educational psychology that the field can connect with as we make our own unique sense of the construct in the specific context of language learning. Empirical work will be needed to flesh out the nature of relationships between processes and specifically between motivation and engagement (see, e.g., Sulis, 2020) as well as at different stages of the process—from WTE, triggering engagement to maintaining engagement; all of which require different design features and which are qualitatively different. As an example, research into the stage of triggering engagement could connect to the growing interest in unconscious processes which suggest that conscious decision-making processes are typically preceded by neural activity which implies that action may begin outside of consciousness (Dörnyei, 2020). In other words, the triggering stage may have especially interesting connections with unconscious processes and the potential to think in such nuanced ways becomes clearer once we begin to disentangle different motivational and engagement processes on different timescales.

While researchers will play a key role in understanding the nature of engagement processes in SLA, I would argue that teachers are especially well situated to be involved in such work. Ushioda (2016) bemoans the fact that very few practitioners get involved in motivation research and that there is an absence of "pedagogically orientated research on motivation grounded in specific contexts of practice" (p. 566). Henry et al. (2019, p. 15) remind us, "good teachers know far more about motivating students than the sum of knowledge that can be gained from research." It would be invaluable looking ahead to proactively also include practitioners in research on learner engagement which is inherently situated in the actions of classrooms in which teachers are the designers of learning experiences.

Finally, the focus of this chapter has been exclusively on learner engagement, but there is a notable gap as, to the best of my knowledge, there have been few studies investigating language teacher engagement (see Hiver, this volume). Given that we know how impactful engagement can be on job satisfaction and well-being (e.g., Hakanen et al., 2006), this would be vital to understand for teachers. However, through processes of contagion, we also know that teacher and learner engagement appears to be interconnected and mutually influential (Gregersen & Al Khateeb, this volume; Skinner & Belmont, 1993). The relationship between those two forms of engagement in class would be a fascinating and critical component of classroom life to understand.

To conclude, engagement is perhaps not as new as it may at first sound. There is much within SLA that connects with and provides background to the construct, and there is work beyond the field in other disciplines that we can draw on and build on. It is an exciting construct that has a close connection to practice and can potentially bridge the gap between theories, empirical work, and practice. It may also add some clarity to the conceptual complexity of motivational research in SLA and enable the connections to specific language developments to be strengthened (Ushioda, 2016). Given its significance for successful learning, "we must make understanding engagement in language learning contexts a priority" (Mercer, 2019, p. 15).

CHAPTER 5

Engaging the Learner: Linking Teaching Practice to Learners' Engagement and Development

Phil Hiver

Introduction

The domain of second language acquisition/development (SLD) that I and many other former protégés of Zoltán Dörnyei identify with most closely is the psychology of language learning (PLL). As many other contributions to the current volume will show, it is a testament to the breadth and sophistication of Zoltán's work in the field (Dörnyei, 2005, 2009a; Dörnyei & Ryan, 2015) that PLL has coalesced into a coherent area of focus. PLL views SLD largely, though not exclusively, as a psychological process and is concerned with how individuals' thoughts and actions in settings of second- and foreign-language (L2) learning and instruction contribute to their meaningful participation and ongoing development in those environments (Gregersen & Mercer, 2022). In seeking to understand how such psychosocial aspects of L2 learning and teaching lead to deliberate effort, attention, engagement, and persistence, it is necessary to foreground the interdependencies between the many cognitive, affective, and behavioral factors at the individual level and between individuals and their environment (Li, Hiver, & Papi, 2021). A central, if unspoken, tenet, too, is that teachers and teaching can play a central role in learners' development (e.g., Hiver, 2017; Lamb, 2017). Yet, as experienced language teachers know, teaching does not cause learning (Larsen-Freeman & Anderson, 2013), nor does it guarantee learner effort, attention, and engagement. This coincides with a hard pivot away from devising positivist plans to motivate or engage learners. Classrooms are complex social systems, and student–teacher interactions are also complex and variable in nature. At its best, teaching can create the conditions necessary for learning to occur by engaging and involving L2 learners in compelling tasks, interactions, and opportunities for development (Mercer, 2019). In this chapter I examine aspects of this agenda and discuss how it might lead to future work in the field.

Dilemmas in Language Teaching

Concerns about the effectiveness of classroom pedagogy have been central to the field for decades (Long, 2015) and are not exclusive to PLL. Instructed second language acquisition (ISLA) research, for example, aims to understand how systematically manipulating the mechanisms of learning and the conditions under which they occur enables or facilitates learners' development in instructional settings (Ellis & Shintani, 2014; Sato & Loewen, 2019). However, while "the two are inextricably linked" (Dörnyei & Kubanyiova, 2014, p. 3), the message coming out of the field is clear: even the most effective instructional method or technique cannot be expected to work in all situations or to engage all learners (Larsen-Freeman, 2012). Given the complexity of what transpires in L2 classrooms, engaging teaching can be seen as challenging and complex; a dynamic process characterized by critical moment to moment decision-making for building engaging L2 classroom environments. In his recent review of the motivating aspects of teaching, Lamb (2017) also comes down firmly on this side, cautioning that "it is simply not possible to reduce highly complex issues to pedagogical 'dos or don'ts'. The [engaging practitioner] somehow learns when, where and how to deploy them in particular lessons" (p. 305). Engaging L2 classroom teaching relates to an attempt to doing the right thing in the right way and at the right time in response to the needs of particular learners in particular places on particular occasions (Duffy, Miller, Parsons, & Meloth, 2009). This way of framing language pedagogy reveals the inherent unpredictability of L2 classroom settings (Hiver et al., 2019; Hiver et al., 2021) and leads to a more nuanced perspective of what engaging teaching entails—one that insists on the importance of context and respects change and variability (Hiver et al., 2020; Mercer, 2016).

The landscape of language teaching in the twenty-first century can inform our understanding of the adaptive ways in which language teachers think and operate in their work and lives (e.g., Mercer & Kostoulas, 2018). While engaging practices are a necessary vehicle for accomplishing particular instructional goals, adaptivity of teacher thought and the ability to regulate that thought in real time, rather than a stock toolkit of techniques, are what allow practitioners to incorporate and respond to the needs of learners. This adaptive capacity constitutes an important aspect of building classroom environments that are engaging, demanding, and supportive of learners' L2 development because it moderates the quality of the interactional and improvisational work that are part of teachers' professional practice. Without considering teachers' adaptive expertise, focusing on practices alone for engaging classroom pedagogy would gloss over the complexities of learning contexts and once again narrow the role of teachers to mere technicians (Zeichner, 2012). Managing the unpredictability of instructional settings requires teachers to draw on adaptive capacities as they combine "attention to technical skill with attention to professional judgment and improvisational capability" (Forzani, 2014, p. 9). For this reason, engaging language teaching entails critical moment to moment decision-making in understanding what engages whom (i.e., which students), under which circumstances, and why (Al-Hoorie, Hiver, Kim, & De Costa, 2021). Let me now elaborate on the details of this proposition.

Engagement: Defining of All Learning

While differing in approach, scholars agree on one definitional aspect of engagement: engagement refers to action (Lawson & Lawson, 2013). This action dimension is believed to be the most important characteristic of engagement, distinguishing it from other related constructs such as motivation, which relates more closely to desire or intent (Mercer, 2019). This idea is embraced by Skinner, Kindermann, Connell, and Wellborn (2009), who describe engagement as "energized, directed, and sustained actions" (p. 225). Under this rubric of energy in action, in classroom settings specifically engagement is conceived of as "constructive, enthusiastic, willing, emotionally positive and cognitively focused participation with learning activities in school" (Skinner & Pitzer, 2012, p. 22). Language learning scholars too, such as Bygate and Samuda (2009), see engagement as the extent to which learners participate in the objectives and content of a learning task, as well as gather and utilize resources to complete it. This resonates also with Reeve's (2012) definition of engagement as "the extent of a student's active involvement in a learning activity" (p. 150).

Engagement defines all learning. Learning requires learner action, and action is a defining characteristic of learner engagement. An engaged learner is actively involved in and committed to their own learning. The predominant line of thinking in many theoretical understandings of language development (e.g. socio-cognitive theory, sociocultural theory, and complexity/dynamic systems theory) is that learning, in both naturalistic and instructed settings, occurs most readily through meaningful use of the language (see Poehner, this volume). Specifically in language learning, the notion of learner action for learning is deeply embedded in the dominant pedagogical paradigms of communicative language teaching, which sees interaction and language use as critical for language development. Attention is also critical to engagement—that is, a learner must direct their attention to the task and attend to features of the language, what those features mean, and how they are used in order to be truly engaged (Philp & Duchesne, 2016, p. 51). The field of language learning is divided regarding the role of deliberate attention and awareness in language development (Rebuschat, 2015), but there is broad agreement that engagement is "the major force of learning" (N. Ellis, 2019, p. 48) and is linked to implicit and explicit learning mechanisms and knowledge. Without engagement, therefore, meaningful learning is unlikely.

While there is a connection between engagement and motivation in learning contexts, motivation should be thought of as an antecedent or precursor of engagement (Reschly & Christenson, 2012) while engagement is the subsequent step in which learners convert this proactive drive into action to complete specific learning goals. In other words, a learner may be fully motivated (i.e., desire or intend to act) but still not engaged in learning, unless they subsequently apply the energy of motivation and proactively get involved through engagement. Definitions of engagement also point clearly to the fact that it is multifaceted and closely related to the demands of particular tasks and learning contexts (see Mercer, this volume). As Reeve (2012) argues, "it almost does not make sense to refer to 'student' engagement because it cannot be separated or disentangled from the social context in which it occurs" (p. 152). Others also agree that engagement is connected more to learners' relationships and responses to the learning environment (Järvelä & Renninger, 2014).

Scholars posit at least three (though sometimes four or more) core dimensions within engagement. Fredricks, Blumenfeld, and Paris (2004), for instance, refer to three central dimensions of engagement: (a) a behavioral dimension, which refers to individuals' qualitative behavioral choices in learning; (b) an affective dimension, including learners' emotional connections and responses to the learning tasks and peers; and (c) a cognitive dimension, which relates to learners' active thinking in the learning process. In contexts of language learning and use, Larsen-Freeman and Cameron (2008, pp. 201–4) contend that how individuals engage shapes how their engagement develops and that researchers should carefully examine the complex interdependent relationships among various dimensions of learners' engagement. S. Mercer (2019) takes this one step further in proposing that "true engagement necessitates all three components" (p. 4). In real-life learning, it is possible that students are only partially engaged in learning (e.g., they are behaviorally engaged and on-task but are merely going through the motions to look busy), whereas they lack cognitive and emotional involvement in the learning. In relation to this, Nystrand and Gamoran (1991) underscore the difference between procedural engagement and substantive engagement. The former refers to learners complying and following instructions for the purpose of going through the motions of learning—a sort of superficial, pseudo-engagement. The latter refers to an authentic, intrinsic, and sustained commitment to learning.

In the domain of language learning, Svalberg (2017) proposes that the social dimension is a crucial additional component of engagement because it is linked to interaction, negotiation of meaning, and attending to formal features. This idea has been embraced by other scholars, for instance Philp and Duchesne (2016), who define engagement as "a state of heighted attention and involvement, in which participation is reflected not only in the cognitive dimension, but in social, behavioral, and affective dimensions as well" (p. 51). What is apparent from this body of work is that the concept of engagement has gone beyond the purely learner-internal psychological conceptualization of its early days and is now used in descriptions of learners' active connections to the learning environment (Järvelä & Renninger, 2014).

Teaching for Engagement: Adaptive Thought and Action

If engagement underlies all language learning, looking at what makes a learning experience or context engaging becomes a new priority, and teaching is a large part of the equation in many instructional settings. Methods no longer lie at the heart of the second- and foreign-language (L2) teaching enterprise. When separated from individuals and the experiences that give rise to them, they encourage a mechanical and decontextualized uniformity that ignores the situated and dynamic reality of L2 classrooms (Mercer, 2018). As teachers and scholars we often expect student engagement from conditions, tasks, and experiences that are not engaging, and we do this through practices that are uninspired and not sensitive to the immediacy of the context. L2 pedagogy, however well informed it may be by theory and research, can remain unengaging if it is not attuned to the individuals in the classroom and the moment to moment interpersonal exchanges that occur between them (Mercer, 2019). The present state of L2 pedagogy is one that is sensitive to contexts of learning and values the sociopolitical purposes of L2 education, in addition to relying on insights from instructed language learning research (Kubanyiova & Crookes, 2016). Current understanding of classroom contexts and post-methods L2 pedagogy leads us to adopt a situated and dynamic perspective (e.g., Larsen-Freeman, 2017) within which language teachers, by necessity, "will need to wrestle with the fact that there are no 'right' answers, only appropriate choices" (Johnson, 2019, p. 172) as they decide what constitutes engaging practice, for whom, when, and under what conditions. Beyond merely encouraging teachers to practice principled eclecticism, it has also emphasized the interdependence of teacher thought and action by promoting language teachers' capacity to mentally revisit and deliberately evaluate their teaching practice (Kubanyiova & Feryok, 2015).

Furthermore, being able to see things from multiple perspectives at once and to track others' understanding and "sensemaking" (see e.g., Fitzgerald & Palinscar, 2019) marks engaging teaching as a cognitive activity with relational objectives. Being able to recognize others' ways of thinking and shifting ideas, including partial understandings and eventual misconceptions, involves the "bifocal capacity to understand ideas and to see them from the perspectives of others who are first encountering them" (Ball & Forzani, 2010, p. 10). This adaptive capacity is key to the process of creating order from complex experiences and encounters as teachers work with students to achieve engagement (Hiver et al., 2019; Hiver et al., 2021). There is widespread agreement that engaging teachers make a crucial contribution in creating the conditions for classroom learning and fostering the educational opportunities for which schools are responsible (Hattie, 2012). Engaging instruction is based on deliberate teaching practice shaped through experience and continuous loops of adaptive thought (Al-Hoorie & Hiver, this volume; Ball & Forzani, 2011). Conventional methods fail to capture the necessary elements of such direct and adaptive attention to deliberate teaching practices, which is why a greater awareness of real-time instructional events and settings is required (Lampert, 2010). Such conscious thought can enable the teacher to be proactively aware of whether, when, and how to adapt to situational demands, as well as which demands to attend to (Johnson, 2019). It can also aid teachers in responding with effective classroom decisions that provide the conditions for learner engagement at the appropriate time and place.

As very recent work on the topic shows, language teachers do engage in adaptive thought and action (e.g., Mercer & Kostoulas, 2018). When looking at how teachers respond to the high-dimensional demands of the language classroom, it is clear that teachers often rely on well-rehearsed practices and schemas as a way of maintaining and optimizing performance (Gao, 2019). For teachers who find themselves in professional settings characterized by situational constraints and reduced instructional autonomy, a tempting default is to adopt classroom practices that are routinized and habitual, utilizing adaptive thought in far fewer instances (Hiver, 2017). However, teachers continuously confront unanticipated situations requiring in-the-moment decisions. Non-routine episodes and situations, which reflect the unpredictability that has always been inherent in classrooms but has only recently entered our thinking more explicitly, require more adaptivity on the part of teachers to foster student engagement (Hiver & Whitehead, 2018a). Wrestling with the fact that there are no right answers in instances when students become disengaged, struggle to develop, or are unsuccessful in their L2 learning may result in teachers re-examining their own thinking and making the rationale behind their instructional practices more explicit. By pondering what they are doing in class to contribute to this effect and how they might resolve dilemmas with learner engagement, situations such as these can push teachers to revise how they are thinking or what they are doing in order to create the essential conditions for learning and engagement (Hiver & Whitehead, 2018b).

An Agenda for Researching Engaging Teaching

I turn now to several recommendations for current and future work that has potential to advance our understanding of the landscape of L2 learners' meaningful involvement and active participation in learning, and will undoubtedly add definition to the field, thereby strengthening its utility for practice.

The first of these ongoing tasks is to focus on the nature of engagement and its relation to instruction and learning conditions. As reviews of definitions, subtypes, and strands of engagement research show (e.g., Hiver, Al-Hoorie, & Mercer, 2021), there is still a need for greater consistency and clarity in operationalizing and measuring engagement. The characteristics listed briefly above may be helpful for understanding the nature of engagement. Since engagement defines all learning and is crucial for engineering the conditions for learning, the return on investment for such fundamental work in establishing clear operational definitions and measurement tools will be substantial. Although it may be some time before more consensus is reached between scholars regarding theoretical models, measurement, and definitions, it is possible to reach empirical agreement about the impact adaptive teacher thought and action has on engagement and subsequently on L2 learning and developmental outcomes. In addition to valid and reliable field-specific measures of engagement that will push research forward, other issues that may need sorting out include, for example, how the various dimensions of engagement interact with one another in various contexts of L2 instruction and whether there are phenomenological differences in how individuals experience engagement in various classroom settings.

A second task that is at the heart of understanding the interface between adaptive teacher thought and action and student engagement is to focus on the necessary conditions for learner engagement. There is an increasing awareness throughout much of our field of the complex systems that comprise L2 learners, classrooms, schools, and language communities (Hiver & Al-Hoorie, 2020b). Within these complex systems, research is needed to identify what makes language learning engaging for students both inside and outside of classroom settings (Ibrahim & Al-Hoorie, 2019), what conditions are part of an engaging instructional context and how teachers contribute to these, and how engaging contexts differ across groups of diverse learners with varied levels and learning objectives. If engagement is thought of as the organizing mechanism for greater involvement and higher-quality participation in opportunities for language learning, then amplifying the necessary conditions for it to thrive can help teachers attend to these multiple dimensions of students' participation. In addition to establishing a person–environment fit and identifying disaffected learners, identifying disengaging learning environments may shed light on the policies, practices, and contextual influences that do not have "holding" power or that provide a disincentive for active learner involvement and meaningful participation.

A third area of interest that will help push this agenda forward is to focus on the development of engagement over time. Student engagement is not static—it can change and does (Mercer, 2019). The precise ways that it is dynamic, under what conditions, and for whom are areas for future work to map out. Often student engagement is conceptualized as a desired outcome, and this is a sound design choice in many instances. It is also possible, however, to take more explicit temporal considerations into account, for example, by investigating the role of teachers, peers, and learning tasks on engagement over time and examining how classroom learning opportunities, assessments, and extramural interests and experiences influence learners' engagement. There are also other means to foreground the ways in which engagement is dynamic and emergent. Engagement can be studied as the process or activity through which development occurs (e.g., what happens to the learner cognitively, emotionally, etc., as they are engaging?), as a system input embedded in thinking about what the learners might achieve (e.g., how does engaging provide a vehicle for bridging learners' current performance or competencies with their future goals?), or as a mediator in the mechanisms of learning and development (e.g., what are the ways in which engaging in learning tasks impacts what learners can expect to gain from those instances of participation and involvement?).

Conclusion

Engagement is a kind of "hands-on" and "heads-on" energy for learning (Skinner et al., 2009, p. 227) characterized by enthusiasm, willingness, effortful exertion, interest, and concentrated attention directed toward understanding, learning, or mastering the knowledge and skills necessary to be a competent language user. Research shows that engaged learners reach higher levels of learning achievement and benefit from many desirable "side-effects" such as deeper interest, greater motivation, stronger self-efficacy, and persistence (e.g., Hiver, Al-Hoorie, & Mercer, 2021). Despite a recent surge in interest in how classroom pedagogy can lead to student engagement, a great deal of work remains to be done to understand how engaging teaching contributes to L2 learners' meaningful involvement, expenditure of effort, and desire to engage with learning opportunities—all crucial conditions for L2 development.

Teaching does not cause learning, so while it is overly simplistic to state that teaching and teachers can determine student engagement, it is also clear that teachers' instructional thought and actions can encourage an upward trajectory in students' personal investment in language learning. Involving L2 learners in compelling tasks, interactions, and opportunities for development during their experiences are key parts of creating the conditions for engagement. These are also indispensable to building L2 classroom environments that push and support learners' development. In this chapter, I have outlined the case that in order for L2 teachers to create such conditions, they must draw on an immediate attention to the unfolding L2 classroom events and interactions through adaptive thought and action. Given the complexity of what transpires in L2 classrooms, engaging learners can be seen as a key part of building L2 classroom environments that enable learners' to optimize the rate and routes of their development, and L2 pedagogy can have strong relevance for learners and their development provided that engaging language learners is at its core.

CHAPTER 6

Goal Self-Concordance and Motivational Sustainability

Alastair Henry

Being a researcher of goals, motivation, and well-being has been a very self-concordant activity for me, which has brought me the next best thing to spiritual enlightenment: Something interesting and meaningful to do, something that I am good at.

KENNON SHELDON

PROFESSOR OF PSYCHOLOGY, UNIVERSITY OF MISSOURI (2015, P. 199)

Introduction

Professional goals can provide purpose in life and support sustained action. Even if, for most people, professional work might not approach spiritual enlightenment, pursuing a goal with personal meaning—a goal that feels "right" for us—can generate dedicated striving and enduring happiness in ways that other goals seldom can. While there is now substantial research into the sources of motivation for language learning (Lamb et al., 2019), the goals that steer learning behavior have received little attention (McEown & Oga-Baldwin, 2019). With a focus on how differences in the qualities of learners' goals can influence goal-directed behavior, in this chapter I explore the theory of *goal self-concordance* (Sheldon, 2014). Against the backdrop of Zoltán Dörnyei's (2009a, 2009b, 2020) field-defining work on L2 motivation and vision, I examine how the pursuit of a self-concordant goal can support effective regulation and can underpin perseverance.

All Goals Are Not Created Equal

In motivational science, goal theories have largely focused on goal-setting processes and regulation. Far less work has been directed to the reasons for pursuing a particular goal, or to the significance that different types of goal-pursuit can have for a person's psychological state of being. Yet, as Ryan et al. (1996) have made clear, exploration of these issues is "crucial for understanding the effectiveness, persistence, and experiential qualities associated with goal activity, as well as the functional impact of goal activities on personal well-being" (pp. 7–8).

When focus is directed to the *reasons* why a person pursues a particular goal, the fundamental question is whether goal-directed action emanates from the self (and is autonomously generated), or whether it derives from external forces. When goal *content* is in focus, questions concern the extent to which a goal responds to a person's basic psychological needs (competence, relatedness, and autonomy), and the impact that need-fulfilment has on well-being. With these questions in mind, it becomes clear that "all goals are not created equal" (Ryan et al., 1996, p. 21). As Ryan and colleagues explain, goals that are autonomously generated, and which are aligned with a person's intrinsic psychological needs, promote healthy forms of goal-striving, effective regulation, and are overall better for the individual than goals that are not.

Continuing the investigation of goal qualities in work begun with Ryan and Deci at the University of Rochester (Ryan et al., 1996), but taking an interest in longer-term goal pursuit and regulatory sustainability, Sheldon and colleagues developed the theory of *goal self-concordance* (Sheldon & Kasser, 1998; Sheldon & Elliot, 1998, 1999). This theory suggests that to support sustained motivational endeavor, it is not enough that a goal is autonomously generated (i.e., "self-determined"). Rather, for motivation to endure over time, a goal needs also to be personally meaningful. Goal self-concordance indexes the degree of personal ownership that people experience in relation to a self-generated goal and seeks to explain differences in motivational persistence and long-term striving.

Self-concordant goals are hypothesized to be pursued with greater vigor and to generate enhanced well-being. In work with a focus on idiographic goals—goals that research participants themselves identify as opposed to goals defined and operationalized in research instruments—Sheldon and colleagues (Sheldon & Elliot, 1998, 1999; Sheldon & Kasser, 1998) developed the terms "self-concordant" and "non-concordant" to refer, respectively, to goals that align with aspects of personality generally relevant to personal growth, and those lacking a similar fit.

In two longitudinal studies, it was found that while at the start of a program of study there were no differences in the intended goal-directed energy of participants with self-concordant and non-concordant goals, six weeks into the program the effort of those pursuing non-concordant goals had diminished. While these individuals had believed they would be able to try hard, it appeared that their energies were coerced and steered in directions not of their own choosing (Sheldon & Elliot, 1998; Sheldon & Kasser, 1998). In subsequent studies, it was found that university students with self-concordant goals were more successful in achieving their goals compared to those with non-concordant goals. Moreover, students with self-concordant goals also experienced increased happiness when they achieved their goals. For those with non-concordant goals, similar levels of happiness did not arise, even when goals were achieved (Sheldon & Elliot, 1999; Sheldon & Houser-Marko, 2001; Sheldon & Kasser, 1998). As Sheldon (2014) has remarked, it was almost as if these non-concordant strivers "should not have bothered—with the wrong goals, they were not going to derive much satisfaction even if they managed to obtain those goals" (p. 354).

Because self-concordant goals are conceptualized as representing enduring interests and strongly held values and beliefs, they predict persistence in goal pursuit (Sheldon & Elliot, 1998, 1999). In an intervention study where participants identified goals for a semester, and were subsequently coached on goal-pursuit strategies, findings showed that goal attainment was boosted only for those students whose goals were initially more self-concordant (Sheldon et al., 2002). In another study, physical health was in focus. Here, participants who possessed self-concordant goals when enrolling at a health club were more likely to remain members two years later (Bailis & Segall, 2004).

Longitudinal research has also focused on associations between goal self-concordance and well-being. In a year-long study, Sheldon and Cooper (2008) found that the well-being of participants who pursued goals that were matched with self-construal dispositions increased over the period of goal-striving. As they explained, results suggested that "happiness can be permanently affected through the successful pursuit of life activities that match one's dispositions and talents" (p. 441). In another longitudinal study reported on by Sheldon and Schuler (2011), not only did participants for whom goals were self-concordant describe higher levels of motivation, but goal self-concordance was also found to predict goal-attainment and enhanced well-being. In addition to Sheldon's own work, incorporation of the construct into other researchers' designs has similarly shown how self-concordant goals consistently promote effective regulation and goal achievement (e.g., Higgins, 1996; Koestner et al., 2008; Milyavskaya et al., 2015; Vasalampi et al., 2009).

Goal Self-Concordance and L2 Striving

Acquiring a new language is rarely easy. For most people, it requires stamina and commitment. Just like other long-term endeavors, goal self-concordance can help explain why it is that that some people are able to consistently commit themselves to the challenges of language learning—and experience happiness in the process—while others struggle to maintain momentum and sustain initial enthusiasm. In relation to the long-term challenge of becoming proficient in another language, there may be particular ways in which goal self-concordance supports successful striving. In the sections that follow, I outline three areas of theorizing, all of which indicate how pursuit of a self-concordant goal can be beneficial for language learners.

Motivational Relevance

Goals are the mental representations of desired end-states (Austin & Vancouver, 1996). In early work on unconscious motivation, Yale professor John Bargh (1990) demonstrated how, like any other mental representation, goals are capable of becoming automatically activated by features in the environment. Sometimes, an environmental makeup can be such that certain goals become habitually activated. In such situations, it is not a question of the person choosing to pursue a goal-directed activity. Rather, the goal becomes automatized to a degree that "conscious choice drops out as it is not needed" (Bargh & Chartrand, 1999, p. 468). Goals that have central importance for the individual, and which represent personally held values and beliefs, are those most likely to become automatized. As Bargh (2017, p. 238) explains:

> Your unconscious knows what your important goals are by how much you think about them consciously and how much time and effort you put into them. ... for important goals especially, your values and feelings and choices become slanted in the direction that best helps you to accomplish those goals, literally changing your mind for the sake of that goal.

When an important goal becomes activated in the unconscious, information and events relevant to goal attainment, and which undergird goal-focused actions, are unconsciously processed. As Bargh puts it, "behind the scenes, your mind is working on your future, constantly" (2017, p. 238). However, this does not mean that all personally important goals will always be permanently activated.

In understanding how personally meaningful goals can systematically differ in their effects on regulation, Eitam and Higgins' (2010) relevance of a representation (ROAR) framework provides valuable insights. ROAR builds on Higgins's (2012) explorations of the motives underlying behavior, and his identification of the fundamental desire among humans "to be effective" (p. 14) (for an insightful discussion of this work, see Papi & Hiver, 2020). The contribution of the ROAR framework is in adding a motivational dimension—*relevance*—to understandings of the effects and dynamics of mental representations. As Eitam and Higgins (2014) explain, "[t]he principal tenet of ROAR is that the activation of mental representations (externally or internally stimulated), and hence the accessibility of the concepts they represent, will be a function of the *motivational relevance* of those concepts" (p. 142, emphasis added). Representations that relate to goal concepts with abiding importance have what Eitam and Higgins (2014) term "cross-situational" or "chronic" relevance; that is, they "will operate regardless of a person's current task" (p. 142). Although representations of other goals can also operate in ways that generate consistent and stable behavior, they are situationally sensitive to a greater degree, having only transient relevance:

> Given that relevance determines activation, chronic relevance will lead to chronic activation and hence similar cognitions and actions across situations (consistency). Representations with transient relevance will make their appearance "inconsistently" or, rather, in a manner that is highly dependent on their current relevance to the situation at hand.
> (Eitam & Higgins, 2014, p. 142)

The differential effect of goal representations with chronic and transient relevance is illustrated in work investigating the goal-orientations and regulation of highly motivated adult learners of Swedish (Henry et al., 2015; Henry & Davydenko, 2020). While for many of the participants in these studies, development of L2 proficiency constituted a self-concordant goal, only a few had described the learning process as effortless, and of having experienced a state of more or less continual optimal functioning (Henry, et al., 2015). For these learners, who were caught up in a directed motivational current (DMC), we can understand how representations of self-concordant goals involving TL proficiency had *chronic relevance*; that is, they possessed the potential to be consistently activated (even in situations where L2 learning was not in focus). For the other participants (reported on in Henry & Davydenko, 2020), a DMC was not experienced. For these individuals, learning was generally effortful. Some of these learners (Profile I) also had goals that were self-concordant. For the participants in this profile, however, goal representations had *transient relevance*. While high-intensity, enjoyable, and self-affirming goal-directed behavior was reported, these states appeared to be undergirded by more conscious forms of regulation and arose in contexts directly connected to learning (e.g., willingly doing additional tasks, or reading more than was required).

Episodic Future Thinking

One of the topics currently debated in L2 motivation research involves the contribution of vision in understanding motivated behavior (Hiver & Al-Hoorie, 2020a). A central issue involves the difference between experiencing an image of the self-in-the-future that is pleasant, but potentially ineffective in regulating behavior, and one that can trigger sustained effort in L2 learning (Al-Hoorie & Al Shlowiy, 2020). In an expanding body of work investigating future-oriented mental imagery and the effects on current behavior, Arnaud D'Argembeau and his colleagues in the Department of Psychology at the University of Liège have explored the role played by personal goals in *episodic future thinking* (D'Argembeau, 2016, 2020; D'Argembeau & Van der Linden, 2012; Ernst et al., 2018). A form of mental time travel (Michaelian et al., 2016), episodic future thinking is the simulation of future events expected to occur in one's life. It involves "pre-experiencing" the future in ways that enable the individual to imagine what it is like to be in a particular situation, and to mentally envision the settings, people, and interactions.

In this work, a key idea is that for an imagined event to be experienced as truly belonging to a person's future, and to be effective in influencing current behavior, it is not sufficient that a conjured image is representationally vivid or elaborate. Rather, it needs also to be linked in a meaningful way to personally important goals and life expectations. Further, in addition to mentally constructing the scenario of a future event, the event also needs to be autobiographically contextualized within the person's life story. Because it links goal pursuit with vision, and because it explains the influence of personal goals in the temporal organization of imagined life sequences (Ben Malek et al., 2018), episodic future thinking offers a key to understanding the role that vision can play in supporting L2 motivation (Henry, 2020b).

An important feature of episodic future thinking involves the mental trying out of future possibilities, and the experiencing of actions needed to achieve particular outcomes:

> goal representations are thought to be organized in a hierarchy in which higher-order goals (e.g., becoming an artist) determine the content of lower-order goals (e.g., taking painting lessons). Within this framework, episodic future thinking may be conceived as allowing the detailed representation of specific events, plans, and outcomes that are related to higher-order personal goals. In other words, an important function of episodic future thinking may be to provide a detailed (quasi-experiential) representation or simulation of what it would be like to be in a desired end-state, and to mentally try out various steps and envisage potential obstacles in achieving this state. According to this view, personal goals drive and constrain future event representations.
>
> (D'Argembeau, 2016, pp. 202–2)

The mental mapping of pathways and obstacles encompassed in the notion of episodic future thinking is consistent with observations by Taylor et al., (1998), who stress the importance of process simulation for effective regulation, and the need to envision problem-solving alongside goal-accomplishment. Indeed, this is one of the ways that episodic future thinking differs from simply imagining a fictitious future.

In a study by Ernst et al. (2018), connections between goals and mental representations of associated future events, and the qualities of episodic future thoughts prompted by self-concordant and non-concordant goals, were investigated. Findings showed how goal self-concordance facilitated the imagining of future events, and that it could enhance the "realness" of a mental image. When a future event was connected with a self-concordant goal, there was a stronger sense of pre-experiencing the imagined event, a stronger belief that the event would occur, and a stronger sense that the event was integrated with identity motives such as self-esteem, distinctiveness, belonging, efficacy, and meaning. More so than events associated with non-concordant goals, future events associated with self-concordant goals functioned to more adequately fulfil the basic psychological needs of autonomy, competence, and relatedness (Ryan & Deci, 2020). Equally, and in line with findings emphasizing associations between self-concordant goals and well-being (Sheldon & Houser-Marko, 2001), connection with a self-concordant goal strengthened the emotional loading of imagined events, and the emotional intensity of future thoughts.

These findings prompted Ernst and colleagues (2018) to conclude that "the experience of more intense and positive emotions when imagining self-concordant future events may serve to guide and energize behavior in pursuing desired goal states" (p. 34). In the context of debate on the role of vision in L2 motivation, these and other results from D'Argembeau's lab point to the *adaptive* function that episodic future thinking has in goal pursuit, and the ways that imagining future states can prompt "mental simulation of the steps needed to achieve these states" (D'Argembeau & Van der Linden, 2012, p. 1202).

Self-Concordant Goals and Agentic Identities

Linked to both of the above-discussed areas of theory, a third way in which goal self-concordance can offer insights valuable for understanding effective regulation and motivational sustainability in L2 learning involves how a personally important goal can become part of an *agentic identity*. Consistent with the notion that self-concordant goals represent stable and self-defining interests, and that they are "more enduringly energized [and] not just transitory whims" (Sheldon, Prentice & Osin, 2019), personal goals can become embodied in forms of physical action. That is, people who pursue a self-concordant goal can be more likely to define themselves as the "doer of an activity" than people for whom a goal lacks self-concordance (Sheldon, 2014).

In a study developing the notion of the *self-as-doer*—a construct representing the tendency for a person to define themselves as "doer" rather than a "haver" of a goal—Houser-Marko and Sheldon (2006) explored the ways in which an identity focused on personal agency could facilitate goal pursuit. The central premise of this research was that, upon encountering an obstacle, difficulty or failure, an identity as the "doer" of an action or goal could promote perseverance in goal-focused behavior. To investigate this hypothesis, participants in Houser-Marko and Sheldon's (2006) study were invited to turn goals into "doer" verb-phrases. Yielding formulations such as "good grade getter," "non-weight-gainer," "Bible reader," "positive outlooker," "relationship maker," and "emotion controller" (p. 1040), participants then rated their identification with each "doer" phrase. Operationalized in this way, the "self-as-doer" construct predicted longer-term goal investment and mediated the effect of self-concordance on sustained effort. In subsequent research, a self-as-doer identity has been associated with effective regulation, and greater self-efficacy in overcoming barriers (e.g., Brouwer, 2017).

The linking of cognition and action in the "self-as-doer" construct has clear similarities with *implementation intentions* theory. Developed by Gollwitzer and his associates, this theory suggests that actions are successfully facilitated when the concept of action and the future event to which it is directed are mentally connected. These connections can trigger what Gollwitzer et al., (2004) term "an implemental mindset." This mindset "tunes a person to process information related to the implementation of goals" (p. 224) and facilitates implementation-focused actions. However, while implementation intentions and the "self-as-doer" construct are similar in explaining goal-directed acting, in the latter it is the goal's self-concordance that influences effective regulation and facilitates goal pursuit.

Returning to Dörnyei's (2009b) original theorizing of L2 vision, one of the conditions identified as influencing the motivational capacity of the ideal L2 self involves successful incorporation of procedural strategies. As Dörnyei (2009b, p. 37) has made clear, an ideal L2 self is likely to be effective to the degree that it forms "part of a 'package' consisting of an imagery component and a repertoire of appropriate plans, scripts and self-regulatory strategies." However, this condition has not received great attention, and "little is known about what kind of ideal L2 selves are likely to translate into self-motivated engagement in L2 learning" (Hessel, 2015, p. 104). If to be effective in regulating behavior it is necessary to position the representation of a desired future state within a context of currently pertaining obstacles—as conceptualized in the notion of *mental contrasting* (Wittleder et al., 2020) and captured in the "self-as-doer" construct (Houser-Marko & Sheldon, 2006)—then a factor influencing the motivational capacity of an ideal L2 self is likely to involve the degree of self-concordance of the overall goal of

L2 learning. Indeed, it might be that an ideal L2 self can be fully instantiated only if the goal with which it is associated represents an outcome with a threshold degree of personal importance.

Conclusion

I began this chapter by noting that surprisingly little research has investigated L2 learners' goals. As McEown and Oga-Baldwin (2019) have observed, this means that researchers interested in "translating, localizing, or otherwise replicating the work done on goals [in educational psychology] have an open, but theoretically and empirically grounded, field for exploration" (p. 7). With this in mind, I suggested that one area particularly deserving investigation involves the *qualities* of language learners' goals. Building on the recognition that not all self-initiated goals are personal, and that goals which align with a person's enduring interests, values, and beliefs can promote motivational persistence (Sheldon, 2014), I argued that the theory of goal self-concordance can provide a key to understanding why some people tackle L2 learning in a positive spirit, and are able to maintain energy over time, while others founder and are more easily distracted by competing activities.

It would seem that there is much useful work to be done exploring the nature of language learners' goals, and the effects that goal-quality has on regulation. In his book-length mapping of the innovations and challenges in contemporary L2 motivation, Dörnyei (2020) identifies three frontiers at which exploration seems likely to take place: the development of understandings of unconscious motivation, the continued investigation of the role of vision, and research into long-term motivation and persistence. At each of these frontiers, examination of the quality of learners' goals and their influences on language learning behavior would seem to have central importance. In this respect, goal self-concordance (Sheldon, 2014), and the constructs and theories with which it is related, can make valuable contributions. Motivational relevance (Eitam & Higgins, 2010), episodic future thinking (D'Argembeau, 2016, 2020), and the "self-as-doer" construct (Houser-Marko & Sheldon, 2006) each provide a novel lens through which the influences of goal qualities can profitably be studied. It is hoped that this chapter might promote such research.

CHAPTER 7

Self-Determined Motivation and Engagement in Language: A Dialogic Process

W. L. Quint Oga-Baldwin and Emiko Hirosawa

Background: What's So Funny about Self-Determined Motivation?

A major problem of the twentieth century can be traced back to the use and misuse of the ideas of self-determination. While the details of this rhetological problem are better left to a historical analysis, there remains a holdover reticence in intercultural studies to recognize concepts and constructs related to the idea of self-determination (see Chirkov et al. 2003). Often, the question is whether self-determination theory (Ryan and Deci 2017) can effectively describe the nuances of local culture, with their own unique and often interdependent views and idiosyncrasies (King and McInerney 2014). According to this view, isn't self-determination theory just another peculiarly Western-educated industrialized rich democratic (WEIRD; Henrich et al. 2010) idea, now being imposed on the world through English language education? How does the seemingly "American imperialist" idea of self-determination apply to teaching and learning any new language in Ho Chi Minh City, Moscow, Havana, or Tehran?

For nearly forty years, self-determination theory (SDT; Ryan and Deci 2017) has worked *against* the idea of a zero-sum, "my rights versus yours" approach to the concept of motivating individuals to move in a specific direction. Some would have us believe that the autonomous motivation of the teacher to achieve a goal (completing a curriculum, for example) impinges on the autonomous motivation of students (for instance, to play and have fun). Instead, SDT posits that by properly working with learners' cultural expectations, meeting their needs for positive human interaction and success, and nurturing their desire to learn, teachers can get better engagement and ultimately better learning. A growing body of self-determination theory research from around the globe corroborates the idea that nurturing basic psychological needs and supporting individuals' inner motivational resources can indeed have positive effects across cultural boundaries (Chen et al. 2015; Reeve et al. 2013). Self-determined motivation and its corollary mini-theories form an interdependent whole, much as all parts of the modern world work together. When needs are thwarted and controlled in one area, the negative effects spread throughout the whole system; when these needs are met in one place, this can have similar unforeseen positive effects elsewhere.

Learning a language requires a similar degree of interplay in many parts of the system. As recent work suggests (Papi and Hiver 2020), the motivation to learn a language is complex, nuanced, and the many interworking pieces can influence the whole in unexpected ways. Self-determination theory is consistent with this perspective, offering insight at both the macro-group and micro-intraindividual levels (Ryan & Deci, 2017). Each of the mini-theories offers an empirically based set of assumptions, measures, and hypotheses on how language learners are motivated. According to SDT, language learners' engagement in learning tasks comes at the intersection of prior motives and environmental influences (Oga-Baldwin, Nakata, Parker, & Ryan, 2017). This dialogic process focuses on creating mutual understanding, where learners respond to teachers' instruction, and teachers' in turn match how students respond (Jang, Reeve, & Halusic, 2016; Skinner, Furrer, Marchand, & Kindermann, 2008).

Self-determination theory offers a set of interrelated, interdependent hypothetical relationships among different aspects of language learners, their teachers and peers, and learning tasks. Though not a specific theory of language motivation, self-determination theory offers a number of advantages for studies of language education. Primarily, this generalized perspective allows for the creation of testable hypotheses for the relationships between different aspects of motivation, based on studies of language along with findings from related fields. The key difference between SDT and other language-specific motivation theories is how SDT can draw immediate parallels with other skill learning, such as teaching (Reeve & Jang, 2006), music (Evans, McPherson, & Davidson, 2012), sports (Ntoumanis & Standage, 2009), and coaching (Bhavsar et al., 2019). By integrating this perspective with the existing literature on language learning, we can achieve a deeper and richer understanding of both general human motivation and domain-specific language motivation.

Self-Determination Theory: A Concise Overview

The central ideas of self-determination theory focus on helping learners develop *intrinsic motivation*, that is, motivation coming from an inherent interest and enjoyment of the task (Ryan & Deci, 2017). Intrinsic motivation comes from within the person. The importance of intrinsic motivation in education has been well researched. One meta-analysis on SDT in educational settings (Taylor et al., 2014) indicated that intrinsic motivation was a significant predictor of achievement, a result corroborated in later studies of diverse American high school students (Froiland & Worrell, 2016).

At the same time, not every motive comes from the desire to engage in a task for its own sake; when some tasks are not perceived to be enjoyable, their impetus is likely to come from external sources. The diverse motives that arise from outside of a learner exist on a continuum of *extrinsic motivation* (Ryan & Deci, 2017), described by **organismic integration theory**. This mini-theory describes the different, concurrent motives that may regulate learners' language learning motivation. Fully *external regulation* of motivation is the desire to avoid punishments or gain short-term rewards. In education, this happens when teachers attempt to motivate by giving stickers, stars, and grades for good behavior (perhaps using the target language), or making rules and apply punishments for bad behavior (not participating in class). Other steps on the continuum move from fully external regulation. Motives that come from guilt, shame, or a desire to please others (parents or peers) with their language performance are called *introjected regulation*. More internalized motives may come from a desire to do well, such as being able to use a foreign language, titled *identified regulation*. Finally, SDT describes how learners may feel a sense of integration, in which using the foreign language is a part of their conception of self, labeled *integrated regulation*. A predominance of motivation across each of the above steps moves learners toward more internalized, *intrinsic regulation*. Completely outside of this process, *amotivation* indicates the lack of desire to learn the language, perhaps due to lack of value, excessive difficulty, or burdensome time costs (Fryer, Bovee, & Nakao, 2014; Legault, Green-Demers, & Pelletier, 2006).

As an example of how students experience each form of regulation as the primary form of motive, we offer a vignette of a student who begins learning Spanish in elementary school. He does not have a choice in the matter; classes are held once each week for half an hour. Though he enjoys the Spanish songs they sing in class and likes practicing the vocabulary, he mostly participates so that he can get a gold star in the Spanish learning passport that records students' daily progress (external regulation). In junior high school, he is given a choice of learning French or Spanish, but an older student he looks up to tells him that Spanish is what "cool people" study. He wants to be accepted by those older peers and follows their example. Simultaneously, he wishes to show his family and teachers that he is a good student (introjected regulation). As he reaches high school, he begins feeling a desire to learn the language in order to be able to really use it in real world situations. He sees the language as a tool for communicating with Spanish speakers in various social situations, and travels to a Spanish-speaking country for several weeks during his summer vacation to learn more (identified regulation). Finally, he enters university and decides to pursue a degree in Spanish language, now feeling that the language is part of who he is (integrated regulation). Along the way in his studies, he has had enjoyable experiences that bring him closer to seeing learning Spanish as a worthwhile task in and of itself (intrinsic regulation). Though at each of these points other forms of regulation may also play a role (e.g., this student may also want to get good grades to please his parents all throughout; he may also be aware of school rules about necessary baseline academic performance), these motives are not the primary drivers of his engagement in Spanish class. He has integrated the external motives into his person and made learning the language ever more intrinsically motivated.

This poses a question: what was it that fed this student's intrinsic motivation? In describing more about this student's learning experience, we attempt to show how the six mini-theories (starting with organismic integration theory and continuing below) weave the different interactions between the person and environment together to explain how this student was able to proceed in a positive motivational trajectory.

SDT posits that intrinsic motives arise when learners' *basic need for competence, relatedness, and autonomy* are met (Ryan & Deci, 2017). When learners feel competent at a task, they are likely to continue (Bandura, 1997). When they feel connected with the people around them, they are more likely to engage in learning (Furrer & Skinner, 2003). When they feel a sense of purpose, relevance, and choice in their behavior, they are likely to work willingly (Jang, Reeve, Ryan, & Kim, 2009). Together, these three concepts form the basis for **basic psychological needs theory**. Robust and growing evidence for the validity of the three basic needs in diverse intercultural settings shows their universal nature in promoting intrinsic motivation and well-being (Chen et al., 2015; Chirkov, 2009). While some of the ideas, especially the relationship between choice and autonomy (Iyengar & Lepper, 1999), are controversial, these questions have largely been laid to rest across cultural settings (Chirkov, 2009). Important to recognize here is that choice is not synonymous with autonomy and does not necessarily fortify a sense of autonomy in all settings (Katz & Assor, 2006). Though some studies do indeed indicate differential functions of the needs across cultures (Joe, Hiver, & Al-Hoorie, 2017), findings continue to show competence, relatedness, and autonomy are interconnected and important nutriments for intrinsic motivation (Nicholson & Putwain, 2016).

Taking from the Spanish learner explained above, it can be assumed that he has experienced a sense of competence, relatedness, and autonomy need satisfaction throughout his learning. When he succeeds at Spanish in his elementary school class and correctly produces the songs he is taught, his need for competence may be met. He feels relatedness in junior high school when he is accepted into a group and develops close friendships with students also taking Spanish. Finally, he feels autonomous when he sees value in learning the language in high school and chooses to use the language with a community of native speakers in their own country. These experiences accumulate and provide him with reserves of intrinsic motives for learning the language, while continually experiencing need satisfaction supports his motivation going forward.

As to how language teachers can help students develop intrinsic motivation, the key is in the quality of interaction with their students. These interactions become resources that satisfy learners' psychological needs. Need support, especially *autonomy support*, forms a crucial part of **cognitive evaluation theory**. By providing instruction that nurtures learners' inner motivational resources (Reeve & Jang, 2006), teachers can help learners develop a sense of ownership and integration with a new language. Through *autonomy support*, teachers across the world can work with learners and help their students feel invested and agentic in the process of learning the language by teaching them in a familiar and comfortable fashion (Jang et al., 2016). *Structure* provides the guidance that learners need to succeed in class, helping them stay on task and achieve understanding (McEown & Oga-Baldwin, 2019; Oga-Baldwin & Nakata, 2015). Finally, *involvement* describes how teachers develop quality relationships with students (Furrer & Skinner, 2003). Research has shown that it is not one but all of these elements together that promotes need satisfaction and engagement (Jang, Reeve, & Deci, 2010).

In his high school Spanish classes, our example learner has a teacher who recognizes the class' interest in a Spanish-language musical artist. This teacher chooses a song by this artist as a way to illustrate a particular piece of language. She sets up a fill-in-the-blank activity by listening, and makes certain the students will be able to complete the task with an appropriate word bank. She then helps the students see other uses for this vocabulary and grammar with examples from other related songs. By using this material, the teacher is supporting her students in two ways; first, she is signaling that she recognizes the students' interest, which shows a personal connection; second, she shows that she is willing to support them by teaching in the students' preferred way. This choice of material might signal both involvement and autonomy support. Further, by setting up the assignment in a clear and achievable fashion, she appropriately structures the activity to deepen the class' understanding of Spanish language. At the end, the high school learners in this Spanish class leave feeling that Spanish can be fun, interesting, and worth knowing.

So where can intrinsic motivation in learning a language take us? **Goal contents theory** will help us answer this question. According to goal contents theory, the quality of learners' goals, intrinsic or extrinsic, will largely determine how long learners will persist at a task. Learners' *intrinsic goals* satisfy students' basic needs that will improve their well-being and guide intrinsic motives. In language education they might orient learners toward making friends across cultures, travelling to new places, enjoying movies, music, and other cultural artifacts, or open new avenues for learning (Vansteenkiste, Lens, & Deci, 2006). *Extrinsic goals* are those set on short-term rewards. Learners may follow peer pressure, seek to make money, or want praise from friends and parents. While these goals can motivate in the short term, they also can limit learners' ability to express themselves in the long term. These goals are an outgrowth of the organismic integration process (see above) described in the mini-theory of the same name and nurtured by the other mini-theories (Ryan & Deci, 2017).

From our story of the Spanish learner, perhaps his study abroad experience in high school required him to pass a language test in order to go to the country of his choice. If he does not get the required score, he will not be able to go, making this a high-stakes testing situation. While this motivates him to learn the grammar and vocabulary for the test, he neglects listening and speaking. He achieves the necessary score to go on his study abroad trip, but in the interim between gaining the required score and his flight overseas he has begun to feel complacent. He feels that passing the test meant he had sufficient skill to live in the country of his choice, but learns upon arrival that though he can accurately conjugate all the verbs in all of the tenses, he struggles with daily communication! He now reassesses his goals, not just wanting to pass tests, but also seeking to understand the complex nuances of communicating with Spanish speakers in this country. He creates new goals to be able to effectively survive in this new environment and sets about trying to learn the vocabulary and skills he needs to achieve these goals.

Our fictional learner seems to be quite positively oriented toward the process of learning a new language. His personality is one where he seeks challenges and is guided by an inner compass that pushes him toward learning. He has setbacks and struggles along the way, but largely works with his own initiative to motivate himself. Within the framework of **causality orientations theory** (Ryan & Deci, 2017; Weinstein, Przybylski, & Ryan, 2012), this young man seems *autonomously oriented*. He is not content to be controlled by outside forces and requirements, but instead resets his orientations according to his environment. Language learners of this type prefer to be self-starters, seeking their own path and self-regulating their learning processes (McEown, Noels, & Saumure, 2014). Other language learners tend more toward a *controlled orientation*. These learners are often more passive, preferring to take direction from outside. They are more likely to respond to social pressure or external rewards (Ryan & Deci, 2017). Important for language learning, they may also show less positive attitudes toward other cultures (Duriez, 2011). Finally, an *impersonal orientation* may indicate that the learner does not believe any aspect of learning a language is within their control, perhaps because they feel failure is likely (Amoura, Berjot, Gillet, & Altintas, 2013; Kwan, Hooper, Magnan, & Bryan, 2011). These orientations represent a personality-centered approach to motivation (McAdams & Pals, 2006), where learners' orientations offer a glimpse into their more generalized functioning (Duriez, 2011).

Another essential question of motivation to learn a language is: Who motivates us? What kinds of people in our lives motivate us toward language learning, and what is the nature of our connection to those individuals? **Relationships motivation theory** (Ryan & Deci, 2017) indicates that the relationships that meaningfully satisfy basic needs will help language learners to develop strong, lasting motivation. Given that much of language learning happens through the communication between individuals (e.g., parent–child, friends, teacher–student), it follows that the quality of those relationships will change the way that learners are motivated (Guay, Ratelle, Larose, Vallerand, & Vitaro, 2013; Ratelle, Simard, & Guay, 2012). High-quality interpersonal relationships between individuals and within groups depend upon the individuals' ability to experience not only positivity or regard but also respect for autonomy (Ryan & Deci, 2017). More negatively, sometimes parents and teachers withhold affection when learners do not perform in a specified or desired manner. This practice is labeled *conditional regard*, and is associated with feelings of shame, fluctuations in self-esteem, poor coping skills, low self-worth, and resentment toward parents (Assor et al., 2004). Teacher conditional regard is also negatively associated with perceived psychological need satisfaction (Kaplan, 2018).

From our example, the Spanish language student develops close friendships with the host family during his summer study abroad program. Though he is older than the children, they come to enjoy showing him local customs and helping him achieve greater day-to-day proficiency in the language; he likewise enjoys sharing his knowledge and experience gleaned from greater life experience and school learning. By communicating with the father and mother, he begins to develop an understanding how to interact with different levels of social formality. In this multigenerational household, his younger host siblings model the appropriate forms of address and respect when they address their grandparents. Though he is often out of line with the local culture, his family is tolerant and patient, explaining to him his mistakes and helping him get the appropriate feedback to navigate the sometimes complex social interactions only visible to longtime insiders. Upon returning home, he often talks with his host family online. In university, he credits the connections he forged between himself and this family as one of the reasons why he wishes to pursue a degree in Spanish.

Though an idealized account, the vignettes attached to this discussion of a Spanish learner represent actual experiences of language learners we have known through the years. Each instance of this language learners' life story can be used to represent one of the mini-theories. These ideas overlap and intertwine—throughout, the ideas of each mini-theory can be seen even during the discussions of the other theories. According to self-determination theory, mechanisms by which motivation grows and flowers are all related, forming a dynamic whole that may be used to predict individuals' actions.

Predicting Engagement: Sweet Harmony

The final piece of this puzzle is engagement: the outcome state of action toward learning (see Hiver, this volume; Mercer, this volume). In studying motivation, we often seek to use our understanding of how students' internal states and reactions to the world predict their actual behavior (Oga-Baldwin, 2019). Engagement, the actions that students take to improve their language ability, offers a clear outcome for students' internal, invisible needs, desires, drives, and motives.

Recent perspectives (Oga-Baldwin, 2019) have proposed that engagement is not only an outcome but a dynamic midpoint, acting as an intermediary between the person and their environment. Work within the self-determination theory paradigm (Oga-Baldwin et al., 2017) has shown that engagement results from influences within each student (need satisfaction, intrinsic motivation) and from the social environment created by the teacher (autonomy support, clear structure). At the same time, studies have also shown that what students do in class influences how teachers react; teachers respond positively to more engaged students, and negatively to less engaged students (Skinner et al., 2008). Likewise, more engaged students are likely to feel more intrinsically motivated after they have engaged with the learning material; that is, actions in class predict their later intrinsic motivation (Oga-Baldwin et al., 2017; Oga-Baldwin & Nakata, 2017). More engaged students also show reciprocally higher self-efficacy, need satisfaction, and mastery goal orientation over time (Reeve & Lee, 2014). In all the studies mentioned above, engaged learners achieved higher test scores and grades.

An important dynamic input in the language classroom is how learners make the learning a foreign language their own. Many perspectives focus on the idea of learner agency (Mercer, 2011), and how language learners make the learning environment one that works for them is an important step in this process. The idea of agentic engagement (Reeve, 2013) helps define how learners generally, and language learners more specifically, contribute to make the classroom climate effective for their learning. Both through positively responding to teachers (Skinner et al., 2008) and through attempting to make the classroom environment match their needs (Reeve & Tseng, 2011), learners dialogically influence the classroom learning environments. The dialectical interaction between learners' and teachers' actions can help create the virtuous circles (or vicious cycles) of motivation in classrooms.

By the time the example Spanish language learner described above has reached university, he had experienced numerous positive and negative Spanish learning experiences. What primed his motivation was the sense of activity that came with his earliest memories learning Spanish; his elementary school class was a place where he could use the language and have fun. He willingly participated in class, sang songs and played language games, and developed very basic fundamentals with the language. In lower secondary school, he did his homework and paid attention in class, taking notes and actively practicing when given the chance. In high school, his teacher paid attention to his and his classmates' interest, giving him many opportunities to use the language. When given the chance to study abroad, he took it, and pursued opportunities to learn. Finally, when choosing a major he reflected on his language learning and how it had met his needs throughout his young life. By building a habit of active language learning, he created a path toward success.

Conclusions: The Strong and the Trusted

In this chapter, we have sought to outline the basic ideas of self-determination theory as a general theory of motivation, and illustrate how they apply to language learning. The six interdependent mini-theories relate to learners' engagement in a dynamic fashion, with the numerous elements inside the learners' minds and from the world at large working together to create motivation and action. According to this perspective, learners develop their motivation in response to the environment, to their previous actions and habits, and to their inner worlds. The elements of the intra-individual motives, the learning environment, and their interplay are common to many of the current language learning theories (Dörnyei & Ryan, 2015; MacIntyre & Doucette, 2010). The development of motivation for learning a language shares much in common with education, parenting, child development, and intercultural studies, as well as less obvious fields such as music, physical education and sports, and management, and ignoring findings from these fields is to ignore potentially insightful parallels. Though at first glance it carries the baggage of a culturally specific framework, SDT's range and broad applicability indicate that it can help define mechanisms and hypotheses for how language learners are motivated and thus how languages can be learned.

PART THREE

Selves Approaches

CHAPTER 8

Using the Self as a Basis for a Motivation System: Is It Worth the Trouble?

Peter D. MacIntyre

In 2015 I had the privilege of speaking at a wonderful conference in Adana, Turkey, on the self in language learning. My talk, "The self and its illusions," was intended as something of a caution within the overall theme of the conference. In the present chapter, as in the Adana talk, I want to share my ambivalent relationship with the concept of self, as applied to language learning. On one hand, the self seems to be a necessary concept in any psychology of language learning that discusses how issues of culture, identity, motivation, emotion, and so on influence language learning and use. How can one do that without reference to the self? However, there is more than enough reason to be concerned with using the concept of the self as a centerpiece for language learning theory and research. The conceptualization of the self is, and has always been, complex and problematic (Damasio, 2010).

The Trouble with Self

Psychology takes on subject matter that can be notoriously difficult to define and measure for research purposes. Prime among the offenders would be concepts such as the mind, consciousness, and the self. Recent years has seen application of physiological, and especially brain-based explanations for psychological concepts. In the first footnote to his excellent book *The Self Comes to Mind*, neuroscientist Antonio Damasio (2010) tells a story of his conversation with Francis Crick, the famed geneticist. They were talking about Stuart Sutherland,

> a British psychologist famous for his dismissive and devastating remarks about varied issues and colleagues, [who] had just published in his Dictionary of Psychology a startling definition that Francis proceeded to read: "Consciousness is a fascinating but elusive phenomenon; it is impossible to specify what it is, what it does, or why it evolved. Nothing worth reading has been written about it."
>
> (p. 337)

If Sutherland said nothing worth reading has been written about consciousness, what biting criticism might he apply to the self? I tracked down a copy of Sutherland's (1996) dictionary, eager to see his commentary. To my disappointment, Sutherland either neglected or chose not to define the self as a stand-alone concept. Then a thought occurred to me—I wonder if this is the comment—does Sunderland's omission signify that the self is even more troublesome to define than consciousness? If so, is it really a good idea to turn to the self as the core concept for a motivation theory?

In a way, my own background in motivation for language learning is similar to that of the second language acquisition (SLA) field itself. My PhD supervisor was R. C. Gardner, author of the influential socio-educational model (Gardner, 1985, 2010). The socio-educational model and the theory of motivation that it reflects have been going strong for some sixty years (Al-Hoorie & MacIntyre, 2020). Prior critics of the model argued that it was **too** influential, that it was limiting readers' thinking about the sources of motivation in SLA (e.g., Crooks & Schmidt, 1991; Oxford & Shearin, 1994). One of those critics was Dörnyei (1994b), whose own model, the L2 Motivation Self System (L2MSS), might be considered the dominant perspective at present (Thorsen, Henry & Cliffordson, 2020). Although there has been an expansion of motivation and related concepts (Lamb et al., 2019), it is argued below that the L2MSS itself is possibly too influential.

Dörnyei (2005, 2009a) proposed the L2MSS with three core concepts: the ideal L2 self, the ought-to self, and L2 learning experience. Details of the model are reviewed elsewhere (see Gonzalez, this volume; Papi, this volume). There is little doubt that the model has been successful in orienting the field toward the self (Boo et al., 2015; Csizer, 2020; Dörnyei & Ryan, 2015). As research on the L2MSS was getting under way, we expressed several reasons for caution, including a possible proliferation of "selves" in the field (MacIntyre, Mackinnon, & Clément, 2009a). A meta-analysis by Al-Hoorie (2018) suggests that such a troublesome proliferation is under way, the language motivation field is witnessing more and more selves being introduced, including anti-ought-to, rebellious, imposed, bilingual, multilingual, private, public, possible, and probable selves, but without sufficient attention to their construct validity or their overlap. In fact, it has become fashionable to introduce a new construct and suffix it with a "self" even when existing constructs seem to exist (e.g., anti-ought-to self versus reactance, and feared L2 self versus fear of failure). Adding a new dimension to an existing construct (e.g., L2 reactance) may be more appropriate than introducing yet another "self".

(p. 738)

Although the L2MSS model has proven popular, even dominant, in thinking about language learning motivation, there are questions about its value in predicting language outcomes as well as its theoretical stance.

Setting aside for a moment the strong overlap between the Gardner (2010) and Dörnyei (2005) theoretical models, and concern whether two models restate with different emphasis the same basic idea of identifying with a language community (Claro, 2020), a deeper question is whether it has been worth the trouble to invoke the self as a central concept. For all its explanatory appeal, the self at its core is something of an illusion.

The Self and Its Illusions

There is an image that I (and many other speakers) like to use in talks about the self, a meme of an orange kitten looking into a mirror, seeing his reflected image not as it is but as a full-grown lion (there are dozens of variations on the theme available on the internet). The image is sometimes accompanied by a quote, "what matters most is how you see yourself," meant to inspire confidence and the motivational pull of desirable future possibilities. This is the very foundation of the imagined ideal possible self central to the L2MSS. Given some thought, the image might not be clear-cut and inspirational. It might simply be showing a horribly defective mirror or (reading right-to-left) metaphorically represent the adult lion's window into his past, and it could be showing a psychotic delusion. What if this might not be a mirror at all but a drive-through snack bar for lions—run little kitten, run! Tongue-in-cheek interpretations aside, this meme captures both the utility and frustration of the self as a concept: the self is based in imagery.

Damasio (2010) outlined a serious attempt to deal with the hard problem of defining the self in the context of the mind and consciousness. To summarize his theory, starting from his perspective as a neuroscientist, Damasio sees the self as based on patterns of neuronal activity that create mental imagery. The images are assembled representations of the internalized consequences of the body's reactions to present experience; our brains create integrated imagery based on our interaction with the world around us. These reactions form simple emotions and complex feelings associated with events that become encoded over time as additional imagery, modified on a continuous basis. Through experience we come to remember our past and anticipate our future, constantly interpreting present experience within present, past, and future imagery. To facilitate the process of fusing past, present and future, images are collected into narratives that further combine into our autobiographical sense of self. Our engagements with the world around us are done from a unique perspective or standpoint reflected by, and in, the body. In a healthy adult, there is a sense of continuously being the same person and having the same body we've always had, even as we grow and change over time. This sense of continuity is combined with both feelings of ownership (a sense of what is "me" and "mine") and agency ("me" being the origin of my actions) (see Al-Hoorie, 2015). The composite imagery from past, present and future mixes together continuously, as "(t)he self comes to mind in the form of images relentlessly telling a story" of engagements with the world and its mental representations (Damasio, 2010, p. 216). Because the imagery is built continuously from birth, it becomes complex and multilayered, interpreted, and reinterpreted in the context of the self—even as it is constantly under construction. Further adding to the complexity, the self is both the knower and the object being known. Funder (2010), looking at the self and its role in personality, said, "beneath all of the real, ideal, ought, and relational selves, it still seems that deep down, a single self must be running the whole show ... (e)xternal appearances, attitudes, and behaviors change across situations and over time, but the one who does the experiencing is still in there someplace, watching (and perhaps directing) everything" (p. 687). Markusand Wurf (1987) said that the self, once thought of as a "singular, static, lump-like entity has become a multi-dimensional, multifaceted dynamic structure that is systematically implicated in all aspects of social information processing" (p. 301).

Like the kitten-lion image, the self's imagery is not a recording of one's life events but an interpretation of them. It is made and remade from images and imaginary experience, conflating past and present with future imagery. It is important to note that the self-as-knower is motivated to adapt, defend, and protect the autobiographical sense of continuity. Because it is continuously adapting, the self becomes layered, sometimes contradictory, and extraordinarily complex, wherein everything in memory and imagination may interact with the core sense of self and its strivings. Further, being rooted in one's own specific perspective, subject to layers upon layers of potentially biased interpretation, the self is more than a little prone to error. Damasio (2010) notes Mark Twain's observation that truth is stranger than fiction because fiction must follow a logic to be believable; the self is not so constrained. An individual's autobiography is best viewed as a combination of fiction and nonfiction, part experiential image and part imagination.

I would suggest that most motivation SLA researchers would prefer to think that their theories and observations as non-fiction, making the imaginary elements of self potentially problematic. Every cognitive psychology textbook will list myriad ways in which cognition is biased, but the most comprehensive list I have seen is on a Wikipedia page: https://en.wikipedia.org/wiki/List_of_cognitive_biases.

The page lists approximately 200 cognitive, social, and memory biases. There certainly is overlap and redundancy in the list, and not all biases are equally relevant to the way the self operates. But given potential interactions among two or more biases, there seems to be no end to the ways in which our sense of self and the world is or can be distorted. In SLA, MacIntyre et al. (1997) reported that anxious learners systematically underestimate, and confident learners overestimate, their second language ability. Building these distortions continuously into layers of the self over time, combining past, present, and future imagery, suggests that there is a lot here for researchers to tease out in any study using the self as its cornerstone.

Approximately ten years ago, we searched the PSYCHINFO database found slightly over 100,000 references to the self in the titles of articles (MacIntyre et al., 2009a). That same search today turned up 150,000 references that include the word self in the title. In 2009 we printed 50 concepts related to the self (ibid.); today we could easily offer 100 or more. Not only is the self an impossibly complex concept, it has produced an impossibly complex literature. To prove psychology has a sense of irony (if not a sense of humor), the literature includes the concept of "the impossible self" (Pizzolato, 2007).

Although there has been some proliferation of self-related concepts in the SLA literature, the original tripartite conceptualization of the L2MSS has remained robust over the years, despite a series of issues that remain largely unaddressed. The core motivational process believed to underlie the motivational effect of possible selves is a discrepancy between the present self and an imagined/future/ideal self. This discrepancy remains largely untested in SLA research, even to this day (MacIntyre, Mackinnon & Clément, 2009b; Thorsen, et al., 2020). Instead, research on the L2MSS has focused on the relative positivity of the ideal self-image, leading Al-Hoorie (2018) to suggest renaming it *the imagined self*. Almost all of the available studies use imagined effort as the criterion variable (i.e., the part of language learning that motivation is predicting). Although the imagined self predicts imagined effort very well, the model needs to be more firmly grounded in observable learning behaviors and language outcomes (Al-Hoorie, 2018; Dörnyei & Ushioda, 2011, p. 200; Gardner, 2010). Further, the ought-to L2 self reflects the sense of obligations that a learner believes that important other people (e.g., their parents) have for them. The available evidence suggests that this self-guide is weaker than ideal L2 self and the process of internalizing the beliefs of others is not specified (Dörnyei, 2020). In addition, it seems critically important to assess not only the strength of imagined expectations held by other people but, more importantly, the learner's volitional acceptance of those edicts. The third aspect of the L2MSS, L2 experience, is the most under-theorized component. Originally meant to capture the continuity of experience over time—nothing predicts the future as well as the past—in practice, L2 experience has become almost synonymous with L2 attitudes (Dörnyei, 2020). Although Dörnyei (2020) has not abandoned the L2MSS, future research seems likely to offer it a more circumscribed role in the literature on motivation processes than it presently claims.

Innovations and Challenges

To his credit, Dörnyei (2020) recently has produced an insightful analysis of some of the challenging issues that remain outstanding for motivation theory beyond (but including) the L2MSS. Every theory grows as research moves forward and Dörnyei's (2020) book is well worth reading. In the first half of the book he summarizes eleven motivational challenges and innovative attempts to deal with them. The second half of the book deals with three research frontiers, specific issues that recur in studies of motivation in SLA: unconscious motives, long-term motivation, and the issue of vision. Dörnyei digs into the complexity of motivation but does not arrive at an expanded or reconceptualized L2MSS. Therefore, it is interesting that in the concluding chapter for the book Dörnyei seems to acknowledge the limitations of the L2MSS as a framework by noting taking vision as an overarching concept. "L2 motivation research has opened the door into this direction [vision] and the outcome, the L2MSS, has proved to be successful. However, vision/mental imagery has even more to offer the field of SLA as a whole, from memory enhancement to the teaching of various language skills" (Dörnyei, 2020, p. 167). The text reflects something of a disconnect between the specificity of the L2MSS with its three components and the wide-ranging issues being raised throughout the book; ultimately that is a good thing because it expands thinking about L2 motivation beyond the three familiar elements of the L2MSS.

To move forward, Dörnyei's (2020) discussion of self-concordance theory both addresses the challenge of long-term motivation and helps to contextualize the L2MSS within the description of the self offered by Damasio (2010). Drawing on the work of Sheldon and colleagues, Dörnyei hits the nail on the head in discussing self-concordant goals. Dörnyei (2020) says,

> a self-concordant goal is self appropriate *in a deep sense*, representing a person's enduring interests and passions as well as his/her central values and beliefs (Sheldon & Elliot, 1999). Self-concordance therefore concerns

a *deep-seated* personal meaning that is in alignment with strongly held convictions.

(pp. 137–8, emphasis added)

If we limit the discussion of the self to concerns that fit this strongly worded description, we will have found an enduring role for the self in SLA.

Is the Self Worth the Trouble?

Given all of the above concerns over theoretical and methodological issues, including frustration over the seemingly endless possibilities of proliferating self-related concepts, there is merit in understanding the self. The self provides a reflection of the invariants people have discovered in their own social behavior that actively affects how they process information. In brief, the self is defensive and resistant to change. If theorists such as Damasio (and Freud before him) are correct, and they don't have to be fully correct to have made a good point, the idea of a deep-seated and defensive self that has difficulty separating fantasy from reality can be quite problematic for language learning in some situations but facilitating in other contexts.

As a concept we cannot and should not leave the self behind or ignore it in favor of new flavor of the month concepts. However, we should be realistic in limiting its applicability to the situations in which it is most likely to be appropriate. Specifically, considering the definition of the self described above, the self applies best to those situations in which the past, present, and future all are integrated and highly relevant within consciousness, situations in which one's view of themselves as a continuous entity matters. Researchers using the self as a major theoretical construct should be able to answer the question, "Why would the self, as big and complex as it is, as full of memory, experience, and imagination as it is, be relevant to the situation in which I am doing research?" Where SLA research on motivation is more circumscribed with lower stakes, the self is less relevant because it does not come to mind *in situ* (MacIntyre & Serroul, 2015). In contexts where a study can justify why such a big concept would be applicable, then the self is quite likely to be a topic worth studying.

In our research with musicians playing traditional Celtic music, some of whom were Gaelic speakers, we were struck with the intensity of the experiences they described (MacIntyre, Sparling & Baker, 2017). Both Gardner's concept of integrativeness and Dörnyei's L2MSS offered some explanatory power, but we had to adjust the intensity and expand the breadth of the conceptualization of the concepts, to bring the kind of emphasis Sheldon's (2014) idea of self-concordance brings. In place of discussing beliefs and cognition, we suggested these heritage learners had *convictions*, in place of affect we argued that they displayed *passions*, and in place of the future L2 self we proposed they had a sense of a *Rooted L2 Self* that connected learners' language future to their own past, as well as the past of their ancestors, and the physical place in which they lived. For the musicians we interviewed, language and music are connected to their physical home and its history, as well as their understanding of their own place in that history. They were consciously aware of the relationships among past, present, and future language development, and that their language learning has implications for the future of the language itself because it is spoken by so few people. In other words, for the interviewees, the Gaelic language learning was extraordinarily important to who they are. Their self-concept was front and center. In other contexts, where in one might be completing a language task that is not particularly self-involved or taking a course simply to fulfil a language requirement, the self would not be as relevant and other motivational concepts likely would have better explanatory power.

Conclusion

In conclusion, Dörnyei (2005) proposed the L2MSS with three main constituents: the ideal L2 self, the ought-to L2 self, and language learning experience. The choice to base a system of motivation on "the self" was a bold move; the self is one of the most notoriously nebulous concepts in the social sciences. Early in the development of the L2MSS, my colleagues and I (MacIntyre, et al., 2009a, 2009b) offered some words of encouragement, but also a series of cautions about the self as a central concept in a motivation theory in general, and a language learning theory in particular.

On the one hand, the self has been a central concept in psychology for decades and it generated an enormous amount of research. But on the other hand, in all of psychology, there is hardly a more difficult concept to define and describe in writing. Although this brief chapter outlines some of the concerns about the self, it should be clear that, applied to situations that really matter, where one's core identity is bound to language, the concept provides an important perspective. Dörnyei (2020) opened the door to locating the L2MSS within broader issues, such as vision and long-term motives. There is a lot to work out with respect to the issues raised by Dörnyei (2020), too many interesting possibilities to address here. However, when combining Dörnyei's (2020) recent work with Damasio (2010) explanation of the self, I would suggest L2 motivation research limit the applicability of the L2MSS to situations in which the self obviously becomes a prominent and salient concern to the conscious mind because only under such conditions does the conceptual complexity of the self seem worth the trouble.

CHAPTER 9

The L2 Motivational Self System: Using the Selves in the Classroom

Mostafa Papi

Background

Motivation for second language (L2) learning has been a topic of interest for researchers in the field of second language acquisition (SLA) for over seven decades. Research on this topic was pioneered by researchers in the multilingual context of Canada, where interest in the target language community and culture were determining factors in one's decision and motivation to learn the other language. For instance, if Anglophones were interested in the French-Canadians' community and culture they were more motivated to learn French. If the interest to learn about the French-Canadian culture and community was so intense that the individual wanted to even adopt and blend in with the French-Canadian culture, the individual was assumed to have what was called an integrative orientation toward learning French (e.g., Gardner & Lambert, 1972). This integrative orientation was found to result in highest levels of motivation to learn the target language. In addition to desire to integrate, learners also had another orientation toward learning a second language that included utilitarian goals such as getting a job, passing a course, traveling, and the like. These two orientations, integrative vs. instrumental, were traditionally assumed to encompass language learning goals and motives. However, in the early 1990s and after three decades of the hegemony of Gardner's theory of motivation, many researchers started to question the generalizability of these findings to other contexts where there is no target language community to integrate into, and pointed to the restrictive nature of Gardner's theory. Most notably, Zoltan Dörnyei championed a new wave of research on the topic and proposed that motivation is much more complicated than what Gardner's theory (Gardner, 1985; Gardner & Lambert, 1972) has outlined. Dörnyei proposed multiple theories of motivation each dealing with different aspects of motivation including but not limited to the process of goal setting and motivation, classroom motivation, task motivation, and, more relevant to the present chapter, the notion of L2 selves.

In his L2 Motivational Self System, Dörnyei (2009a) drew on motivation theories from the field of psychology to propose that if knowing the target language is an important dimension of the future self that the person desires to become, this person is said to have a future L2 self. The future L2 self could be an Ideal L2 Self, representing the L2 attributes that the person would ideally like to possess in future, or an Ought-to L2 Self, representing the L2 attributes that the person is expected to possess in order to avoid negative consequences. An example of an Ideal L2 Self is an image of a person who uses the target language fluently and effectively in communication with international friends and colleagues. An example of an Ought-to L2 Self is an image of a person who performs very well in their language classes or at their job and avoids negative consequences such as failure in school or at work, respectively. An Ideal L2 Self and an Ought-to L2 Self could even look like they are the same goal (e.g., using the target language effectively at work) on surface; however, the deeper regulatory focus of the goals could be different. That is, whereas an Ideal L2 Self has a promotion focus concerned with approaching positive end-states such as advancement and accomplishment in one's career, an Ought-to L2 Self has a prevention focus concerned with avoiding negative end-states such as avoiding losing one's job. In other words, whereas the former is about moving from the current state to a more desirable state, the latter is about maintaining the current state and avoiding a less desirable state.

The Ideal and Ought-to L2 Self act as motivators through creating feelings of discomfort associated with the discrepancy between one's current self and their future selves. In other words, individuals are motivated to reduce the discrepancy between their current L2 self and their future L2 selves. This perceived discrepancy creates a feeling of discomfort that results in motivation to reduce the discrepancy. As the learners move from their current self toward their future selves, they experience different types of emotions depending on the type of future self that they are trying to approach. Learners who are motivated to realize their Ideal L2 Self, experience elation-related emotions such as excitement and joy (see Dewaele, this volume) as they move toward this promotion-related self but if they fail to realize their Ideal L2 Self, they experience dejection-related emotions such as sadness and disappointment. By contrast, learners experience the quiescence-related emotions such as calmness as they succeed in moving toward their Ought-to L2 Self but feel agitation-related emotions such as anxiety if they do not make appropriate progress in doing so.

The pursuit of Ideal L2 Self vs. Ought-to L2 Self also results in the employment of different strategies in goal pursuit. Learners who are motivated by their Ideal L2 Self are more concerned about moving from the current state to a more desirable state, therefore, they are willing to take an eager strategic inclination, which involves taking advantage of every opportunity to use the target language without being concerned about the risk of making mistakes. Those motivated by an Ought-to L2 Self, on the other hand, are concerned about maintaining their current state and tend to take a vigilant strategic inclination that involves a cautious and minimal use of the target language in order to avoid making mistakes and risking their current situation.

In sum, learners who are motivated by their Ideal L2 Self experience joy and excitement and use eager strategies in their L2 use when they advance toward their Ideal L2 Self and experience sadness and disappointment when they fail to do so. By contrast those who are motivated by their Ought-to L2 Self experience anxiety and use vigilant L2 use strategies when they fail to realize their Ought-to L2 Self but experience calmness and safety when they succeed in doing so. In other words, the ultimate goal of learners motivated by their Ideal L2 Self is to achieve the feeling of joy whereas the goal of learners motivated by their Ought-to L2 Self is to achieve the feelings of calmness and safety.

Research on L2 Selves

The future L2 selves have been the subject of scholarly research. Studies in this area can be divided to three groups that have explored the relations between the selves on one hand and emotions, motivation, behavior, and achievement, on the other hand.

Some studies have explored the connection between selves and emotions. Papi (2010) found that Ought-to L2 Self increase L2 anxiety whereas Ideal L2 Self decreased L2 anxiety. Papi and Teimouri (2014) found similar results. In another study in the context of Iran, Teimouri (2017) found that Ideal L2 Self predicted L2 learning enjoyment whereas Ought-to Selves predicted L2 anxiety and shame. Similarly, Papi and Khajavi (2021) found that Ideal L2 Self predicted L2 enjoyment positively and L2 anxiety negatively whereas Ought L2 Self predicted L2 anxiety positively.

The biggest group of studies have examined the predictive validity of motivation theories by exploring how the selves predicts motivation and behavior. In the case of the future L2 selves, researchers examine whether the learners who have strong Ideal or Ought-to L2 Selves also show high levels of language learning motivation, behavior, and achievement or proficiency outcomes. Many studies all around the work have been conducted to evaluate the predictive validity of the future L2 selves. For instance, in an international study in the context of English learning in China, Japan, and Iran, my colleagues and I (Taguchi, Magid & Papi, 2009) found that Ideal L2 Self was a strong predictor of motivation; Ought-to L2 Self also predicted motivation but not as strongly as Ideal L2 Self. Csizer and Kormos (2009) tested the model in the context of Hungary and found only Ideal L2 Self to predict motivation. In Hong Kong, Dörnyei and Chan (2013) found that Ideal and Ought-to L2 Selves were associated with both motivation among learners of English and Mandarin but only Ideal L2 Self correlated with the students' grades in Mandarin. In a large-scale study in the context of China, You and Dörnyei (2016) found that in both rural and urban areas Ideal L2 Self and Ought-to L2 Self predicted motivation. Csizér and Lukàcs (2010) found that Ideal L2 Self predicted motivation among learners of German and English in Hungary. Kormos and Csizer (2014) found that Ideal L2 Self predicted motivation among secondary school, university, and young adult learners in Hungary. Papi and Abdollahzadeh (2012) found that Ought-to L2 Self was associated with low class participation. Domakani and Mohammadi (2016) found that Ideal L2 Self predicted the use of self-regulated learning strategies but Ought-to L2 Self did not. Khajavi and Ghonsouli (2017) found that Ideal L2 Self resulted in willingness to communicate in a second language. Papi et al. (2019) found that Ideal L2 Self contributed to eager L2 use strategies representing maximum use of the target language whereas the Ought-to Self resulted in vigilant L2 use strategies concerned with the minimal and cautious use of the target language.

The third groups of studies have also been conducted on the relationship between the selves on one hand and L2 proficiency achievement on the other hand. Papi and Teimouri (2012) found that the learners who had a strong Ideal L2 Self and a weak Ought-to L2 Self rated their English proficiency higher than other groups of learners. Kim and Kim (2014) found that Ideal L2 Self predicted self-reported English proficiency among elementary students in South Korea. Papi and Khajavi (2021) found that Ideal L2 Self predicted English achievement (final course grades) through increasing enjoyment and eager L2 use, whereas Ought-to L2 Self negatively affected English achievement through increasing anxiety and vigilant L2 use strategies. Finally, in meta-analysis of many studies in this area, Al-Hoorie (2018) found that only Ideal L2 Self correlated with L2 achievement.

Applications in the Classroom Context

As the studies reviewed above show, both Ideal L2 Self and Ought-to L2 Self contribute to student motivation. However, whereas Ideal L2 Self enhances learning enjoyment and decreases the negative emotion of anxiety, Ought-to

L2 Self results negative emotions such as anxiety and shame. In addition, whereas Ideal L2 Self results in constructive learning behaviors such as willingness to communicate in a second language and the eager use of the second language, Ought-to L2 Self leads to vigilant and minimal use of the language and low class participation. These findings show that whereas both Ideal and Ought-to L2 Self contribute to the intensity of learner motivation, there are qualitative differences in the emotional and behavioral outcomes of these selves (Papi, 2016, 2018) with Ideal L2 Self appearing to lead to emotional and behavioral patterns more adaptive and constructive to language learning. It is, thus, not surprising that most motivation researchers have emphasized the enhancement of Ideal L2 Self as their focal approach in motivating language learners (see, e.g., Thompson, this volume). Such an enhancement of Ideal L2 Self can lead to learners' experience of positive emotions during the learning process and enhance their promotion-oriented learning behaviors such as eager L2 use and willingness to communicate. Different techniques have been empirically used in a few studies (e.g., Mackay, 2015; Magid, 2011; Magid & Chan, 2012; Munezane, 2015; Sampson, 2012; Sato, 2020) to help learners develop and activate an Ideal L2 Self. These studies, reviewed below, have shown that helping students develop an Ideal L2 Self with specific and clear features could have positive motivational, behavioral and learning outcomes.

Magid (2011) conducted a motivational program consisting of activities to develop students' future L2 selves (Ideal L2 Self and feared L2 self) and help them come up with plans and strategies to achieve them. He had students read or listen to motivational songs. Then the students were asked to close their eyes and listen to excerpts that were developed by the researcher to help students visualize their ideal English selves (e.g., imagine living in a community abroad and using English to communicate with others). The students were also guided to jot down their goals as well as their ideal L2 selves in the domains of jobs, relationships, and lifestyle, and their positive or negative role models for their motivational goals in each domain, and come up with a timeline and strategies to achieve those goals. The researcher reported that at the end of the program, the students' vision of their ideal L2 self, their English learning motivation, oral English proficiency and vocabulary knowledge increased even though it is hard to attribute the linguistic improvements directly to the intervention program.

Magid and Chan (2012) employed sophisticated workshops within two intervention programs on developing an Ideal L2 Self among learners of English in England and Hong Kong that lasted four and three months, respectively. In the England program, students were asked to write about their future professional, personal, and social future including their jobs, relationships, and life styles. They were also asked to make lists of their positive and negative role models and also think about the self they fear they might become. These techniques were intended to help learners to develop a clear and elaborate picture of their Ideal L2 Self. In a following workshop, the learners were asked to create a timeline including paths and steps toward achieving their Ideal L2 Self. This was meant to make the achievement of these goals appear as something feasible and real rather than imaginary. To make it feel even more real and doable, they asked students to develop action plans detailing the steps they need to take to move toward those goals and the date they had in mind to start working on the plans. In the Hong Kong program, students were asked to draw an Ideal Self Tree each with three limbs indicating the ideal English user they want to be, their ideal career, and how they want to use English at work in personal life. After the workshops, the students were given twenty-three audio-recorded imagery situations to listen to and keep their Ideal L2 Selves activated and motivating. The participants also received counseling and feedback on how they were progressing in achieving their goals. The results of the studies showed that these interventions helped the participants develop a vivid and elaborate vision of their Ideal L2 Self, and increased their motivation and self-confidence (see also Chan, 2014).

In an action research study, Sampson (2012) conducted a one-semester program during which the researcher asked students to complete a free writing activity describing their "best possible English self." Based on data collected from the free-writing task, other task-based activities were developed to enhance the participants' Ideal L2 Self explicitly and implicitly. These included ranking pictures of their Ideal Selves (e.g., jobs, lifestyle), discussing the pros and cons of each, selecting role models, developing strategies for goal-achievement, timelines for achieving their ideal selves, and also reflecting on the "failed future self." Students also wrote reflections on their progress throughout the semester, and in the end they presented their reflections through a skit. The study found that by the end of the program the student developed a clear Ideal L2 Self and came to recognize themselves as agents of their own learning process.

Mackay (2015) employed three types of visualization activities. The first type included positive visualization, through which students using breathing and relaxation techniques and were guided on how to use visual stimuli to trigger mental images. The second type of activities included visualizing the future L2 self they identified with the most. The third type included students interviewing successful language learners on the strategies and plans they used to realize their future L2 selves, and developed a learning timeline and a list of strategies and plans to realize their own L2 selves. Based on the qualitative results, the author reported that the intervention helped students form clear, detailed, and personal visions of their Ideal L2 Selves.

Munezane (2015) examined the effects of a similar intervention on learners' willingness to communicate in a second language (L2 WTC). The students were asked to visualize their Ideal L2 Self with the desired proficiency in English and share them with their classmates. Next, they drew pictures of their Ideal L2 Selves, wrote about them at home, and presented them in class. While imagining themselves as future specialists in their own field, the students discussed important global issues and gave class presentation on the issues. One group of the students were asked to jot down and discuss their goal for the next twenty years, the next year's goals, and the current semester's goals. The students were then guided to reflect on how English proficiency can help them reach those goals. The study showed that visualization increased students L2 WTC; in addition, students enjoyed the content of the interventions and found themselves to be more competent in reaching their motivational goals.

Safadri (2021) employed a six-step program on a small sample of participants in Iran. The program included activities such as creating a vision of learners' Ideal English Self through reflection, discussion, and scripted imagery, strengthening the vision through creating their future autobiographies, interviewing successful English learners, and doing mini-projects. The authors reported that these activities enhanced learners' motivation and Ideal L2 Self.

Finally, Sato (2020; see also Sato & Lara, 2019) had a group of Chilean business-major students complete language learning tasks that required envisioning their ideal selves as internationally successful entrepreneurs and emphasized the important use of English. The students also had to reflect on the potential obstacles that they might have in the pursuit of their ideal selves. More specifically, they were asked to watch an interview with a very successful Chilean entrepreneur who spoke English with a Chilean accent. They were asked to pay special attention to the person's English skills. They were then asked to envision themselves just like the person in the video and as highly successful people and pay attention to the role of English in their success. A control group watched a similar video of a successful Chilean entrepreneur without who spoke Spanish and did similar worksheets without any attention to the role of English. The results of the study showed that the intervention led to improvements in Ideal L2 Self but not in Ought-to L2 Self or intended effort. In addition, the students in the intervention group used English more frequently and Spanish less frequently in their classes.

The studies reviewed about employed interventions based on the conditions that Dörnyei (2009a) considered necessary for the future selves to have motivational power. That is, the studies tried to (a) create an Ideal L2 Self if students didn't have one, (b) strengthen the vision through imagery enhancement, (c) make the Ideal Self appear plausible, (d) activating the Ideal Self through different communicative tasks, (e) operationalize the ideal vision by developing action plans and strategies, and, finally (f), making the Ideal L2 Self more desirable by considering the possibility of failure. Even though these preliminary studies might lack empirical rigor, they provide promising evidence that classroom activities developed based on Dörnyei's proposals provide the motivational content that many language classes seriously need. They also confirm Papi's (et el., 2019) proposal that enhancing the Ideal L2 Self can lead to more eager behavioral outcomes such as WTC and the eager use of the target language.

From a motivation-as-quality perspective (Papi, 2018; Papi et al., 2019), designing experiments that enhance both the ideals and the oughts, and measuring the effects of those interventions not only on the ideal and oughts but more importantly on the quality of learning behaviors and outcomes could be theoretically more meaningful and lead to more validity in the results and interpretations of such studies. In addition, both immediate and long-term benefits of such interventions should be explored in order to better understand the real value of such interventions, which can only be valid if the sample size is large enough to allow for sufficient statistical power in the analyses, the participants are blinded to the purpose of the study, and there is a control group that is involved in equally instructional learning activities. Keeping the principles laid out by Dörnyei (2009a) and Papi et al. (2019; see also Papi & Khajavy, 2021) in mind, teachers can creatively develop numerous ideas that can not only provide communicative, task-based, and enjoyable activities for language teaching but also implicitly or explicitly enhance learners' motivation to achieve the highest levels of proficiency in the language they desire to learn.

CHAPTER 10

Language Learning in Rural America: Creating an Ideal Self with Limited Resources

Amy S. Thompson

Introduction

My foray into language learning started in the small town of Monroe, Louisiana, when I was introduced to French at Grace Episcopal Middle School. While Louisiana does have French influence, this cultural nuance primarily pertains to the southern part of the state. The northeast, where Monroe is located, is largely separated from this French culture, except for the inclusion of a small Mardi Gras (Fat Tuesday) celebration, which embraces consumption of copious amounts of King Cake during the weeks leading up to Ash Wednesday, culminating in a bead-throwing, purple-, green-, and gold-themed parade on Louisville avenue. To illustrate the separation of Louisiana culture from French culture, when I recently described the Louisiana version of a King Cake, a cinnamon roll circular cake topped with purple, green, and gold icing, to a French colleague, she assured me that it decidedly had no relation to the French Galette des Rois which, in France, is not eaten on Mardi Gras, but on January 6th for the celebration of Epiphany.

So why did I, a young woman living in Monroe, Louisiana, a predominantly rural community, best known for Coca-Cola and the inception of Delta airlines as a crop-dusting enterprise, become obsessed with French? I immediately found joy in the different sounds and structures of the language. I loved trying to construct unique phrases with newfound words and would even take my verb conjugation and vocabulary notecards on my distance runs to use every moment I could to absorb the language. Long before Dörnyei's (2009a) L2 Motivational Self System (L2MSS; see Papi, this volume) introduced the second language acquisition (SLA) world to the connection of visualization and the concept of an ideal language learning self, I was imagining a variety of situations in which I could use French, making up scenarios and acting out all roles in my mind. Although I do not have digital versions of pictures that I look on my first visit to France in the early 1990s, Figure 10.1 is a picture I took in 2007 that helped sustained my vision as a French speaker.

FIGURE 10.1 *A trip to Paris in 2007—Notre Dame and the Seine River.*

This chapter is an overview of some of the aspects connected to learning a language other than English (LOTE) in rural contexts in the United States. Using data from different contexts, by the end of the chapter, the reader will have information about such contexts, as well as ideas of how to overcome perceived language learning barriers present for language learning in contexts similar to rural America.

An overview of Language Learning in a Rural Setting

There is a dearth of SLA research focusing on language learning in rural settings, potentially because population density facilitates data collection in a variety of ways. However, research on rural settings in the field of sociolinguistics is more common, with a recent work collected in the edited volume *Rural Voices: Language, Identity, and Social Change Across Place* (Seale & Mallinson, 2018), which spans a variety of contexts worldwide. In this volume, there is a chapter about language shift in Appalachia (Hazen, 2018), which pertains to the topic at hand. Hazen paints a picture for his readers regarding the reality of living and working in Appalachia, noting that "West Virginia does not have truly urban areas" (p. 80), sentiment substantiated by WorldAtlas.com. According to the 2010 census data, Charleston, the state capital, was the largest city in WV with a population of 51,400; Clarksburg was noted as the tenth largest city with a population of 16,578. Morgantown, the home of West Virginia University, was listed as a population of 29,660, although during the academic year, the size of the town effectively doubles with a student population of about 30,000 students per year. Most West Virginians live in areas or towns of 2,500 people or fewer. Hazen also notes that since the 1970s, most people in the state live in rural areas and commute to non-rural areas for work.

Additionally, Hazen addresses various stereotypes about West Virginia, including the unfounded notion that most people in this area are uneducated. Although the view of Appalachia as a whole is that of a region that is "isolated, homogeneous, and stuck in time" (Hazen, 2018, p. 77), the reality is that since 2010, West Virginia has been on par with the national average of 80 percent of the population earning a high school diploma. It should be noted, however, that West Virginia has relatively little racial or ethnic diversity, according to the U.S. Census Bureau, with the population composted of 92.1 percent "White alone, not Hispanic or Latino," 1.7 percent "Hispanic or Latino," and 3.6 percent "Black or African American." It is also the case that 97.5 percent of the inhabitants are L1 English speakers; however, Hazen is quick to point out that the regional varieties of English that exist in the state are rich indeed. Figure 10.2 is an image of our front field in a rural setting that is common in West Virginia.

FIGURE 10.2 *Our front field, Spring 2020, Reedsville, WV (current population, 608).*

This overview of West Virginia, the only state whose entirety is in the Appalachian region, along with the description of Monroe, Louisiana, in the introduction, sets the stage for the point of inquiry of this chapter, namely: How does a rural environment with primarily L1 English speakers affect learning a LOTE? Specifically, how can learners accurately create ideal language selves when there is a dearth of role models and/or target language input in the immediately accessible area? Using Dörnyei's (2009a) L2 Motivational Self System (L2MSS) as a motivational framework, along with ideas of the interconnection of self and context (Mercer, 2016; Ushioda, 2009), this chapter provides insights to language learning in a rural context.

Although there are many different motivational frameworks, this chapter will utilize the L2MSS. The L2MSS was conceptualized using Higgins' (1987) Self-Discrepancy Theory (SDT) and Markus and Nurius' (1986) concept of possible selves. Essentially a two-part theory (Thompson, 2017b), the L2MSS has the conceptualization of selves (ideal and ought-to) coupled with the contextualized learning experience. With a promotion focus, the ideal self is the self that the learner would like to become in terms of language use, and with a prevention focus, the ought-to self is the self that the learner feels he or she should become in terms of language use. Formation of a strong idea self is dependent on a learner's ability to visualize themselves using the language in question. The learning experience is formed by the language learning context with all of the interactions and events therein. Additional selves have emerged in the literature; the type of self that is especially relevant in this chapter is the self that forms as a reaction to doing the unexpected or thriving in challenging situations. Thompson (2017a) refers to this self as the anti-ought-to self, and Lanvers (2016) refers to this type of self as a rebellious self. Both authors have argued that such a self is prevalent in Anglophone settings when there are oftentimes no expectations to learn a language other than English (LOTE), and even suspicion or resentment toward those who do. The concept of an ideal teacher self, especially those that develop in rural settings (i.e., Gao & Xu, 2014), is also a relevant concept for this chapter.

Gao and Xu (2014) discuss data collected from English teachers in rural China. Their ideal selves are shaped in part by student interactions that lead to student progress. Also important in their ideal self formations are the previous English teachers or family member that influenced their feels toward English. These teachers indicated that they wanted to continue to improve their English; however, several indicated that the rural context did not offer substantive prospects to improve their English: "In rural schools, English teachers had no environment for learning [...] In the villages, there was no money for us to have any professional development [...] We just could not keep teaching with the world shut to us" (p. 163). Another participant indicated that "English competence ... has been consistently at the core of her visions of 'ideal self'" (p. 164) and teaching in a rural context did not allow her to maintain the competence that she gained in her master's program.

The language learning context, which can be operationalized as the learning experience aspect of the L2MSS, is indispensable to the formation of a language learner's ideal self. As Mercer (2016) insightfully argues, context is not monolithic but refers to "multiple levels of contexts stretching from micro-level interactional contexts to macro-level cultures" (p. 13, see also Serafini, 2020). The dynamicity of contexts, as well as the variation at the micro- and macro-levels needs to be taken seriously: "At times, cultures and contexts appear to be presented as static, monolithic, external entities which affect individual characteristics in a simple unidirectional manner. Such simplistic views of cultures or contexts risk distorting the nature of an individual's relationship with them and potentially leading to unintended stereotyping and over-generalisations" (Mercer, 2016, p. 12). Connecting this concept to the stereotypes of West Virginia, it cannot be assumed that everyone's experiences in and interactions with a specific context are going to result in the same outcomes. Relatedly, it cannot be assumed that creating an ideal self in a LOTE will be a logical impossibility in a rural context, although, as the participants in Gao and Xu (2014) indicated, resources play an important role in affording experiences and creating selves. As Ushioda (2014) indicated, both learner agency and context are important actors in language learning; learners have the capability to create their own micro-contexts in rural settings in which language learning can be successful: "In short, there is no doubt that context matters in SLA, yet what matters just as much is the individual agency of L2 learners, inherently part of and actively shaping the developing contexts of learning, input and interaction in which they are situated" (p. 189).

Facing Resistance: A Tale of Two Cities

Taking into consideration the context, and all external influences therein, do students in rural America face more resistance to learning a LOTE than those in urban settings? This query can be addressed by comparing at data from a large urban center in Florida ($N = 230$, Huensch & Thompson, 2017; Thompson, 2017b) to recent data collected at a large public university in West Virginia ($N = 1305$). The state of Florida is more diverse than West Virginia, according to the U.S. Census Bureau, with the population composed of 53.5 percent "White alone, not Hispanic or Latino," 26.1 percent "Hispanic or Latino," and 16.9 percent "Black or African American." Almost 30 percent of Florida residents speak a language other than English as an L1, which is in stark contrast to the 2.5 percent of those in West Virginia who speak a language other than English. The data point analyzed between these two contexts was open-ended question asking if any resistance had ever been encountered in terms of language study (i.e., the anti-ought-to self).

Certainly, the overall data sets had differences in terms of size, scope, and overall purpose of the data collection; nonetheless some insights can be drawn from looking at the open-ended answers in both sets. In terms of percentages of participants who felt external resistance to LOTE study, 28 percent of participants in Florida felt pressure to study a different LOTE or not to study one at all; in WV, it was 8 percent. One possible rationale is that in a context like West Virginia, the topic of LOTE study simply does not come up as much in conversation, potentially because of lack of experience, as one participant notes: "Not directly, but none of my friends, family, or the people I am surrounded by study or have studied a foreign language." Looking at the open-ended questions, similar salient themes emerged: languages are hard (either in general or in reference to a specific language), advisors discouraged language study, friend/family provided opinions about language study, language is useful/important, Spanish is the most useful language, and English should be spoken in America. Table 10.1 provides illustrative examples of these themes from the rural and urban contexts in question.

One difference in this qualitative data is that the students in Florida talked more specifically about Spanish being present in their surroundings and how it was a more familiar language: "It [French] intimidates me, which is another reason I was pulled towards Spanish. I've heard Spanish my

Table 10.1 Comparison of student experiences with resistance to language learning in two contexts

Theme	West Virginia	Florida
Languages are hard	Some people have questioned my choice in Japanese, seeing as it's much more difficult than Spanish or French. I continued because I love the language and knew I would be more motivated to learn it than any other language.	I have felt an obligation not to study Chinese or any language that is not a Germanic language because I have been told they are too difficult to understand.
Advisors discouraged language study	My advisor has [discouraged me] on multiple occasions, but that's because I will be graduating late to fulfill my minor. I continued because it's something that I want to learn, nobody's opinion or graduating late will affect that.	My advisor tells me not to study Japanese since it is an extra class every semester, but I am passionate about Japanese and I love languages, so I will continue to study.
Friend opinions about language study	My friend Travis says I'm wasting my time and money, but he's been working at a local grocery store in our small town and living with his mom since high school, so what does he know?	Some of my friends and family thought French was silly and would poke fun.
Family opinions about language study	My dad says French is useless.	Many have discouraged me, family telling me there was no point, or people saying that it was too hard.
Language is useful/ important	Sometimes people will ask "What good does a Spanish minor do for your Accounting major?" I always ignore this because I know the benefit it can have in any field.	Sometimes I feel as if society does not put as much emphasis on learning another language as much as they should.
Spanish is the most useful	My dad wanted me to take a Spanish class instead of a French class. He says that the Spanish language could be more easily applied in everyday life.	When I was studying French growing up many people told me it was a waste of time and the only language worth learning is Spanish.

Theme	West Virginia	Florida
English should be spoken in America	A former roommate said, "We are in America they need to speak English." I continued because it's what I want to do and out of spite because that was the stupidest thing I have heard. America is considered The Melting Pot so we have all races, cultures, languages, and ethnicities; what we don't have is a national language.	I have felt strong resistance from family and co-workers to NOT study anything but English. Some of the people closest to me have made fun of my language learning both directly and indirectly. Directly I have been told that "this is America and we only need to speak English." Also, indirectly I have heard people make jokes about language learning in English but with a foreign accent with the intention of belittling speakers of other languages.

whole life and am more familiar with it." Another Florida participant called Spanish "too common to learn and too easy," while another commented on the context-specific characteristic of Florida, where they were discouraged from studying French: "My family was adamant that I would be better off studying Spanish due to living in Florida where a lot of Spanish speakers live." The participants in West Virginia talked more vaguely about how languages would be useful for their future, but did not comment specifically about using a LOTE in the context of West Virginia, for example, "They wondered what I would need it for but I explained that it will be needed in the future" and "Sometimes people question why I would want to major in another language because they don't see how that will get me a job." Although there are contextual differences regarding resistance to LOTE study, participants are indicating similar themes in both the rural and urban contexts. Looking at language enrollment data by state (Thompson, 2021), it can also be seen that enrollment in university language classes can be predicted neither by size nor by diversity of the state population. For example, in West Virginia, 3.2 people per 1,000 inhabitants are enrolled in postsecondary language classes. In Florida, this number drops to 2.1 enrollees per 1,000 inhabitants. Looking at examples of qualitative data in the two contexts and general enrollment data gives an overview of LOTE study in different contexts. Certainly, there are differences in attitudes and trends when digging deeper, but on the surface, it appears that students in rural contexts are faced with similar challenges and motivations as those in largely urban contexts. With this in mind, the question becomes how teachers in rural contexts are able to foster language learning motivation and ideal self creation in areas where access to target language input is less readily available.

Teaching in a Rural Context: Insights from Experienced Teachers

The students represented in the data above were all attending a large public university in one of the larger cities in West Virginia. Having had insights from these language learners, I also wanted to have the K–12 teacher perspective, as many language teachers in West Virginia teach in the small towns described in the first part of this chapter. I have had the fortune to be involved with language teachers around the state via a professional organization: West Virginia Foreign Language Teachers Association (WVFLTA). Through my interactions, I worked with several aspects of the organization, including the language advocacy subgroup. Four teachers, all L1 English speakers, who were involved in this sub-group, agreed to provide me with information about their language learning and teacher experiences. None of these teachers spoke a LOTE at home growing up and were introduced to learning a LOTE at school. While a full analysis of the experiences of these teachers is beyond the scope of the current chapter, a brief discussion of their initial experiences with learning a LOTE will be presented, as well as examples of how these teachers helped their students envision themselves as speakers of Spanish, the primary language with which these teachers had teaching experience. These teachers, we will use the pseudonyms of Barbara, Lowery, Laura, and Michele, had an extraordinary amount of teaching experience—approximately forty years each. They have all recently retired but are still active in WVFLTA and language advocacy for the state and for the nation.

All of these teachers became interested in language learning for a variety of different reasons. For Michele, it was a good friend of her parents of Italian descent who convinced them to try to learn Italian. Michele often fell asleep listening to the Italian language lessons, repeating everything in her head. In college, she at first wanted to learn a LOTE to get a job as an interpreter for the United Nations, but deciding to take some education classes, she "fell in love with the students and never thought about the UN again." Lowery grew up in New York City and "heard a bit of Spanish." He was also motivated by an anti-ought-to self and wanted "to be the first in [his] generation to speak another language and travel the world." He was also further motivated by "a professor at the Universidad de Madrid who told [him that he] would never learn to speak Spanish well. [He] was a pretty strong-minded and determined young man ... who took that up as a challenge!" Barbara grew up on a farm in rural northwest Ohio and "had absolutely NO EXPOSURE (sic) to LOTEs." She first took Latin in school, as it was a "typical college prep course at the time." When her family moved two weeks into her freshman year of high school, she was placed into a Spanish class in her new school. According to her, "After about two days [she] was completely engaged with Spanish and decided that [she] would become a Spanish teacher. After that [her] course never wavered." Laura was first exposed to Spanish in an after-school program at a church in Morgantown, where she grew up. She also indicated that growing up in Morgantown, a college town with a non-student population of about 30,000 people, "gave [her] an experience that others in more rural areas of WV did not have. [She] had classmates from different countries and was exposed to varied cultures and cultural events." Her early exposure to Spanish "fueled [her] curiosity" and she was lucky to have parents who "were world travelers and encouraged [her] to continue my studies and travels."

As all four of the teachers have extensive experience, it is not surprising that they had a multitude of ideas regarding helping students envision themselves as Spanish speakers. For example, Laura, who taught Spanish in the eastern panhandle of West Virginia, an area rife with peach and apple orchards that employed Mexican workers on the farms, volunteered with her students "to provide activities for children at a local Hispanic Festival." She also organized a variety of events herself, such as a concert featuring the Argentinean singer, Justo Lamas, which attracted students from over three hours away, a foreign language week, and a Spanish immersion program for the eastern panhandle with the support of West Virginia University faculty. Michele, who taught in West Virginia's northern panhandle, organized field trips for her students to Pittsburg restaurants to expose them to Spanish speakers and to traveling shows to expose her students to the target culture. Barbara and Lowery, who both taught at the same school in eastern West Virginia on the Ohio border, primarily talked about the importance of making the language classroom its own immersion experience. Lowery credits Barbara with the creation of the immersion experience, who "had established a rigorous, no-nonsense program that was almost a totally natural immersion from day one on in Spanish I." Barbara describes how an immersion environment is crucial to language learning: "When students walk into the room, they need to feel this room is 'special'—this is where we learn through doing—demonstrated by activities, not an oral explanation." She continues to explain how she utilized realistic scenarios for role play, debates, and authentic materials such as advertisements to help her students transform into Spanish speakers in her classroom. Abundantly creative, these ideas worked with the resources that were available to them and relied very little on travel to create these immersion experiences. As Michele stated, even after she was able to take some students abroad starting in her sixth year of teaching, she "continued the other activities because not everyone could afford to go on the bigger, more expensive trips abroad," which is a common concern for students with relatively fewer monetary resources.

Concluding Thoughts

This chapter is a reflection of language learning attitudes and trends; certainly, there are other issues, such that of proficiency levels that have not been addressed, which is out of the scope of the current chapter. Reflecting on the contexts in which I have had my language learning and teaching experiences, the question of resources, in terms of money, as well as in terms of potential contact with the target language in question, has consistently been raised. As we saw in the Florida versus West Virginia student attitudinal data presented, living in an urban setting does not make anyone immune to negative attitudes toward LOTEs; however, there is no doubt that access to LOTEs in big cities is easier to come by. Living in Tampa, I was able to listen to the radio in a variety of different languages, Spanish being the most common. Since moving to West Virginia, I have had to work harder to maintain some target language input, downloading podcasts, reading, and watching television in languages other than English. However, with availability of Internet, which admittedly is not available in some of the most remote settings, target language resources are available to those who want them. As discussed by these experienced teachers, traveling abroad is not a realistic expectation for exposure to a target language for many people; instead, energy spent on target language exposure via immersion and interactive activities is what will help students have a concept of self in a LOTE in rural settings everywhere. Perhaps especially salient to rural contexts is the ability to use language learning as an escape, a sort of inner adventure created out of wanderlust, or even out of a sense of necessity. In my case, moving to Monroe as a young child was difficult; perhaps unconsciously, similar to Lvovich (2013), I threw myself into learning French as an escape: "A French personality, after all, was much less confusing and safer than being a Jew in Soviet Russia. It was a beautiful Me, the Me that I liked" (pp. 8–9). While I was not facing any sort of overt discrimination as was Lvovich's situation, I was also an outsider, and French was my window into another world, a world in which I could conjure up visions to suit my fancy in a language that I loved. My first experiences with French started me on a path of a lifelong language learner of multiple languages, leading to travel and other experiences that have enriched my personal and professional life beyond measure.

Certainly, in whatever context potential language learners find themselves, the context will inevitably shape the language experience. As Mercer (2016) reminds us, the context will also affect different learners in unique ways. In rural contexts, exposure to people from different cultural and linguistic backgrounds is oftentimes more limited than in urban settings, and, as stated in the conclusion of Lanvers et al. (2021), "While we cannot naively think that learning a LOTE would single-handedly solve certain non-inclusive tendencies, facilitated learning of a language certainly creates awareness, understanding, and connections to people different from oneself." Taking into consideration the connection of language learning and tolerance (i.e., Thompson, 2021), language learning in rural contexts is imperative. Reflecting on the wisdom gained from many years of teaching, Lowery indicates that language learning "takes you to a whole new world of learning, enrichment, and joy—while giving you a much more objective view of your own language and culture."

CHAPTER 11

Using Technology to Harness the Power of L2 Selves

Flordelis González-Mujico

Introduced in social psychology to explain human motivation, the construct of "possible selves" allows L2 learners to be viewed as active producers of their own development and conceptualization of their as-yet unrealized potential, drawing upon their hopes, wishes, and dreams. In this sense, possible selves function as future self-guides that shed light on how individuals are moved from the present toward the future, forming an explicit link between the current self-system and self-regulated behavior, a process within which vision and imagery play a pivotal role. From this perspective, a recent development in the field of L2 motivation and language acquisition has been to examine the power of possible selves using technology. It is against this background that this chapter examines research conducted in the last decade on the use of technology-assisted language learning in the construal and activation of L2 selves, and their subsequent impact on L2 motivation and learning.

The Relationship between Technology and L2 Selves

Technology-enhanced language learning (TELL) is a term proposed by Garrett (2009) to describe efforts made to incorporate technology in language education through the use of computer-assisted language learning and/or handheld communication devices that facilitate mobile-assisted language learning. Within TELL, the complex and rich media landscape of new technologies such as the Internet and Web 2.0 tools (e.g. blogs, wikis, social media spaces) have significantly altered human communication (Williams, 2009). The fact that learners seem to communicate more and in greater numbers with this type of digital technology makes it increasingly important for L2 education to attend to the literacy practices of students and the diverse ways of making meaning in these multimodal contexts (Jewitt, 2008). As a medium of self-expression, a foreign language is a tool we can personalize as a means to expand and express our identity or sense of self in novel and interesting ways and with different people in new contexts (Ushioda, 2011). The fact that TELL can expand to include sounds, images, and hypertexts, within one environment, has incremented affordances for L2 learners to try out different ways of constructing their own L2 identities as a means for self-representation. In doing so, language learners can enter a dialogue with their L2 self and develop a personal voice that scaffolds their transportable identities in an L2 learning context. The question remains as to whether this can heighten L2 motivation and learning.

Motivation continues to be considered a critical determinant in L2 learner engagement and achievement (Lamb, 2017). The L2 Motivational Self System (L2MSS; see Papi, this volume), often referred to as future self-guides, is proposed by Dörnyei (2005) as a way of making sense of the complex relationship between motivation, the learner's concept of self, and the learning context. Based on the concepts of "possible selves" from social psychology (Markus & Nurius, 1986) and Self-Discrepancy Theory (Higgins, 1987), Dörnyei's L2MSS describes motivation as a tripartite construct consisting of the ideal L2 self, the ought-to self, and the L2 learning experience. Within this system individuals are motivated by the image they have of their L2 selves using the target language. The ideal L2 self refers to a desirable self-image of what language learners would ideally like to become in the future. The ought-to self concerns the attributes that L2 learners believe they ought to possess to meet the expectations of others and to avoid possible negative outcomes when learning an L2. Target language proficiency is assumed to be an integral aspect of one's ideal or ought-to self; however, the ideal L2 self appears to exert a more pronounced impact on our motivation to learn a language due to the desire to reduce the discrepancy between our actual and future ideal L2 selves (Ushioda, 2009). The L2 learning experience represents situated and executive motives related to the immediate learning environment and experience that can help the learners successfully conceptualize an ideal and/or ought-to L2 self. These environments extend to both structured and naturalistic language learning experiences such as TELL.

Despite scholarly recommendations (e.g. Ushioda, 2011), and its predominant position in studies of L2 motivation, the L2MSS has yet to have a significant impact on TELL. Nevertheless, the current literature reports a great potential to engage and motivate students in a manner that links their language learning experiences beyond the classroom. Although these studies mostly probe English language learners, it also broadens to the use of TELL underpinned by L2 selves among learners of less commonly taught foreign languages such as Japanese (Nakai, 2016), Mandarin (Cai & Zhu, 2012), Cantonese (Lai, 2019), Icelandic, and Serbian (Ros i Solé, Calic & Neijmann, 2010). Broadly speaking, models or frameworks for the effective construal, activation, and sustainability of L2 selves using TELL systems are explored in two ways. A handful of studies have examined the effects of synthesizing informal and formal TELL activities based on the L2MSS framework. More recently, however, scholars have started to explore how these effects might be enhanced by the digital visualization of L2 selves. It is against this background that fifteen studies (Appendix) are discussed, in an effort to better understand how this interdisciplinary field has unfolded over the past decade.

This chapter begins by examining the relationship between informal and formal TELL contexts in relation to the construal and activation of L2 selves, followed by how recent developments in the visual digital projection of the L2 self can contribute to this process. Each section discusses the implications of the findings in these studies for L2 motivation and learning. The chapter continues with an overview of the current directions and limitations of using TELL to harness L2 selves, upon which four directions for future research are proposed, before presenting a final conclusion.

Pushing the Boundaries of L2 Learning in the Digital Era

That classroom practice accommodates what learners are doing outside is a common thread that unifies the current literature from the very outset. Both the Internet and Web 2.0 technologies are employed to develop and integrate TELL activities in the L2 classroom and beyond, through which the L2MSS is examined. Three underlying patterns can be woven from this pool of research. To begin with, the ideal L2 self appears to have a greater impact on motivation within TELL environments. Several studies report a positive correlation between online language learning activities and the ideal L2 self. As a starting point, Sundqvist (2015) and Nakai (2016) describe how the construal of an ideal L2 self among learners can trigger and scaffold online self-directed learning. Over a seventeen-week training program, elementary learners of L2 Japanese, in a study by Nakai, were asked to create professional role plays in the classroom, prompting them to imagine an ideal L2 self as a caregiver working in Japan. Subsequently, students felt motivated to create a private group page on Facebook so as to share their interests and L2 learning doubts, thereby extending the boundaries of the learning space and connecting the language learning to their real lives outside of the classroom. Albeit limited to one participant, Sundqvist illustrates how the desire to become an ideal L2 self gamer spurred years of persistent English foreign language (EFL) learning via self-access to games. In order to understand what was happening in the game, this learner spent a number of years observing, reading, listening, and trying to connect visuals with audio, describing his experience as "three years of informally learning English by trial and error" (p. 359).

From the opposite direction, research shows that informal online language learning can help to foster images of the ideal L2 self. In a Jakartan EFL context, Lamb and Arisandy (2019) identify entertainment-oriented and L2 self-instruction-oriented activities as capable of nurturing the ideal L2 self, while also reporting a positive correlation with attitudes to learning English. In a similar manner, Lai's (2019) analysis of South and Southeast Asian ethnic minority secondary school students in Hong Kong reveals interesting findings on the regular use of social media. Engaging with social media in daily life increased students' ideal L2 self and motivated effort in formal learning of Cantonese and traditional Chinese script, both directly and indirectly, via positive bicultural integration identity and bicultural competence. The more frequently participants used Chinese social media, the more likely they were to perceive their ethnic culture and Chinese culture as blended together and coexisting in their identity. In turn, this heightened positive future projections of themselves and what they perceived their bicultural competencies to be were, which again bolstered participants' ideal L2 self and L2 learning.

Searching for answers, Zheng, Liang, Li, and Tsai (2018) provide a possible explanation for the ideal L2 self's positive activation within digital learning environments. Based on two online learning management systems that provided teaching, learning, and assessment materials, the authors identified the ideal L2 self as having the most significant power for positively predicting self-regulatory capacity. Participants with positive promotional goals and future L2 selves were more likely to plan their own learning with specific objectives, select proper task strategies, and conduct frequent self-evaluations when learning English online. In a four-week online learning community project conducted by Cai and Zhu (2012), however, even though some activities were designed to fortify the participants' self-images in learning Mandarin, they only promoted motivation in the aspect of the L2 learning experience. An outcome attributed to it being a more fluid and dynamic aspect of motivation that may change noticeably even within a relatively short period of time. Although participants' reflective journals commented on the motivating features of the learning resources and tools provided, and the opportunities to interact with other Mandarin learners made available by the project, demotivating features largely focused on technology issues (e.g. difficulty in navigating the forums and problems with sound recording programs), and the time and work required by the project, which may have been detrimental to the credibility and confidence of L2 selves.

This brings us to the second emerging theme that relates to the production of online media, specifically the implications of the implicit critical gaze and assessment of real or imagined audiences. Although the act of reviewing spoken and written language through TELL environments is again positively correlated with the ideal L2 self, the impact and external demands of participation that feels threatening bring to the fore the ought-to self. Ros i Solé et al. (2010) were the first to use the MP3 player/recorder as a means to integrating a sense of self in the L2 educational environment. Over a period of two years, at a British university, learners of Icelandic and Serbian/Croatian had the opportunity to use technology for their day-to-day practices in a variety of situations. By hearing their voice recorded and sharing their own recordings with other fellow students and the teacher, participants were confronted with the sound of their L2 self and a perception of how they were positioned by others. As the listening and discussion sessions progressed, students began to get used to their own L2 voices, to project their desired L2 selves, and to feel more at ease when listening to themselves in front of an audience.

As a means of self-representation through writing, three papers present interesting findings on the relevance of legitimate peripheral practice when using Web 2.0 tools. In these studies, EFL participants ranged from secondary school students being asked to write blogs (Henry, 2019), to university students communicating via websites, Wikispaces (Chen & Brown, 2011) and social spaces such as Twitter, Instagram, and YouTube (Little & Al Wahaibi, 2017). Similar to the participant in Sundqvist's (2015) study, effective L2 selves seem to have been generated through a perceived obligation to emulate aspects considered to be ideal, and necessary, among experienced and target language users of these online spaces. Ito and colleagues (2010) use the term "genres of participation" to describe the modes and conventions that structure patterns of engagement within particular media forms. Users become part of the genre's shared cultural system, their engagement constituting a particular form of specialized and collective social action. In these studies, learners had to reconcile their own desires to communicate effectively in English via the ideal L2 self, while the ought-to self appears to have guided legitimate peripheral practice in terms of the characteristics learners believed they should be able to exhibit as producers of the English language, with the perceived and explicitly stated needs and expectations of their audience. On the same assumptions, Chen and Brown, and Little and Al Wahaibi argue that the L2MSS needs to consider the influence of media-influenced perceptions and cultural variation. These authors observed that participants' L2 selves were based on their motivation to provide a bridge to overcome misconceptions and dogmatic opinions of participants' religion and culture. The desire to reduce the discrepancy between how participants regarded this imposed identity in relation to the L2 self they wanted to show the world appears to have fueled the motivation to carefully curate cyber interaction.

Digital Visualization: Seeing Is Believing

Recent developments in the visual digital projection of the L2 self have allowed language learners to experiment with self-representation not only through audio and written format but also through vision, the third and last trend to emerge from the current literature. The ability to visualize a clear and vivid image of a future L2 self as a competent target language user may serve as a positive stimulus for learners to reach their L2 goals. This functional link between visual and mental imagery is related to the fact that the same brain regions that encode incoming sensory information are involved in mental imagery (Pearson & Kosslyn, 2015). Imagining a scenario can evoke an emotional state that is as powerful as physically experiencing the same scenario (Adolphs et al., 2018). This correspondence has caused a number of scholars to examine the viability of creating desired L2 selves that EFL learners can see and hear. On the whole, these studies endorse the visual projection and subsequent curatorship of a digital ideal L2 self, when a balance exists between the realism and relatability of the images. A condition that resonates with learners' aforementioned need for authentic and legitimate digital L2 learning interaction.

Toward the end of the last decade, Adolphs and colleagues (2018) offer a good starting point on digital visualization, specifically, on language learners' preferences in the construal and projection of digital L2 selves. In this study, Chinese EFL higher education learners displayed a preference for 3D virtual avatars in combination with real-life contexts. Digitally embellished 2D images held little value for further investigation, while the process of facial overlay that blended learners' facial appearance onto one of the protagonists in the video dialogue was considered too unrealistic, particularly the quality of movement in features such as the mouth and eyes, which the authors attributed to technical difficulties. Given the many common goals shared by English language learners, these authors suggest keeping a library that curates or films a selection of real-life context videos that will be of relevance to a considerable number of language learners, which learners can then personalize when creating their own L2 avatars. That same year, Ockert (2018) reinforces this idea of visual curatorship. In this study, keeping a library of videos provided snapshots of participants' progress over time, which learners could review, and in turn triggered motivation. Using a tablet computer, the act of videoing and viewing oneself successfully speaking English to be understood by classmates heightened the ideal L2 self among Japanese EFL high school learners. These recordings allowed participants to notice skill development and to alleviate the self-consciousness associated with public speaking, which led to a stronger self-image as a speaker of English and increased the realism of attaining L2 language goals. Although less conclusive, participants in a study by Gleason and Suvorov (2012) who were asked to submit three live videotaped presentations, and then provide asynchronous peer feedback and self-evaluations on the same, also reported a higher increment on the ideal L2 self. However, these authors were unable to link this increment with oral proficiency.

Imaging L2 selves digitally are further scrutinized in two intervention studies published at the end of the last decade. Sojourned EFL Asian university students were invited to complete three phases of L2 selves' visionary training programs outlined by Dörnyei and colleagues (Dörnyei & Kubanyiova, 2014; Hadfield & Dörnyei, 2013). To anchor the ideal L2 self in a sense of realistic expectation, participants were encouraged to create the L2 self vision, substantiate this vision, and keep the vision alive in a curatorial manner using photo narrative journals and digital portfolios. Learners in Fryer and Roger's (2018) longitudinal study reflected on their ideal, ought-to, and feared L2 selves before, during, and after their study abroad experience in Australia. By keeping a photo journal, these participants registered an increased clarity and specificity of their L2 self visions. This increased the levels of motivational energy directed at language learning goals, with the capacity to regulate study behaviors, and continued to fuel motivation even six months after the participants had returned home to Japan. These authors concluded that the vision of an L2 self needs to be created before students commence their sojourn in the target language context. A caveat that is not sustained in González-Mujico and Lasagabaster's (2019) paper, which describes a six-week intervention in a UK higher education English for Academic Purposes context. Despite completing the first phase of Hadfield and Dörnyei's visionary training program in the UK, experimental students that completed and submitted a multimedia e-portfolio in its entirety reported significant progressive gains on intended learning effort, ideal L2 self and post-test attitudes to English, and exhibited significant L2 listening gains. This is significant as it demonstrates that, contrary to previous findings, digital visualization can boost the ideal L2 self within a relatively short period of time. In line with the current literature, this study also noted a positive correlation between the ideal L2 self and self-regulation, and the detrimental ramifications of technical issues and legitimacy to L2 motivation and learning.

Current Directions, Limitations, and Future Research

The current literature highlights the opportunities that TELL systems offer for harnessing L2 selves. Bridging informal and formal language learning contexts, digital technologies can serve as a platform for students to embody and practice an L2 with endless possibilities. This interaction with technology appears to provide a fertile environment for boosting motivation via the ideal L2 self. Not only do learners seem motivated to use TELL in an attempt to reduce the discrepancy between their actual and desired L2 selves, but the regular use of TELL can help students to perceive this variance fostering an ideal L2 self that serves as an incentive to continue learning. Indeed, the ideal L2 self proved to be the most significant component when predicting motivated learning behavior and self-regulation within TELL settings, irrespective of the target language. Although TELL can effectively extend L2 learning beyond the classroom, only two studies corroborate a positive correlation between the ideal L2 self and self-regulation. If we want language learners to become meta-cognitively, motivationally, and behaviorally active participants in their own learning process (Zimmerman, 1989, p. 4), in a way that connects to their lives outside the educational environment, further light needs to be shed on how integrating learners' ideal L2 selves in these contexts can nurture self-regulated learning.

Online digital media production is part of an ongoing process of social evaluation and practices driven by desires for recognition and validation, which places high demands on digital self-projection (Henry, 2019). An experience that is influenced by a complex combination of the learner's present self-concept and their aspirations for the future (Dörnyei & Ushioda, 2009). For digital tools to function as a form of prosthesis (Ros i Solé et al., 2010) that allows individuals to review and adjust an L2 self based on the present self, the theme of curatorship needs to be addressed. Defined as an essential life skill, self-curatorship allows users to control, select and publish aspects of their performed, recorded self in digital media, emphasizing the need to remain focused on "human rather than technological determinism" (Potter, 2012, p. 5). To achieve this, learners need to know how to manage resources and assets made for, by, and about them in a range of online media. This extends to both the praxis and the theory. Keeping a digital library of language learners' development over time in visual, audio, and written format would support students' transition from the present toward the desired future L2 self. The challenges of using new technologies, however, may hinder this transformation at times. This means that in order to curate effective L2 selves using TELL that heighten L2 motivation and learning, practitioners need to ensure learners feel comfortable and confident using the hardware and/or software, and that they understand the modes and conventions applicable to the genres of participation. To continue examining the full potential of harnessing L2 selves using TELL, the theme of self-curatorship needs further scrutiny. This includes greater clarity on the symbiotic relationship between the ideal L2 self and the ought-to self within online genres of participation, and the cultural implications of membership within this process, particularly whether the desire to dispel online media misconceptions can serve as a catalyst to the L2MSS. Only in doing so will it be possible to identify useful strategies that can help learners to acquire curatorship skills in the target language. To what degree this can be further developed with L2 avatars in real-life situations is another interesting line of inquiry.

Whether these conditions can accelerate L2 acquisition should also be considered. Listening proficiency was the only skill to register a significant increment among participants in one study. On the one hand, this finding confirms the power of L2 selves when projected visually, while it adds further strength to the claim that learners' ideal L2 selves are positively associated with both visual and auditory components of imagery (Dörnyei & Chan, 2013). Nevertheless, evidence in terms of language gains remains scarce. Whether a boost in motivation via L2 selves underpinned by TELL improves language competency remains unclear and warrants attention in future investigations. Even though digital visualization was able to activate the ideal L2 self in a short period of time (González-Mujico & Lasagabaster, 2019), and sustain these effects long-term (Fryer & Roger, 2018), longer interventions may be necessary to improve language development all-around. On the flip side, the question as to how language competency can be measured requires further analysis and draws attention to methodology, a final aspect that should be borne in mind. While future interventions need to include control groups to increase the validity of the results (Magid, 2014), more quantitative studies should be undertaken in an effort to analyze generalizable patterns and relationships across a large dataset, thereby rendering a broader picture of the relationship between TELL and L2 selves.

Final Remarks

In the current digital era, how technologies can play a role in motivating learners continues to be a prolific area of study in the field of language teaching and learning. As technologies become more sophisticated, the extent to which students can use these tools in the L2 classroom and beyond increases the potential for enhanced learner engagement. The L2MSS (Dörnyei, 2005) has been significantly conducive to the scientific community's further understanding of the construct of motivation and L2 selves, as it ascribes the language learner a central role through which we can investigate what heightens or abates motivation, a prerequisite for any language student. Despite the dearth of research, the last decade provides some empirical evidence on the benefits of integrating language learners' possible selves within TELL. To broaden the conceptual horizons of L2 selves and TELL, it is necessary to continue examining these epistemologically divergent fields in symbiosis. Be that as it may, setting up these necessary mixed-expertise researcher groups can pose considerable motivational and logistical challenges, which may explain to some extent why digital innovations tend to be slow in the domain of L2 acquisition (Adolphs et al., 2018). Needless to say, the results of both fields converging in a manner that exploits its full potential remain undetermined.

Appendix

Table 11.1 Current literature on L2 selves using TELL

Author & Year	Research objective	Methods/Sample	Findings
Ros i Solé et al. (2010)	Relationship between TELL and L2 selves	Two case studies on Icelandic and Croatian/Serbian L2 learners in UK higher education (HE) over a 2-year period	TELL enables an extension of the self that explores perceptions of L2 selves
Chen and Brown (2011)	Relationship between written online media production and L2 selves	A 16-week qualitative study on six international EFL HE students in the United States aged between 18 and 33	Ought-to self guided task completion in the presence of an authentic audience, while ideal L2 self reconciled students' own communicative goals and desires
Cai and Zhu (2012)	Impact of an online learning community project on the L2MSS	A 4-week mixed methods study on 44 L2 Mandarin HE students in the United States aged between 19 and 31	Online learning project had a significant positive impact on L2 learning environment only
Gleason and Suvorov (2012)	The role of asynchronous oral TELL tasks in L2 motivation and the development of L2 selves	A 17-week mixed-methods study on 10 Asian EFL HE students in the United States aged between 20 and 30	Perceptions regarding L2 selves increased, albeit higher for the ideal L2 self but unable to link to oral proficiency
Sundqvist (2015)	Relationship between L2MSS, mindsets and English language acquisition through online gaming	A case study on a 14-year-old EFL Bosnian student in Sweden over 2–3 years	Positive correlation between informal EFL online learning and the ideal L2 self

Author & Year	Research objective	Methods/Sample	Findings
Nakai (2016)	Relationship between online self-directed learning, learner autonomy and L2 selves	A 17-week qualitative intervention on 10 adult upper elementary Philippine female learners of Japanese in Japan aged between 23 and 31	Online self-directed learning correlated to the construal of the ideal L2 self
Little and Al Wahaibi (2017)	Explore learners' identities and self-perceptions when using social digital spaces through the L2MSS	A qualitative study on 14 Omani EFL HE students aged between 21 and 22	Association between using social digital spaces, the ideal L2 self and cultural identity
Adolphs et al. (2018)	Examine the viability of 2D and 3D digital visualization in the construal and activation of the ideal L2 self	A qualitative study on 9 Chinese postgraduate students studying in the UK	3D animation offers the best approach—finding the balance between the realism and relatability of the images, and situated context main challenge
Fryer and Roger (2018)	Exploring changes in the L2MSS through photo narrative journals	A longitudinal qualitative intervention study on 8 EFL Japanese HE students during a 1-month compulsory sojourn in Australia	Reflecting on the ideal, ought-to and feared L2 selves increased clarity and specificity of future L2 self vision, and levels of motivational energy directed at L2 learning goals even six months after the intervention
Zheng et al. (2018)	Relationship between the L2MSS and self-regulation in online learning environments	A quantitative study on 293 Chinese EFL HE students	Positive correlation between online language learning self-regulation and the ideal L2 self

Author & Year	Research objective	Methods/Sample	Findings
Ockert (2018)	Examining the effects of videoing and viewing via a tablet computer on the ideal L2 self	A quantitative intervention on 18 Japanese EFL junior high school students—survey based with a control group	Positive self-review of the successful production of EFL via a tablet computer may bolster ideal L2 self
González-Mujico and Lasagabaster (2019)	Exploring L2 selves and self-regulation using digital portfolios	A mixed-methods intervention on Asian EFL HE students in the UK—control group included	Digital L2 selves boosted intended learning effort, ideal L2 self, attitudes to English and language listening gains
Henry (2019)	Exploring online media creation and L2 motivation through an EFL blog project	A 5-week qualitative intervention on EFL seventh-grade 13-year-old students in Sweden	In L2 activities that involve online media creation, motivation can be enhanced when space for genreexploration is provided
Lai (2019)	Relationship between social media use, bicultural identity and L2 motivation	A quantitative study on 141 secondary school ethnic minority students in Hong Kong learning Cantonese and Chinese traditional script	Chinese social media use influenced the ideal L2 self and motivated effort in Chinese learning indirectly via bicultural integration identity and bicultural competence
Lamb and Arisandy (2019)	Exploring the link between online informal learning of English (OILE) and the motivation to learn English in class	A mixed-methods study on 200 Jakartan compulsory EFL HE students and 108 voluntary evening language students aged between 14 and 52	Positive correlations between OILE and the ideal L2 self with students favoring entertainment and self-instruction, which correlated broadly with a positive attitude to classroom learning

PART FOUR

Emotions and Affect

CHAPTER 12

Research on Emotions in Second Language Acquisition: Reflections on Its Birth and Unexpected Growth

Jean-Marc Dewaele

Introduction

Looking back at the history of SLA and the emergence of certain fields within it, it is easy to fall into the trap of predeterministic thinking. In other words, a certainty that events could only unfold in the way they did because they were destined to happen, driven by God, fate, or some unknown force (McKewan, 2009). In this view Lambert, Gardner, and Dörnyei were destined to introduce motivation in SLA research and occupy a central position in the field just like Moses was meant to lead the Israelites out of Egypt. We picture Wally Lambert and Robert Gardner coming down the stairs of the Psychology Department at McGill University in Montreal clutching the fresh off-print of their paper in 1959 like Moses came down from Mount Sinai holding the stone tablets with the Ten Commandments. Little did they know at the time that this paper would be considered the pioneering study of motivation research in SLA. Thinking back of the time, Gardner (2020) writes: "In 1959, no one would have thought that the Gardner and Lambert paper would eventuate in the publication of an anthology referring to it and the research that can be associated with it. I did not" (p. 5).

Similarly, it is easy to imagine Zoltan Dörnyei basking in the sunshine in front of the building of the Psychology department at Eötvös University in Budapest where he obtained his PhD, triumphantly holding an off-print of his 1990 paper in *Language Learning*.

It is equally tempting to see these groundbreaking papers as having descended from heaven through a process of divine inspiration, just like Moses had written down God's words. Nothing is further from the truth. Zoltan Dörnyei (personal communication 2020) pointed out that his highly cited 1994a paper in which he challenged Gardner would have been rejected straight away in today's world as one reviewer recommended a straightforward reject, a second reviewer was lukewarm, and only the third reviewer was more positive. The editor, Sally Magnan, decided to ask for revisions and invited the two negative reviewers to write response articles. The resulting debate attracted widespread attention. Also, the paper that provided the empirical foundation for the L2 Motivational Self System, Csizer and Dornyei (2005) was rejected by a major journal on statistical grounds before being resubmitted and published elsewhere. It is crucial for (young) researchers to remember this. The peer review system is fallible (though there is no better alternative), and good papers may get rejected for a wide range of reasons, including those who challenge the orthodoxy and are judged negatively by reviewers who wish to maintain the status quo. As editor myself, I know how difficult it is to weigh conflicting reports of reviewers, and to estimate the citation potential of a paper—because one of the main indicators of an editor's performance is the journal's impact factor.

Beside the fact that nobody has a crystal ball to predict the citations a paper will receive, a regular source of tension between researchers is the ownership of a new concept, and the publication date. One could, of course, argue that these researchers picked up things "that were in the air" and were somehow lucky to be the first to put it on paper. My argument is that new theories do not appear *ex nihilo*: predecessors and teachers prepare the ground on which young researchers use their free will to produce something original that might end up reshaping the trajectory of a discipline. Of course, they do not know it at the time and all researchers hope that their work will be noticed and may have some impact. A new idea may at the time of publication feel like nothing more than the flapping of the wings of a butterfly in the sense that it is impossible to predict whether it will cause a turbulence or a storm somewhere in the tortuous future, or sink in a sea of global indifference.

The Lift-off of Emotion Research in SLA

Considering to what extent research into emotion and SLA has taken off in recent years (Dewaele, 2019a; Dewaele & Li, 2018; Prior, 2019; White, 2018), it might be equally tempting to believe that this was meant to happen.

Psychologists had been studying emotions for decades and several journals are uniquely devoted to emotions. Some language learning researchers referred to emotions as "affect" (Arnold, 1999; Schumann, 1997). One could thus argue that it was inevitable that at some point SLA researchers would become interested in affect/emotion. An intriguing question is why this had not happened earlier. The main reason that has been advanced so far is that SLA was long dominated by a cognitive perspective that dismissed emotions as "irrational" (Dewaele, 2019a; Prior, 2019). These cognitive researchers defended the position that SLA was scientific research in search of the truth because it focused on observable units in learners' speech: phonemes, morphemes, lexemes, speech acts, and so on. It did so in a rigorous manner and subjected them to quantification and statistical analysis. As John Schumann (personal communication 2020) pointed out: "If one used sophisticated statistics in one's research then one was doing scientific research, one could consider oneself a scientist, and one's field could legitimately be considered a science." Because emotions have no observable physical referents in the world, they fell outside the remit of traditional SLA research. John Schumann (personal communication 2020) wondered: "Can we do scientific research on nonmaterial non-observable concepts? Science emerged to explain the physical world. Are we inappropriately overextending it to the nonphysical world? Can we get scientific truths when we work with non-material symbolic entities?"[1] The winds of change in applied linguistics started to blow with the advent of qualitative research that legitimized research on L2 learners' subjective side that fell outside the scope of sociopsychological research: their emotion, investment, duty, love, desire (Kramsch, 2003; Pavlenko, 2007). John Schumann argued that SLA is not a hard science but rather a "Wissenschaft in the sense of inquiry, study, scholarship" that is unlikely to uncover Truth (personal communication 2020).

One could of course wonder why SLA researchers seemed unaware of long-standing solid research carried out by psychologists on emotion. One possible explanation is that most SLA researchers had graduated from modern language departments, where they typically had been immersed in the literature of the target language. Emotions are at the heart of novels, poems, and plays, and I personally remember how the woolly, emotional, and hermetic language of literary criticism put me off as an MA student and drove me to the unemotional philological and linguistic courses that looked at facts that professors did not try to embellish. It is possible that (applied) linguists associate(d) emotion with the literature courses that they left behind and resolutely opted for the study of the cold observable facts.

Luck played a part in what would become my lifelong interest in emotion. I met Aneta Pavlenko in the early 2000s and she went on to become a figurehead for emotion research in applied linguistics. She studied emotion concepts in Russian–English bilinguals and tracked their conceptual restructuring as a consequence of socialization in the L2. My own interest in emotion was triggered indirectly by two separate events in 2001. The first was a purely personal event: a beloved aunt of mine who worked in palliative care and whose belief in social justice and charity is unsurpassed asked me what my job at Birkbeck consisted of. I answered happily that I taught university students about SLA and multilingualism and did research on these topics. "Could you give an example?" she asked. Proud of my recent study on gender agreement in French interlanguage (Dewaele & Véronique, 2001), I explained to her that we had uncovered a mysterious pattern of correct gender agreement and a startling lack of agreement in the same sentence by my Flemish learners and that we tried to pinpoint the psycholinguistic causes. She looked at me quizzically, and asked gently, "isn't that splitting hair?" I was taken aback by the brutal honesty of that comment. Of course, solving a little psycholinguistic riddle was a perfectly legitimate enterprise for an academic, but it was not going to have any social impact. So I told her that I felt it was amazingly fun to do and, moreover, that I got paid to do it. A distinct feeling of unease swept over me as I uttered these words. Did it matter, really? The second event was 9/11 and its wide-ranging sociopolitical consequences. I realized that there was an urgent need to promote peace, tolerance, and positive thinking. I felt that as applied linguists we have a moral duty to do some good for society beyond our ivory tower and our classrooms (Dewaele, 2004). I was in this frame of mind when I met Aneta Pavlenko, whose own multilingualism, persecution, immigration, and research had made her aware of the central role of emotion in language and life (Pavlenko, 1997).

Communicating Emotions in a Foreign Language

Aneta Pavlenko and myself were surprised to discover that very little research in SLA had ever focused on emotion in a foreign language (LX), so we decided to collaborate on a joint paper in which she would look at variation in the use of emotion words in her corpus of advanced English interlanguage by Russian L1 users and I would do the same in my corpus of advanced French interlanguage by Dutch L1 users. We managed to produce and finish the paper over email before having ever met, and we presented it at the Third International Symposium on Bilingualism in Bristol in 2001 (Dewaele & Pavlenko, 2002). She continued her work on emotion concepts in her Russian bilinguals and how L2 socialization could cause conceptual restructuring of emotion categories (Pavlenko, 2005). We soon realized the limitations of our early joint work and decided that to capture the complexities of emotions in multilingualism, triangulation and a broader interdisciplinary perspective were needed. Organizing panels on emotion at international conferences allowed us to bring together colleagues from various disciplines with different ontological and methodological backgrounds who shared our interest in how multilinguals communicated their emotions in different languages, how their preferences evolved, and how it affected their identity. This group of cognitive psychologists, specialists in autobiographies of bilingual authors, psycholinguists, educational psychologists, psychotherapists, and applied linguists contributed to our special issues (Dewaele & Pavlenko, 2004; Pavlenko & Dewaele, 2004) and to an edited book (Pavlenko, 2006). All contributors agreed that a better understanding of multilingualism and emotions might lead to better practices in environments where monolingualism was the norm and where it never occurred to people that using a LX to talk about profound feelings and private, complex emotions was not a fact that could be swept under the carpet. Wierzbicka (2004) and Pavlenko (2007) also made a powerful point that autobiographical data from multilinguals is a rich and legitimate source of data for researchers. Aneta and I agreed that future research needed a combination of etic and emic perspectives, of quantitative and qualitative data to understand both general trends and unique experiences of multilinguals (see also Dewaele, 2019b). It led to the development of what was the first online questionnaire in applied linguistics, the Bilingualism and Emotions Questionnaire (BEQ) (Dewaele and Pavlenko 2001–3). It was put on a dedicated webserver at Birkbeck, with the technical help of an expert in informatics, and it allowed us to collect data from 1,579 multilinguals with more than 71 different L1s from all over the world. The dataset was used for multiple articles and chapters, and two monographs (Dewaele, 2010; Pavlenko, 2005). The BEQ has since been adapted and reused by multiple scholars.

The sudden interest in our early research on multilingualism and emotions led to some unexpected pressure from established colleagues about our positioning in the field and our theoretical and methodological (not to say tribal) allegiances. We decided not to join any particular camp to avoid power plays and to maintain an open and welcoming attitude toward anyone with an interest in emotions.

Classroom Emotions

My interest in the communication of emotions in individuals' multiple languages had always been complemented by an interest in the personality and the emotions of LX language learners and users (both aspects were combined in Dewaele, 2010). This interest arose from my experiences as an instructor of French at the Vrije Universiteit Brussel. I had been struck by the differences in oral performance of my students during informal conversation classes and during the formal oral exam. It became the topic of my PhD dissertation (Dewaele, 1993). The smell of students' sweat during the exam could become overpowering on a hot summer day. I opened the windows, added an extra table between the student and myself, made sure to break the ice, and put the students at ease, to no avail for some students. I became interested in the sources of anxiety (Dewaele, 2002). Around the same time, I attended my first conference of the American Association of Applied Linguistics and ended up meeting Zoltan Dörnyei, Peter MacIntyre, Elaine Horwitz, and John Schumann at the receptions and conference dinner. The impact of these face-to-face meetings was profound and sometimes unexpected. Discussions ranged from the theoretical, ontological, methodological, even theological, to the esthetical and purely personal. I discovered that these researchers had a wicked sense of humor, an amazing sense of purpose, a willingness to listen and to give constructive criticism. Moreover, they had outstanding work ethic and could be relied upon to act as reviewers or contributors. The prevailing view at the time was that emotions were peripheral in SLA. We later demonstrated the strong link between motivation and emotions (MacIntyre, Dewaele, Macmillan and Li, 2020). This was reflected in Dörnyei's (2005) book where there are a mere thirteen occurrences of the word "emotion," mostly linked to personality traits and emotional control. The author's increased interest in emotions in SLA was reflected in Dörnyei and Ryan's (2015) revised version where a whole section in the introduction is entitled "Emotions" and starts as follows:

> Perhaps the greatest omission of the classic ID paradigm is that it barely acknowledges the central role of emotions in human thought and behavior, even though affect is an unavoidable component of any attempt to understand the nature of learner characteristics. Feelings and emotions play a huge part in all our lives, yet they have been shunned to a large extent by both the psychology and the SLA literature. "Shunned" does not mean fully "ignored," though, because there is a significant body of research looking at emotions in both fields; but affect has been considered at best a poor relation to rational thinking, a disposition that originates from the deeply rooted tradition in Western thought that has separated reason from emotion. (p. 9)

The authors acknowledge the existence of previous work on anxiety (cf. Horwitz, 1986) and add that "there are also other, more positive emotions, such as excitement or hope, that are integral to learning a language, and we need to consider these aspects too" (p. 10). The section concludes with an admission that the previous edition of the book had omitted emotion:

> Thus, it is fair to conclude that past research on learner characteristics has suffered from a general "emotional deficit" and the 2005 version of our book reflected this trend fully: Affective issues were only discussed under the rubric of "emotion control strategies" within the chapters on motivation and learning strategies. (p. 10)

Unsurprisingly, the word "emotion" appears seventy-three times in Dörnyei and Ryan (2015), and I am confident that it will be even more frequent in the next edition of the book.

The arrival of positive psychology in SLA led to a boom of interest in learner emotions. MacIntyre and Gregersen (2012) introduced Fredrickson's (2001) broadening-and-building theory that highlights the distinctive functions of positive and negative emotions. Adapting the theory to the FL classroom, MacIntyre and Gregersen (2012) argue that learners' positive emotions can counter and overcome anxiety and shame, enhancing acclimatization in the classroom and boosting the ability to catch more language input (see also Gregersen & Al Khateeb, this volume). MacIntyre and Gregersen (2012) linked Fredrickson's approach with Dörnyei's L2 Self System (Dörnyei, 2005), arguing that it is possible to use L2 learners' imagination to provoke a positive reaction. Teachers could thus focus on introducing activities that are emotionally arousing and have an inherent positive-broadening direction (p. 202).

I realized that I had always behaved as a positive psychologist in my interactions with students without having ever heard of positive psychology. Judicious praise and honest feedback about areas for improvement had been my motto from my language teaching days to my current PhD supervision. Having met Peter MacIntyre at a number of AAAL conferences, I was impressed by his combination of professionalism, knowledge, and a great sense of humor. Being an expert curler and a proud Nova Scotian added to this uniqueness. As a psychologist teaching courses on human sexuality at Cape Breton University, he could regale us, applied linguists, at conference dinners with the type of assignments he would set for his BA students (description of a form of deviant sexuality with the exception of pedophilia). Around 2010 we discussed the need for a widening of the range of classroom emotions in FL classes using a mixed-methods approach. We devised a new 21-item Foreign Language Enjoyment (FLE) scale. Using an online questionnaire, we collected data from close to 2,000 FL learners worldwide. In two contributions that triggered interest in this approach, we juxtaposed FL Classroom Anxiety (FLCA) (Horwitz, 1986) and our own measure of FLE (Dewaele & MacIntyre, 2014, 2016). The main finding was that despite a moderate negative correlation, these two dimensions were independent of each other. In other words, they do no fluctuate in a seesaw manner. This was supported by qualitative data in which participants reported experiencing high levels of anxiety and enjoyment simultaneously in public speaking tasks. Further research showed that FLE is much more linked to teacher characteristics (Dewaele & MacIntyre, 2019; Dewaele, Witney, Saito & Dewaele, 2018) while FLCA is more dependent on learner-internal variables such as neuroticism (Dewaele & MacIntyre, 2019). Research on FLE and FLCA blossoms, especially in Asia (for general overviews, see Dewaele, Chen, Padilla & Lake, 2019; Dewaele & Li, 2020).

How Emotion Research Fed into a Social Justice Agenda

The lack of interest in emotion in SLA was reflected in the absence of emotion in textbooks. As a consequence, FL learners were left woefully unprepared to use their newly acquired language skills in emotionally loaded situations (Dewaele, 2005, 2011). I have thus argued consistently for textbook writers and teachers to pay more attention to emotional language in the target language, preferably using authentic audiovisual material to show students how the presence of a hedge preceding an emotion word, how the inflection of word of the volume and pitch at which it is uttered, how the dramatic pausing, the facial expression, and body posture all contribute to the correct interpretation of the illocutionary force. A swearword can thus become more or less offensive depending on these multiple verbal, vocal, and visual factors. It is crucial to prepare FL learners for real-world interactions where emotion wielded wrongly can have painful social consequences.

One of the interesting aspects of publishing research is that it causes a spark in readers, who might get in touch to pursue one specific aspect of the research. This was the case for Beverley Costa, who was then chief executive and clinical director of the charity *Mothertongue*, a multiethnic counselling service that provided therapeutic support that was culturally and linguistically sensitive to Black and minority ethnic communities. Beverley realized that too little was known about multilingualism in therapy and that trainers of psychotherapists in the UK seemed to assume that language was no more than a technical issue. Together we used online questionnaires to gather data from psychotherapists and clients (using snowball sampling) on their awareness of the language status of patients and on their eventual use of code-switching (Costa & Dewaele, 2012; Dewaele & Costa, 2013). This research received the Equality and Diversity Research Award from the British Association for Counselling and Psychotherapy in 2013. We have since continued to raise awareness among therapists about the issues that clients face in having to discuss their emotions in an LX and how code-switching is highly relevant in understanding how the client feels, as it typically occurs in moments of heightened emotional arousal (Costa & Dewaele, 2019). This work on multilingualism in psychotherapy inspired young researchers to dig deeper and in different directions. Rolland, Dewaele and Costa (2017) reported that a large majority of her multilingual participants who were in psychotherapy had not had the opportunity to discuss their multilingualism and multiculturalism despite the fact that it was a central element of their identity. They also avoided any code-switching. Cook and Dewaele (2021) used an interpretive phenomenological approach to investigate the lived language experiences of refugees in the UK who had endured sexuality persecution and who were part of a therapeutic community. They found that the use of English (an LX for all participants) facilitated disclosure of trauma in the individual therapy sessions. It also acted as a tool to reinvent themselves, freeing them from the shackles of shame deeply embodied in their L1, and it enhanced their self-awareness, self-esteem, and confidence.

Some Concluding Remarks

Doing research is a lonely exercise, as you sit for hours in front of a computer imagining and polishing new research questions, designing new research instruments, harvesting and cleaning data before moving to the analysis, calculating, sorting, double-checking, looking for trends, for unique life experiences told by participants, for an original storyline, turning fledgling incomplete provisional pieces of research into tentative conference presentations, or a first draft of a chapter or paper. It takes courage, optimism, and a fair amount of self-belief. The first exposure to critical feedback from supervisors, reviewers, editors, audiences is like launching a newly built boat from the dry-dock into the water: Will it float? Can it be improved? Will people want to read it? This experience is shared by all researchers. Sometimes fresh ideas have more chances of getting published in journals that are not the flagships journals of the discipline and that are less conservative in their preferences. Those of us who presented our research on emotions at mainstream applied linguistic and SLA conferences will remember the early indifference more than the hostility. I imagine that we could have shifted to different, safer topics that might have speeded up our career progression. However, we cherished our academic freedom and we shared our passion with a growing group of friends and colleagues. We could not have foreseen that twenty years later, most major SLA and applied linguistic conferences have panels on emotions.

CHAPTER 13

Enhancing Emotional Engagement in Speaking Tasks: A Cognitive-Behavioral Theory Approach

Kate Maher and Jim King

Engagement in L2 Learning

The amount of practice needed to develop communication skills in a foreign language means language learning is unlike other classroom subjects. Going through the motions of participating in classroom speaking tasks is rarely enough to develop spoken proficiency. L2 motivation research has shown how language acquisition is enhanced when learners actively immerse themselves in making it count. The journey of this research began with the work of Gardener and his colleagues (see e.g. Gardener & Lambert, 1972) examining French- and English-speaking communities in Canada, focusing on motivational factors from a social psychological perspective. More recent theories have centered on motivation at the classroom level, focusing on the thinking processes of individual learners, and have been influenced by Dörnyei's (2002, 2019b) ideas surrounding task motivation and the dynamic nature of L2 motivation in the form of directed motivational currents (DMC) or sustained flow (Henry, Davydenko, & Dörnyei, 2015; Ibrahim & Al-Hoorie, 2019). This latest dynamic perspective reiterates the complexity of L2 learning by revealing the multitude of factors that can influence motivation. Most lay people intuitively know what motivation is but would probably encounter difficulties if asked to provide a clear definition of the construct. The ambiguous nature of motivation has become even more apparent by viewing it through a dynamic lens, making identification of L2 motivation's component parts tricky to pin down.

The fuzziness of motivation can lead to challenges in the practical application of this research. Motivational theories do not explain the actions of every learner all of the time; even a motivated learner does not participate as expected occasionally. Building on the insights of motivation research, engagement offers a more practical approach to the pursuit of getting learners positively involved with classroom practice, focusing on positive action rather than the energy behind it (Mercer & Dörnyei, 2020). Engagement incorporates the interlinked facets of cognition, emotion, and behavior. When a speaking task emotionally engages a language learner, they cognitively attend to it, investing effort to participate, resulting in L2 output (Cho, 2018). Dörnyei and Kormos (2000) define engagement as the "initial condition" for cognitive and linguistic processing. Studies by Dörnyei and Kormos (2000), Egbert (2003), and Aubrey (2017) have tested L2 task conditions found to facilitate engagement and flow. In essence, the learner needs to perceive an appropriate balance of challenge for their language ability, the task is relevant and interesting to them, they have opportunities for focused attention, and chances to control the task. Although it is unrealistic to expect learners to be engaged in every task or even class, these conditions provide clear-cut ideas for teachers to incorporate into lesson planning. The "apex" of engagement is a heightened emotional state called "flow" (Csikszentmihalyi, 1990) or "optimal task experience" (Dörnyei & Ushioda, 2011). The learner is so immersed that they focus all their energy and action on the task meaning that the "motivational drive has succeeded in cutting through the complexity of the surrounding multitude of distractions, temptations and alternatives" (Dörnyei, 2019b, p. 60). Motivation theories remain relevant but as part of a cohesive approach. Rather than targeting something allusive, teachers can invest time in creating situations that encourage learners to become absorbed in their practice.

A further role of engagement and flow in language learning is helping learners reduce experiences of L2 speaking-related anxiety. Like the interdependent facets of engagement, cognition, emotion, and behavior also feature in the cognitive-behavioral cycles of anxious learners (Figure 13.1; Maher, 2020). The negative emotion of anxiety can cause learners to have negative thoughts about their language skills and ability to perform in the social environment of the classroom. They may also experience unwelcome physical sensations such as blushing and shaking, which confirm that they are nervous and lead to negative behaviors, which in this context is avoidance of oral participation. Approaches from cognitive-behavioral theory (CBT) for reducing anxiety, including performance anxiety, have applied the concept of engagement and flow. Taking part in enjoyable activities such as art and music can act as a positive distraction from negative thoughts

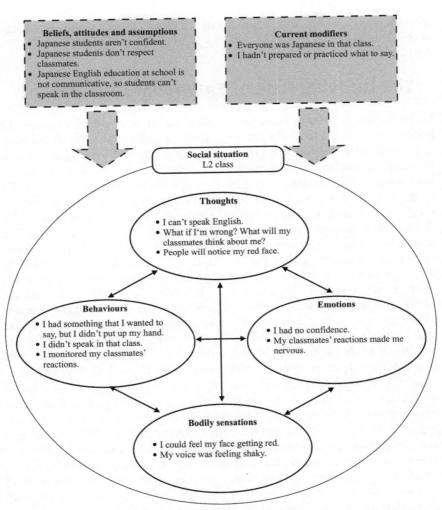

FIGURE 13.1 *CBT model of not initiating talk due to speaking-related anxiety (Maher, 2020).*

(Csikszentmihalyi, 1990). If an anxious language learner can engage in a speaking task, they may forget any nervous feelings they had, making it more likely they will enjoy speaking and want to try similar activities again.

However, even with optimal task conditions, L2 speaking anxiety can lead to emotional and social disengagement in the classroom, making it difficult for some students to reach anywhere near a level of flow. The purpose of this chapter is to demonstrate the types of barriers there are to engagement for language learners, placing emotional distractions at the center of the issue, and to suggest activities to promote both positive emotional and social engagement based on elements of CBT to support learners to engage in speaking tasks.

The Unifying Role of Emotional Engagement

In the foreign language classroom, teachers facilitate cognitive engagement because they want to help learners think more clearly about learning tasks and speak more in the target language while performing these tasks. However, if teachers are too focused on this, they may become distracted from what is the antecedent of engagement as a whole: emotional engagement (Pekrun & Linnenbrink-Garcia, 2012). For a learner to give attention to a speaking task and participate with their peers, attention must be given to the learner's emotions related to speaking and the task (Cho, 2018). If a learner experiences positive emotional engagement such as happiness and enjoyment, engagement has the potential to enhance learning by making the learner feel that they want to try speaking again and reduce emotional disengagement such as boredom and anxiety (Egbert, 2003). In the case of negative emotions such as anxiety, understanding emotional engagement as the central facet is key to facilitating engagement in nervous speakers (see Dewaele, this volume). While the task may have the four necessary conditions to facilitate engagement, anxiety can become a distraction that prevents them from enjoying speaking and interferes with their attention.

In the foreign language classroom, there is a myriad of emotional distractions originating from the learner's characteristics and the learning environment due to the cyclical relationship between emotional and social engagement. L2 speaking tasks can cause learners to doubt their proficiency and ability to do the task successfully in front of others. This self-doubt often arises from fears about performing in the social context of the classroom, which can cause them to negatively compare themselves with their peers and risk embarrassment if they fail the task. Emotional engagement may also relate to learners' feelings of connection or disconnection with their peers and, particularly, their interlocutor in a speaking activity (Pekrun & Linnenbrink-Garcia, 2012). So, even if a learner is motivated and cognitively able to participate, negative emotional distractions endemic to L2 classroom speaking situations can often lead to the silence of disengagement.

Emotional Distractions in the Foreign Language Classroom

This section considers examples of emotional distractions in a Japanese university language classroom context. The examples are presented using a cognitive-behavioral model of silent L2 learners' social anxiety (King,

2014; King & Smith, 2017) to illustrate the role of distractions in limiting engagement focusing on L2 in-class speaking situations. Using this cognitive-behavioral model, we will demonstrate how learners can become trapped in a negative cycle of cognition, emotion, and behavior, impacting on their oral participation and pulling them toward silence. The model also highlights the role of immediate contextual factors and higher-level sociocultural factors. These factors form part of a complex dynamic system that can include the learner's mental characteristics, previous learning experiences, the task, social groups, relationship with the teacher, and the physical characteristics of the classroom (King, 2013a, p. 128). Factors that frequently came up in interviews in our studies were related to interpersonal relationships with peers, especially the fear of the "ever-watching other." Rather than stand out, participants described how their anxiety about having their performance negatively evaluated resulted in avoiding speaking up, meaning they prioritized peer over academic evaluation. Although other common factors appeared in the data (e.g., the washback effect of English as a subject in high-stakes exams and sociocultural expectation of learner silence in academic settings), peers' influence exemplifies the cyclical relationship between the emotional and social facets and their integral role in engagement.

Cognitive-Behavioral Model of Silent L2 Learners' Social Anxiety

How an individual interprets their environment determines how they feel about and what action they take. Not all language learners perceive events that can happen during speaking tasks—making a grammar mistake or misunderstanding what their partner said—as negative, and therefore, are less likely to experience anxiety about participating. Cognitive-behavioral approaches for reducing anxiety emphasize cognition and CBT activities work by showing the person how their thoughts impact what they feel and do, and how to control them. CBT differentiates a person's thoughts into core beliefs, negative assumptions, and negative automatic thoughts (NATs) (Kennerley, Kirk, & Westbrook, 2017). Knowing about and recognizing NATs can be helpful for learners. NATs take over the person's thoughts, causing them to interpret their environment negatively automatically. If an anxious learner has to speak with a partner, they may become distracted by their fears about participating even before the task begins.

In the cognitive-behavioral model of silent L2 learners' social anxiety (Figure 13.2), the specific types of negative thoughts are "feared predictions" and "self-focus image," which the next sections will discuss with examples. Interlinked with these are "somatic and cognitive sensations" that can occur because of the negative thoughts, but also feed into how the learner interprets their situation and intensify their negative thoughts: "I'm shaking

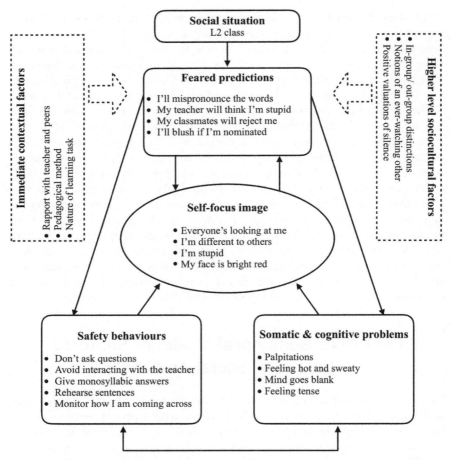

FIGURE 13.2 *A cognitive-behavioral model of a silent L2 learner's social anxiety (King & Smith, 2017, adapted from King, 2014).*

so I must be nervous." The "safety behaviors" in the model are the resulting actions of the learner due to their thoughts and sensations. Safety behaviors can reinforce the learner's negative interpretation of the situation; if the learner always avoids speaking, they will not be able to have any positive experiences that would make them want to try again. Figure 13.2 is a summary of commonly occurring thoughts, behaviors, and sensations in the Japanese L2 classroom context.

Feared Predictions

Learners that are anxious about speaking can perceive the classroom as an "emotional danger zone" with plenty of potential for undesirable

Table 13.1 *Examples of feared predictions*

Type of feared prediction	Learner	In-class L2 speaking situation	Observed behaviors	Thoughts (reported in interviews)
1) Excessively high standards for social performance "My opinion must not upset others. I have to be careful what I say so that I fit in with my partner."	Yuma	Sharing opinions about a reading passage with his partner in English.	Both Yuma and his partner remained silent at the start of the task. Yuma was looking down at his desk, smiling. After about one minute, his partner initiated the discussion in English. Yuma responded in Japanese.	"I worry about upsetting my partner with my opinion. I don't want my partner to misunderstand my opinion, so I'd rather say it in Japanese because I can't say it clearly in English. I don't want to cause trouble with my partner if my opinion is strange or different. They might feel confused and then it would be awkward."
2) Conditional belief about social evaluation "If I speak English, my partner will think badly about me because of my poor English skills."	Mami	Discussions in groups of three to four people. All groups were given the same discussion questions.	Mami's group used Japanese for most of the discussion time. Mami sat back in her chair, sometimes writing notes, and giving a few short responses in Japanese. She repeatedly covered her face with her hand.	"If I speak English, my partner will think I am strange or showing off. They will think that I am not good enough to use English." "My partner will be bored if I speak. They don't want to listen to me. They will just tolerate me and my poor English." "Even if my partner is my friend, I feel nervous about speaking. What if they think differently of me?"

Type of feared prediction	Learner	In-class L2 speaking situation	Observed behaviors	Thoughts (reported in interviews)
3) Unconditional belief about the self "I have to be perfect when I speak English. I must not make mistakes."	Natsuki	Teacher asking questions to the class, waiting for volunteers to respond.	Natsuki remained silent.	"I think my English is not perfect but they expect it to be ….. I worry about if I'll make a mistake. If I make a mistake, I'll be embarrassed so I don't want other students to expect my English is perfect."

consequences such as negative evaluation—by peers and the teacher, and feeling embarrassment and shame (King & Smith, 2017). For some learners, discomfort from making a mistake, for example, might be outweighed by the learning opportunity it brings. However, anxious learners may actively want to avoid it, concerned that their lack of ability will be exposed. A learner can become distracted by automatically predicting and listing up all the things they fear will go wrong for them *if* they participate. In weighing up the risks, they may decide it is not worth it and remain silent. Feared predictions can be distinguished into three categories: (1) excessively high standards for social performance; (2) conditional beliefs concerning social evaluation; and (3) unconditional beliefs about the self (Clark & Wells, 1995). Table 13.1 provides some examples from our studies of English-majors (all names are pseudonyms) in this setting and use data from class observations and interviews (studies include King, 2013b, 2014, 2016; King & Smith, 2017; King, Yashima, Humphries, Aubrey, & Ikeda, 2020; Maher, 2020).

Self-Focus Image

In addition to negatively interpreting the classroom environment, anxious learners can put themselves at the center of what is going on around them, focusing on how they are performing and coming across in this social situation fueled by self-doubt about their language ability and managing peer relationships. This focus makes it hard for them to objectively interpret the environment and look for cues that would contradict their negative thoughts. Self-focus image is understandably a ubiquitous distraction in the foreign language classroom. Some learners reported how they feel the center of attention when they speak because other people are listening and watching: "I think that to speak in front of everyone means you would probably become a model," "You're judged because other people are watching you, you have to be perfect," (King, 2013a, p. 115). Self-focus worries are not always limited to self-doubt about how they use their L2. Sometimes learners can feel that they are under a spotlight due to concerns about using the L2 at all: "When my partner was using Japanese during the task, I worried about whether using English would look strange, even though I wanted to speak English. I kept thinking 'What should I do?' The pressure was on me" (interview from unpublished data by Maher). While a more confident learner might have ignored their partner's behavior and used English, this anxious learner connected their partner's actions back to their performance. Table 13.2 contains further examples of self-focus image of a single learner from unpublished data by Kate. During our interviews, it became apparent that the participant, Haruna, was highly cognizant of her situation, putting herself in the center, which intensified her feeling of being watched. Her thoughts often resulted in her speaking less to avoid being under the spotlight.

Table 13.2 *Haruna's self-focus image thoughts*

In-class L2 speaking situation	Observed behaviors	Thoughts (reported in interviews)
Free-talk time with a partner, students could choose the topic they spoke about	Haruna asked her partner a question at the start: "What's new?" and remained quiet for the rest of the activity just nodding or smiling.	"I feel a lot of pressure on me to start talking, to choose the topic. The topic has to be fun and interesting, but how can I do that if I don't know what my partner likes? I worry 'What are they thinking about me? Why is my partner using their smartphone? Am I boring?'"
Timed-speaking for 90 seconds about a topic given by the teacher and followed with peer feedback, all in English	When it was Haruna's turn to give feedback to her partner, she smiled and gave a short comment in Japanese, before looking down or away until the teacher told them to change roles.	"My English has to be perfect to give my partner advice, otherwise they will think 'How can she give me advice? I don't want her advice because her English isn't good.'"
Discussions in a group of six people	For most of the activity, Haruna took on the listener role, and when she spoke, she quickly passed to another group member. Her eyes were moving up and down from her group members to her lap.	"I saw some people in the group whispering and laughing when someone was speaking. I was thinking 'What are they whispering about? Is it me? Why are they laughing?' When I was speaking, I didn't want to look at their faces."

To further demonstrate how an anxious learner's thoughts, behaviors, and sensations can form into a negative cycle of distraction, Figure 13.3 provides an overview of another learner, Mari. During in-class observations, Mari often remained silent or only contributed short responses in English. In follow-up interviews, she described how she spent a lot of time outside of class preparing for speaking tasks; planning what she would say by writing scripts, getting friends to check those scripts for mistakes, and

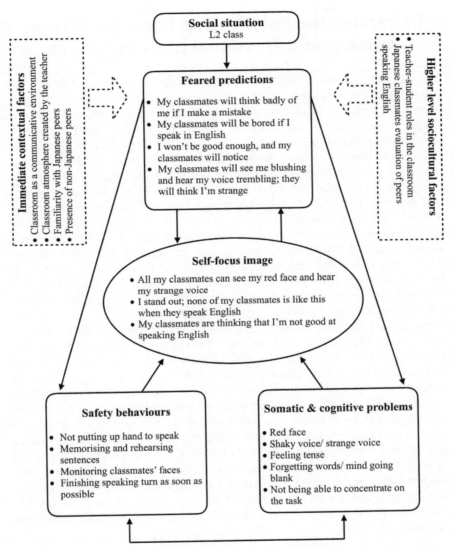

FIGURE 13.3 *Cognitive-behavioral model of Mari's silence and anxiety in the foreign language classroom based on King (2014) and Maher (2020).*

rehearsing. Despite these efforts, she remained quiet when her speaking turn came, about which she expressed deep disappointment in herself. By looking at the model and distractions of an individual, it is clear to see how and why some learners may struggle to become engaged in an L2 speaking task.

Reframing the Relationship between Silence, Anxiety, and Emotional Disengagement

One of the reasons behind the emergence of engagement research in educational psychology was as a response to concerns about learners who disengage and drop out of education, with one of the main lessons learnt being increased consideration toward promoting enjoyment in the classroom (see Hiver, Al-Hoorie & Mercer, 2021). Perhaps because of how engagement became a key concept, its description tends to be limited to positive emotions, such as enjoyment and interest. Likewise, emotional disengagement is often described with negative emotions, such as boredom and anxiety. With anxiety being categorized under "disengagement," there is a risk of it being associated with boredom and dropping out. Particularly if an anxious learner displays silent behavior, which could be interpreted as behavioral disengagement. In the case of learners like Mari (Figure 13.3), their observable behaviors would indicate that they are disengaged because of their low oral participation. Yet, Mari was motivated and engaged until when she had to speak. By examining engagement through a cognitive-behavioral model, it is arguable that anxious learners are overly engaged or negatively engaged, rather than disengaged. Their minds are racing with distractions that prevent them from engaging behaviorally. Of course, anxious learners can also be bored and withdrawn from their learning, having to participate in a task that is not interesting and risking negative peer evaluation may also result in feeling nervous. The issue with describing the emotions of engagement and disengagement in an essentialist manner is that assumptions could be made about a learner's motivation and interest in language learning. Enhancing emotional engagement requires more than increasing enjoyment and interest in the class. Some learners will also need support to manage their emotional distractions. We believe that both teachers and learners can benefit from an awareness of the cognitive-behavioral cycles shown in this chapter. In the next section, we suggest CBT-based activities to help control negative thoughts to enhance emotional engagement.

Suggestions for CBT-based Activities to Enhance Emotional Engagement

The activities in this section are intended to show learners how their thoughts can affect their engagement and performance in speaking tasks and show them that anxiety is dynamic and (usually) not related to every aspect of language learning. The activities can be done independently or as part of a course. Having students share their worries about speaking with their peers can act as a bonding exercise, but also be a confidence booster if they realize that feeling nervous is normal and a common experience. We recommend briefly explaining the cognitive-behavioral model (Figure 13.1) to introduce the purpose and potential benefits of the activities. Using language learning-specific examples from your teaching context will increase the relevancy of the activities for the students too. A further recommendation is to model the process of each activity first, then ask the students to try an example as a group, before asking them to try it individually. We recommend that you follow the order of the activities, building up to 3 and 4. Activities 1, 2 and 3 are adapted from Stallard's (2002) cognitive-behavioral therapy workbook. The activities in this book are designed for young people, so they are kept simple and visually attractive. Stallard provides easy-to-understand activity guides to show how the theory and skills can be applied.

Activity 1: Thought Diary

After students understand the influence that thoughts can have on feelings and behaviors, have them record what negative thoughts they have during in-class L2 speaking situations. As previously described, NATS can be a constant source of distraction source and have a harmful influence because the person is often unaware of them, making it impossible to manage them. This activity is a first step to enhancing emotional engagement or increasing positive emotional engagement, by students recognizing what negative thoughts they often have, when they have them, who they have them with, as well as the effect they have on their performance. Here are some suggestions for using thought diaries with students (see Figure 13.4):

- The thought diary is an independent activity that they can do outside of class, but, depending on the atmosphere of the class group, encourage students to share some parts in class with a partner to get feedback and advice. Make sure to reassure students that there is no pressure if they feel uncomfortable about sharing their diary.

- Encourage students to fill in the diary for at least one week. After that, move on to Activity 2: Balanced thoughts (see Figure 13.5).

- You may also want to encourage students to record positive thoughts as well. This can build their confidence by reminding them of successful moments when they felt engaged and that they can repeat their success in the future. It can also be useful for them to compare what occurred when they had negative thoughts and positive thoughts to see if they can understand some of the causes behind their negative emotions and how to feel more positive.

Date and class	Speaking situation (Make a note of details about the situation: what type of task, who did you speak with etc.)	Thoughts (Make a note of what negative or positive thoughts you had)	Behaviours (What did you do before, during and after the speaking situation?)	Feelings (How did you feel before, during and after the speaking situation?)
- Example -				
20th Oct. Fri Eng. Spking Skills	- Group discussion about AI - 4 people in my group - We had to speak in English for 10 minutes - The teacher chose the groups randomly. I didn't know anyone in my group. - One girl spoke a lot and was very confident.	I liked the topic, but after I heard that girl speaking, I didn't want to speak anymore because she was so good.	I listened to that girl. I tried to understand what she was saying.	Before the task, I was excited to speak because I like this topic, but during the discussion I felt ashamed of my English compared to hers. Afterwards, I felt sad that I didn't try.

FIGURE 13.4 *Thought diary.*

Activity 2: Balanced Thoughts

After trying the thought diary, students should be more aware of what types of negative thoughts they have and in what situations they occur. Once students can recognize their negative thoughts, they can use this activity to try to break the negative cycle by being more objective and challenging their thoughts. In this activity, students are asked to find evidence that supports their negative thoughts and evidence that contradicts them. This process encourages looking for alternative interpretations and practice a more neutral assessment of situations before jumping to negative conclusions. The following are recommendations for trying this activity with students:

- If it is possible to do this as a class activity, have students work in pairs taking it in turns to share one of their negative thoughts and think of an alternative interpretation. It can be hard to contradict long-held beliefs and reoccurring thoughts, so getting another person's perspective can be helpful.

- Encourage students to fill in the diary for at least one week. Doing this as an ongoing activity for a term will be more beneficial as the more data they collect about themselves, the more practice they will have in balancing their thoughts.

- Tell students that this is not about just being a positive thinker. Not all the situations they face can be given a positive spin, for example, if they have received negative peer evaluations. Pushing themselves to be positive may put pressure on them and dismisses the reality of the situation.

Date and class	Thoughts (What was your negative thought?)	Support (What evidence supports this thought?)	Challenge (What evidence contradicts this thought?)	Alternative interpretation (What is a more balanced way thought?)
- Example -				
14th Dec. Mon Debate class	My classmates think my English is really bad.	When I said my opinion, they were whispering and laughing.	I've never heard them say anything bad about me or my English skills. They are friendly when we speak after class.	Maybe they were laughing at a joke or something else. I didn't hear what they were whispering, so I don't know 100% it was about me.

FIGURE 13.5 *Balanced thoughts.*

Activity 3: Planning for Positive Engagement

Once students have practiced balancing their thoughts, use this activity to plan how they can apply this skill for managing emotional distractions to engage more positively in classroom speaking situations (see Figure 13.6). This activity is similar to behavioral experiments used in CBT sessions. The CBT method encourages people to take an active approach to test out their fears. Furthermore, by actively seeking out "risky" situations, there is the possibility that they will have a positive experience which will make them want to try again. This activity can also help anxious students to focus on the experience of participating, rather than the pressure of trying to achieve an end goal. By redirecting the mind to focus on the process of doing a task rather than just aiming to complete it, there is more chance of entering a state of flow (Csikszentmihalyi, 1990). Here are some points to consider when introducing this activity to students:

- Encourage students to choose small achievable goals at first; putting up their hand to volunteer an answer once a class can be a big step for some. Also, try to guide students toward choosing goals that focus on sustained engagement, such as "When I worry about what my partner is thinking, I will keep calm and finish what I wanted to say," rather than end goals with consequences, such as getting a good score on a speaking test.

- The reward element of this activity is crucial for reinforcing the positive experience and encouraging them to want to keep trying.

- A good way to model this activity and to help students make an achievable goal is using an upcoming speaking activity that you have planned for the class. Explain what they will do in the activity, and then, if appropriate, put the students into groups to discuss possible goals and how they could apply balanced thinking. It could also be fun to decide on a reward as a class to keep everyone motivated. After modeling the activity, encourage students to do it independently.

Activity 4: Engagement Diary

This activity is adapted from Aubrey's (2017) intervention study on measuring flow in inter- and intracultural tasks. After completing speaking tasks, the students completed a learner diary to evaluate their performance and do a post-task reflection. The diary provides data for the teacher on students' perceptions of task enjoyment and interest, task success, social connectedness, and intentions for skill improvement. This data can also be

What is your goal?	
Example	I will not stop in the middle of a sentence when I get nervous. I will finish what I want to say.
What do you need to do to achieve this goal? (How will you use balanced thinking?)	
Example	I need to remember that if my partner looks bored, it could be for many reasons that aren't related to me.
When will you try to challenge yourself? (Make a note of the date, class and what type of speaking situation)	
Example	Next Tuesday in English Conversation class. We always start with free-talk, so I will try then because I usually just listen to my partner, or ask a question.
What reward will you give yourself for doing this challenge?	
Example	I will buy myself a cookie!

FIGURE 13.6 *Planning for positive engagement.*

useful for students to notice how they engaged they were in a task and recognize how they overcame any distractions. We recommend adding a CBT component to the diary. Activities 2 and/or 3 could be done before the speaking task to prepare the students, and then use the learner diary post-task to reflect on their engagement, performance, and managing their thoughts and whether that helped them to engage (see Figure 13.7).

Note: Care should be taken when introducing these activities to learners as some of the terminologies—anxiety, CBT and emotions—are sensitive and may cause alarm due to their mental health implications. It is better to use terms that are less intimidating, such as "confidence-boosting" and "controlling your nervous feelings."

Conclusion

Facilitating engagement and flow is partially dependent on the teacher creating optimal task conditions. But in a class of individuals who interpret their environment differently and bring different language learning baggage

1. How well do you feel you did the task?	
Example	I guess it went quite well because my partner and I kept talking mostly in English.
2. How did you feel about your performance during the task activity?	
Example	Not that good. My partner had to help me a lot.
3. Would you like to do this activity again? Why/ why not?	
Example	Yes, because I enjoyed speaking about this topic and it was good to use the vocabulary we learnt in class.
4. Did you like working with your task partner/ group? Why/ why not?	
Example	Yes! She was so kind and helped me a lot. But I felt bad because she had to wait for me a lot to find the right word.
5. How well did you feel you managed your thoughts? How did this influence your performance?	
Example	I tried to stay calm and remembered that she is a kind person, so she was just helping me. I don't think bad things about people when they need my help, so she probably wasn't thinking bad things about me. I remembered these points when I couldn't say the word I wanted and she was waiting for me. It helped me to laugh it off and keep trying.

FIGURE 13.7 *Engagement diary.*

with them (Mercer & Dörnyei, 2020), meeting the conditions for as many students as possible is demanding. Our hope in writing this chapter is to demonstrate that positive emotional engagement is a central facet that determines cognition and behavior in tasks; however, aiming to make classes "fun" is unlikely to be sufficient to facilitate student engagement. If a learner is highly anxious, they will be distracted and less able to find enjoyment. CBT-based activities can be a practical way to provide students with tools to minimize the harmful effects of distractions in their learning environment. CBT can give learners skills that they can apply independently, making them autonomous in the pursuit of enhancing their language learning.

CHAPTER 14

Motivation Contagion: The Reciprocal Influence of Language Teachers and Learners

Tammy Gregersen and Ahmed Al Khateeb

Do highly motivated language teachers beget highly motivated learners? Vice versa, do motivated language learners foster motivation in their teacher? Is there such a thing as "motivation contagion"? According to Roffey (2012), teacher and learner well-being are two sides of the same coin, but does this translate into greater reciprocal motivation? According to Mercer and Gregersen (2020, p. 2),

> Happy teachers make for happy pupils. Interestingly, the reverse is also true. When pupils are happy, it is usually more rewarding and motivating to teach them, thus, teachers are also more likely to draw positivity from their learners—such a mutually reinforcing positivity is a win-win for all.

Motivation appears from feelings of attachment to others (Deci & Ryan, 2000, 2012). We feel motivated when we interact positively in relationships. In the language classroom, motivation is critical not only for the well-being of teachers, but it also plays a significant role for that of their learners. Because teachers are protagonists in their learners' engagement and motivation (Hill & Rowe, 1998), teachers' satisfaction in teaching and the confidence they exhibit positively influence these same feelings in learners (Frenzel & Stephens, 2013). Motivated and passionate teachers tend to have learners who will be, too, and so begins a positive upward spiral. Furthermore, a vital source of motivation for teachers emanates from their learners, the connections that bind them and savoring students' growth (Papi & Abdollahzadeh, 2012). "The motivation of teachers and learners is tightly intertwined in a reciprocal relationship" (Mercer & Gregersen, 2020, p. 2).

The model of reciprocal causation posits that teachers' emotions have a mutual influence on their ability to stimulate motivation and create supportive social environments, which consequently influences learners' motivation and social-emotional development (Frenzel, Goetz, Stephens & Jacob, 2009). Because educational outcomes as well as social and emotional well-being are unequivocally shaped by the quality of relationships forged among teachers and learners, emotionally intelligent language teachers place less importance on controlling learners and more on skills to connect meaningfully with them (Murray-Harvey, 2010).

According to Izard (2007), emotions may be the foremost motivation system that human beings possess. Such prominence has significant implications in the "crossover theory" that suggests that emotions can be evoked from the emotions of others either openly or ambiguously (Hartel & Page, 2009). During crossover, teachers and learners, on an inter-individual, dyadic level, transmit their states of well-being (Bakker, Demerouti & Burke, 2009). In a study by Becker et al. (2014) learners' perceptions of teachers' emotions significantly predicted those of the students. That is to say, teachers' emotions are as important as their instructional behaviors—a notion that carries with it theoretical implications for crossover theory and practical implications for teachers (see also Dewaele, this volume; Maher & King, this volume). Becker et al. (2014) suggest, "Teachers need to acknowledge the power of their emotions and that teaching involves more than just instructional behavior. The emotions that teachers bring to the classroom have important effects on their students' emotions" (p. 25). Such crossover is not a general, static phenomenon, however. Their study also indicated that teachers influence learners' emotions at the lessons-to-lesson level and that their own emotions should not be disregarded in their daily and often busy teaching schedule—not only for their students' sake but also for their own well-being as well.

Learning theories on social cognition as well as social construction (Bandura, 1977; Pekrun, 2000; Wild, Enzle, & Hawkins, 1992; Wild, Enzle, Nix, & Deci, 1997) also offer context for the conveyance of emotions from teachers to students. Learners intuit via comments and observation of teachers' enjoyment that a topic or task is valued, which thus positively influences students' own enjoyment of learning (Pekrun, 2000). Similarly, "appreciation-oriented modeling" is a situation in which teachers communicate their enjoyment "in savoring the experience and aesthetic satisfaction of learning tasks" (Brophy, 2004, p. 266). Such teacher enthusiasm is one of the essential teacher qualities positively affecting learner motivation (Brophy & Good, 1986).

The purpose of the present study is to examine the dynamic interconnectedness of language teachers' motivation and that of their learners—to ascertain whether "motivation contagion" exists between language teachers and learners. To do this, the researchers adopted a methodological approach that was composed of eight teachers and their learners recording their level of motivation at the outset of every class and then again upon its completion over the duration of six to ten classes, depending on the schedule of the classes. By using this data gathering methodology, the researchers were able to eliminate limitations that often arise with recall inaccuracies and cognitive and memory imprecisions that often occur with one-time recall-based self-report ratings (Carson, Weiss, & Templin, 2010; Robinson & Clore, 2002). Much like experience-sampling procedures that are less vulnerable to biases, especially recall inaccuracies, the participants in this study self-rated their motivation directly in the situation and evaluated their real-time degree of motivation rather than their beliefs about it. Second, one-time motivation assessments are prone to focus on relatively stable habitual motivation (i.e., trait-based) (Frenzel, Goetz, Lüdtke, Pekrun, & Sutton, 2009, p. 712), but they are relatively incapable of evaluating the micro-processes involved in "motivation crossover." Conversely, the multi-measures over weeks can account for the dynamic nature of motivation that vary according to situational factors such as the changing motivational levels and relational idiosyncrasies of teacher and learners at a given time (i.e., state-based emotions). Finally, our approach of sampling teachers and learners in the moment of beginning and ending a class produced data of ecological validity as the construct of motivation is assessed within its naturally occurring, "in-situ" context (Carson et al., 2010).

Methodology

After consenting voluntarily, eight university professors and their English learners (total $n = 221$) who were preparing to become English language teachers or translators in a public university in Saudi Arabia made up our sample population. Class sizes ranged from eight to forty-one students; five of the classes were male ($n = 148$) with male professors and two were composed of female students ($n = 73$) with their female professors. Starting during the third week of the semester, and over a period of eight to ten weeks (depending on the course schedule), professors and their learners self-reported their level of motivation before and after class on a scale from 1 (not motivated at all) to 10 (extremely motivated) and placed their responses on a chart specifically created for this purpose. Table 14.1 summarizes the demographic and class information of the sample population.

Table 14.1 Demographic and class information of sample population

	#/gender of participants	Level in four-year degree	Years teaching	# of classes completed	Course
Prof A	26/male	Level 8/ year 4	>15	8	Short Story
Prof B	24/male	Level 2/ year 1	10–15	6	Vocabulary Building
Prof C	41/male	Level 2/ year 1	>15	8	Introduction to Translation Studies
Prof D	8/male	Level 6/ year 3	5–10	10	Modern Novel
Prof E	22/male	Level 4/ year 2	5–10	10	Introduction to Literature
Prof F	27/male	Level 4/ year 2	10–15	9	Semantics & Pragmatics
Prof G	32/female	Level 4/ year 2	5–10	10	Academic Writing
Prof H	41/female	Level 1/ year 1	10–15	8	Composition/Listening & Speaking

After collecting the data from each professor and his/her students, we obtained our results by finding the mean of each professor's level of motivation at the beginning and end of each class, the difference between them and the standard deviations. We also calculated the average. initial and ending level of motivation for the totality of students in each class, the difference and standard deviations. The results are presented in a series of tables containing the number of classes taught by the eight professors and the average level of motivation of their students before and after each class.

Results

To assess the dynamic interplay of language teachers' and learners' motivation, we will focus on two sets of numbers that reflect two different interactional processes and timescales. The first corresponds to the motivation of participants as each class commences. Because teachers and learners had already established relationships and expectations of the class based on over three weeks of previous interactions, this data would tend to reflect a longer-term state-like measure concerning how enthusiastic teachers and learners are about the class in general. The second aspect, centering on the difference between average motivation at the beginning and ending of each class, will reveal in-the-moment changes that are most likely inspired by interactional processes between teachers and learners during the specific class period.

Let's begin by assessing the data one group at a time. In Professor A's classes, evidence from Table 14.2 demonstrates the same positive trajectory between the teacher and the students, in terms of both the self-reports at the commencement of the classes and the average differences between the levels of motivation before and after class of the professor and students. The professor began his class with an average motivation of 7.4 on a scale of 1 to 10, while the students began with a group average of 7.5. As the classes terminated, the professor saw an average positive difference of 1.7, with the students reporting almost the same: 1.6. If this were the only group in our sample, it would be easy to say that, indeed, teacher and learner motivation are reciprocal and have a tendency to mirror one another. But then, we have seven more groups to inspect.

Professor B's initial motivation rating was higher than Professor A's, but in the end, Professor B's average difference had a negative trajectory—in fact, the lowest of the eight professors in the sample. That is to say, in five out of six classes he was less motivated when his classes ended than when they began. The sixth class was neutral—beginning and end both reported seven, that is, zero difference. However, this downward tendency did not seem to have an adverse effect on his students, as their total average group difference was +1.3. This might lead one to suggest that the link between teacher and learner motivation found with group A was a glitch, but when careful notice is paid to individual classes, another tendency emerges. For example, Table 14.3 shows that Professor B certainly had a bad day during

Table 14.2 Beginning and ending of self-reported level of motivation by Professor A and the average of his learners

	Professor A			Students (n = 26)		
	Beginning	End	Difference	Beginning	End	Difference
Class 1	7	9	2	6.6	8.6	2.0
Class 2	8	9	1	7.3	8.9	1.5
Class 3	8	8	0	7.0	9.3	2.1
Class 4	8	9	1	7.5	8.4	1.8
Class 5	7	9	2	7.3	7.7	1.9
Class 6	7	10	3	7.7	8.1	1.4
Class 7	6	9	3	8.0	8.4	1.3
Class 8	8	10	2	8.6	8.9	1.1
M	7.4	9.1	1.7	7.5	8.5	1.6
SD	0.7	0.6	0.96	2.0	0.4	0.6

Table 14.3 Beginning and ending of self-reported level of motivation by Professor B and the average of his learners

	Professor B			Students (*n* = 24)		
	Beginning	End	Difference	Beginning	End	Difference
Class 1	9	8	−1	6.2	7.7	1.5
Class 2	10	8	−2	7.2	8.1	1.4
Class 3	8	5	−3	7.3	8.7	1.4
Class 4	7	5	−2	7.0	8.6	1.6
Class 5	8	4	−4	7.5	8.6	1.1
Class 6	7	7	0	7.4	8.7	1.3
M	8.2	6.2	−2	7.1	8.4	1.4
SD	1.1	1.6	1.2	1.8	1.2	1.6

class #5. As class began, he rated his motivation with an 8, but upon its completion, his motivation fell by 50 percent, to a 4. At the same time, Table 14.3 indicates that, in comparison to other class periods, the students' gains from beginning to end of class in terms of their motivational level was their lowest (1.1) of any time during the study, so even if students were still on a positive trajectory, something happened to their motivational level that did not allow it to rise as high as during other classes.

Professor C is the most consistent teacher of our sample. Table 14.4 shows that he taught eight classes and rated both his incoming and outgoing

Table 14.4 Beginning and ending of self-reported level of motivation by Professor C and the average of his learners

	Professor C			Students (*n* = 41)		
	Beginning	End	Difference	Beginning	End	Difference
Class 1	9	9	0	6.6	8.2	1.5
Class 2	9	9	0	7.2	8.3	0.9
Class 3	9	9	0	6.9	8.0	1.1
Class 4	9	9	0	6.7	7.7	1.0
Class 5	9	9	0	6.4	7.0	0.7
Class 6	9	9	0	6.9	7.6	1.1
Class 7	9	9	0	6.8	7.9	1.1
Class 8	9	9	0	6.9	7.6	0.7
M	9	9	0	6.8	7.9	1.0
SD	0	0	0	2.0	2.1	1.6

motivation at 9, making his average difference zero and the standard deviation zero. Because 9 on a scale of 1 to 10 is so high, we must consider the ceiling effect as we discuss this sub-sample. Such remarkable stability is also mirrored in the average difference of his students' beginning and ending scores. With the exception of Professor E's students whose average difference was 0.7, Professor C's students had the second lowest difference between motivational beginning and ending levels (1.0). This number is even more significant given that this class is the largest of the population with an enrollment of forty-one students.

To discuss the motivational contagion between Professor D and his eight students, we would like to draw attention to classes 7, 9, and 10 in Table 14.5. Note that with the exclusion of class 9, which must have been a horrible day for Professor D, the majority of his initial self-ratings of motivation were between 8 and 10—that is, very high. Also observe that on two occasions (classes 7 and 10) the difference between beginning and ending classes was negative. How did the classroom reality that accounted for this adverse evidence influence his students' motivation? The answer is that it created the lowest positive average difference from among the ten classes: 0.4, 0.1, and 0.4. Most other classes saw a rise in motivation from 1.0 to 2.6. That is to say, although students still maintained a positive trajectory during Professor D's low motivation classes, the degree to which higher motivation was experienced was less.

In comparison to other professors in the study, Table 14.6 demonstrates that Professor E had low initial motivation (7 out of 8 professors) with a

Table 14.5 Beginning and ending of self-reported level of motivation by Professor D and the average of his learners

	Professor D			Students (n = 8)		
	Beginning	End	Difference	Beginning	End	Difference
Class 1	10	10	0	7.4	8.6	1.2
Class 2	10	10	0	6.8	8.7	1.0
Class 3	9	10	1	5.6	8.2	2.6
Class 4	8	10	2	8.7	9.2	0.5
Class 5	8	9	1	8.0	9.5	1.5
Class 6	8	8	0	7.0	8.6	1.6
Class 7	10	9	−1	9.1	9.5	0.4
Class 8	7	7	0	7.7	9.5	1.7
Class 9	1	2	1	8.9	9.0	0.1
Class 10	8	5	−3	9.0	9.4	0.4
M	7.9	8	0.1	7.8	9.0	1.1
SD	2.5	2.4	1.3	1.2	0.9	1.7

Table 14.6 Beginning and ending of self-reported level of motivation by Professor E and the average of his learners

	Professor E			Students (*n* = 22)		
	Beginning	End	Difference	Beginning	End	Difference
Class 1	10	8	−2	6.6	8.1	1.5
Class 2	10	10	0	7.4	8.2	0.8
Class 3	5	4	−1	7.4	8.0	0.7
Class 4	7	6	−1	6.9	7.5	0.6
Class 5	8	5	−3	7.3	8.2	0.9
Class 6	5	5	0	6.8	7.9	1.2
Class 7	7	8	1	7.4	8.0	0.9
Class 8	6	7	1	7.7	7.3	−0.3
Class 9	5	5	0	7.8	8.2	0.4
Class 10	8	9	1	8.1	8.8	0.6
M	7.1	6.7	−0.4	7.3	8.0	0.7
SD	1.8	1.9	1.2	2.0	1.7	1.3

score of 7.1 and experienced a negative overall trajectory in the difference between his rating at the beginning of class and at the end (−0.4). He was more motivated going into class than in coming out. This may be part of the reason that Professor E's students saw the smallest difference between their pre- and post-class motivational levels (0.6), too. That is to say, learners came into class with relatively average levels of motivation as compared to other language learners in other groups in the study, but they also left within the same somewhat mediocre range.

Like Professor E, Table 14.7 shows that Professor F also had a negative motivational trajectory, but much larger (−1.3), only surpassed by Professor B (−2.0). Although Professor F's students may have found his classes motivating as evidenced in their positive differences between the beginning and end of classes (2.2), they tended to initially enter the class with the lowest level of motivation (5.6) than any other group in the study—in fact, the next group up had an average difference of 6.0.

Professor G's students' mean motivation level was 6.8 at the beginning of class, roughly average when compared to that of the rest of the groups, which increased to 8.3 showing a positive rise in their level of motivation with a difference of 1.5. In fact, Professor G's students had the largest standard deviation of all the eight student groups in the study 2.7, as expressed in Table 14.8. Indeed, Professor G had a minor positive difference in his motivational level (0.5) as he began with a high rate. Nevertheless, his standard deviation was one of the lowest of the professors with 0.8. That

Table 14.7 Beginning and ending of self-reported level of motivation by Professor F and the average of his learners

	Professor F			Students (n = 27)		
	Beginning	End	Difference	Beginning	End	Difference
Class 1	4	6	2	3.7	7.7	4.1
Class 2	7	4	−3	5.4	7.7	3.8
Class 3	8	5	−3	5.1	7.3	2.2
Class 4	8	7	−1	5.3	8.3	3.0
Class 5	6	4	2	6.4	7.8	1.4
Class 6	9	8	−1	5.7	7.1	1.5
Class 7	9	9	0	5.8	7.2	1.4
Class 8	8	7	−1	6.9	8.2	1.3
Class 9	7	4	−3	5.8	7.4	1.5
M	7.3	6	−1.3	5.6	7.6	2.2
SD	1.5	1.8	1.6	1.8	1.8	1.6

Table 14.8 Beginning and ending of self-reported level of motivation by Professor G and the average of her learners

	Professor G			Students (n = 32)		
	Beginning	End	Difference	Beginning	End	Difference
Class 1	10	10	0	7.0	8.5	1.5
Class 2	9	9	0	6.8	8.5	1.3
Class 3	9	10	1	6.3	8.4	1.7
Class 4	10	10	0	6.7	8.0	1.3
Class 5	8	10	2	6.6	8.1	1.5
Class 6	9	10	1	6.8	8.1	1.3
Class 7	10	10	0	6.8	8.2	1.4
Class 8	10	10	0	5.8	8.2	2.4
Class 9	10	10	0	7.3	8.2	0.9
Class 10	8	9	1	7.6	9.1	1.5
M	9.3	9.8	0.5	6.8	8.3	1.5
SD	0.8	0.4	0.6	2.7	1.6	1.8

is to say, of the thirty-two students in the class, nine indicated an initial self-rating of motivation of less than 5, while eleven students self-reported motivational levels over 9 as the class was about to begin. The nine students whose motivation was rated below 5 was enough to bring the entire average

Table 14.9 Beginning and ending of self-reported level of motivation by Professor H and the average of her learners

| | Professor H | | | Students (*n* = 41) | | |
	Beginning	End	Difference	Beginning	End	Difference
Class 1	8	6	−2	6.5	8.4	1.9
Class 2	5	7	2	6.6	8.2	1.6
Class 3	6	9	2	6.6	8.2	1.6
Class 4	7	7	0	7.0	8.2	1.2
Class 5	9	8	−1	6.4	8.2	1.8
Class 6	9	7	−2	7.1	8.3	1.2
Class 7	6	7	2	7.1	8.6	1.5
Class 8	8	9	1	7.3	8.6	1.3
M	7.2	7.5	0.2	6.0	8.3	1.5
SD	1.4	1	1.7	2.4	1.9	1.1

down to a point where their initial motivation levels fell in the middle of the pack. The important takeaway from this finding is that psychometric data used to analyze group tendencies is not as effective as individual-level studies that would allow researchers to track the idiosyncratic highs and lows of the relationships among language teachers and their students.

Like all the other student groups in the study, Professor H's learners self-reported a positive motivation trajectory between their beginning and end rankings in all eight classes, but their professor perceived the same tendency only 50 percent of the time, having assessed feeling higher motivation at the beginning of four classes than at the end of them as shown in Table 14.9. Professor H also fell within the bottom three professors considering her self-ranking of motivation at the beginning of classes (7.2). Although the average students' difference between the initiation of the class and its completion demonstrated an upward tendency, the scores they assigned at the beginning of the class put their average as the second lowest of all student groups.

Discussion and Conclusions

In terms of teacher motivation as classes commenced, two professors self-reported high scores between 9 and 10 (Professor E, 9.3; and Professor C, 9.0), two professors rated their initial motivation between 8 and 9 (Professor D, 8.8; and Professor B, 8.2), and the remaining four language professors ranked their initial motivation as falling between 7 and 8 (Professor A, 7.4; Professor F, 7.3; Professor H, 7.2; and Professor E, 7.1). That is to say, half of the professors sampled began teaching their classes feeling a level of motivation above 8; while the other half fell below 8, but never less than 7.

In comparing that to students, the averages of the students' initial motivation never exceeded 8 (compared to half of the professors whose did), only four groups (D, B, A, and E) had an average between 7 and 8 (compared to the other half of the professors whose did) and the other four groups (G, C, F, and H) had an average initial motivation lower than 7 (a situation which no professors reported).

As far as the general findings concerning the differences between the beginning and ending self-reports that reveal more in-the-moment findings, student groups invariably had positive differences—that is, not even one instance arose wherein the average of the students revealed a downturn in their motivation from the beginning to end of class. This is substantially different from their professors who experienced much more variability. In fact, results show that three professors (A, G, and H) showed positive gains, two remained relatively the same (C and D), and three actually self-reported lower levels of motivation after their classes had ended compared to the time they had begun (B, F, and E).

Upon observing these general findings, one might conclude that teachers' and learners' levels of motivation are not tightly linked, but such observations are somewhat deceptive, because a close analysis of the details reveals some hidden contradictory results that are glossed over by lumping data into groups. For example, Professor A's motivational levels and that of his students were closely aligned: both the self-reported levels of motivation at the beginning of the class and the difference between motivational levels at the commencement and conclusion of classes were off by a mere 0.1. Professor's B very bad day during class 5 (his end self-reported motivation was four points less than the beginning) aligned with the lowest average difference among his group of students. For Professor C, his consistency in his motivation both among and within his classes was mirrored in his students' relative stability between self-reports of the difference between beginning and ending levels of motivation. Furthermore, Professor D's students showed less increase in motivation during class when the professor's self-reports between beginning and end were negative. As for Professor F, his negative emotional trajectory as evidenced in the difference between his self-reported levels of motivation at the beginning and end of class was reflected in students whose ratings upon entering class were the lowest of all the groups. The standard deviations that represent the variability in the responses of Professor G's students provide the strongest rationale for taking an individualized approach to motivation data as some students' responses aligned closely with their professor while others did not—reinforcing the dynamic nature of motivation and the presence of other variables that influence the system. Finally, the data reflecting Professor H's and her students' level of motivation at the initiation of classes demonstrate that both were equally low in comparison to other groups in the study.

To conclude, motivation is a dynamic variable that fluctuates on different timescales in language learning. This study looked at it on two different levels: the degree to which teachers and learners entered each class—suggesting a more state-like phenomenon—and the degree of difference between the beginning and end of the class—reflecting a more momentary fluctuation. Our research using eight groups over eight to ten classes demonstrated the dynamic nature of motivation contagion, with many instances of teachers' and learners' motivation aligning and just as many times when other variables may have entered the system to cause greater disassociation. While our group level analysis revealed where the data came together and spread apart, individual data provided a more nuanced perspective.

CHAPTER 15

Group DMCs and Group Emotion in the L2 Classroom

Christine Muir

Language teachers stand in front of groups of language learners every day. Similar scenes can be found in schools all across the globe: regardless of geographical location, demographics of the learners, the age, or suitability of the physical environment of the classroom itself alongside a multitude of other varying factors, all these diverse contexts are connected in the very basic sense that teachers are standing up in front of class *groups*. While it is certainly the case that some language teaching does take place one-on-one with individual students, the vast majority of teaching worldwide occurs in these social settings. Such teaching is not always an easy task. Each student brings with them into the classroom personalized goals, individual preferences, unique personalities, different motivations. Indeed, with this in mind one may wonder why it is that group dynamics tend to form such a minor part of many language teacher training courses. The two Cambridge international English language teaching qualifications, for example—the CELTA/Certificate in teaching English to speakers of other languages and the DELTA/Diploma in teaching English to speakers of other languages—do not have any overt focus on teaching and managing learner *groups* at either level. Although there is a modest literature on group dynamics in the context of SLA, it would be difficult to argue that sufficient work has been done in this area to date to be able to tell the full story. The acknowledgment that managing some class groups can be so challenging may account for why, when things do seemingly fall "magically" into place, the positive experiences that can follow often become so highly memorable.

The motivational framework in which this chapter is rooted encapsulates a very specific "coming together" of exactly this kind.

A *directed motivational current* (or a DMC) is a powerful, goal-directed stream of energy aimed toward the achievement of a personally highly valued aim. The energy contained within this self-propelling current of energy can often support individuals in achieving more than they had initially anticipated, and sometimes even more than they may previously have believed to be possible. The experience is characterized by a *highly charged, positive emotional tenor*, which individuals often retain strong memories of even many months (and even years) after its conclusion. DMCs can emerge in diverse contexts, language learning among them. For example, someone might experience a DMC in studying to attain the necessary qualifications and proficiency to be able to study for postgraduate qualifications in an L2, or to obtain a visa (as in the cases of Shirin and Alan in Ibrahim, 2017), or while training to become an English language teacher (as for both Tuba and Zahra in Zarrinabadi & Tavakoli, 2017). DMC emergence can occur not only individually but also in groups. In instructed classroom contexts, it has been argued that group DMCs emerge via *intensive group projects*, and, more specifically, from project designs "*with DMC potential*" (for it is certainly not the case that *all* projects are likely to be capable of inspiring and supporting group DMC emergence; see Muir, 2019, 2020).

I have recently reflected elsewhere on this unique type of *group-level motivational emergence*, specifically from a complexity approach to research and understanding, and with a view to considering future research avenues and possibilities (Muir, 2021; see also Sampson, 2016). To date, research exploring the experience and purposeful facilitation of group DMCs in instructed language classrooms remains at its very early stages. The limited research on group DMCs can largely be attributed to the fact that DMC research itself is an emergent area of inquiry (begun still not a decade ago: Dörnyei et al., 2014, 2015, Henry et al., 2015, Muir & Dörnyei, 2013). Yet, the majority of research into language learner motivation across the field of SLA as a whole, too, has historically tended to concentrate focus on *individual* rather than *group* levels of understanding. The study of group-level motivational emergence continues to be an area ripe for further research.

Although the emergence of group DMCs in language classrooms is likely to be a relatively rare occurrence (certainly they are not descriptive of the "normal" engagement exhibited by students), our understanding of the significance of DMCs is rooted in their being comprised of *the same building blocks* as other experiences of long-term motivation more broadly (Dörnyei et al., 2016). Even if a group project, after being introduced into an instructed classroom context, does not lead to the emergence of a group DMC, the productive and engaged group work that can be facilitated may nevertheless lead to highly positive student experiences and development. With this in mind, recently developed research tools, such as that designed to investigate *group work dynamics* (GWD)—defined as "the socioemotional climate that exists within a small work group and the degree to which it exhibits a genuine sense of warmth, trust, cheerfulness, and accomplishment" (Poupore, 2018, p. 351; see also Poupore, 2016)— although designed to investigate group work dynamics in the context of discrete language learning *tasks*, as a methodological tool may equally be able to contribute to understanding of the experience and manifestation of group DMCs. The instrument is designed to measure multiple contributing factors, both verbal and nonverbal, with each variably weighted. Examples of positive GWD characteristics include positive remarks and providing help (verbal) and touching and speaker/listener eye contact (nonverbal); examples of negative GWD characteristics include impersonal or superiority responses (verbal) and yawning and sighing (nonverbal). Initial empirical studies utilizing these tools have been able to document, among other things, the ways in which common group members can perform entirely different functions when engaged in activities with different group members (see the interesting study of Mina in Poupore, 2018, foregrounding the importance of robust positive group dynamics to productive group work in education), and a clear relationship between GWD and group motivation and emotion.

In this chapter, I focus on a fascinating aspect of group DMCs that has so far received scant research attention. Research into positive language learner emotions have gathered significant steam in recent years, as has evidence that positive emotions in language learning can also affect cognitive processing (see Forgas, 2008; Storbeck & Clore, 2007; in the context of SLA, e.g. Dewaele & MacIntyre, 2014; MacIntyre & Gregersen, 2012). The affective experience of individual DMCs has received some, albeit limited, dedicated investigation (for an exception see e.g. Ibrahim, 2016), yet, a parallel focus on the emotional experience of group DMCs has yet to take its turn center stage.

I begin by offering a slightly more detailed introduction to DMCs, foregrounding in particular the important role of this positive emotionality experienced by individuals. I introduce the notion of *emotional contagion*, and use this to explain how positive (and negative) emotion can sometimes be "infectious." I then go on to introduce the notion of *group emotion*, highlight its relevance in the context of group DMCs, and its importance as a site for future investigation. Although I root discussion in this chapter in the context of group DMCs, as I have touched upon already, these principles and ideas may be equally as relevant to the investigation of collaborative learning and group-level motivational emergence more broadly. By way of underlining the relevance and importance of this novel line of inquiry, I conclude by highlighting some of the positive outcomes demonstrated as emergent as a result of positive group emotion and of group DMCs.

Emotion in Individual and Group DMCs

The highly marked, positive emotional tenor of DMCs is one of several key characteristics. In individual DMCs, this is rooted in an individual's perception of progress, not only to a desired goal, but to one that is truly *self-concordant*. Self-concordant goals are ones that are wholly *identity-congruent*, and so which "belong to the self in a deeper sense" (Sheldon & Elliot, 1999: 494). These are goals that tap into the core of who we are, the way in which we understand and see ourselves, and our deepest desires for future achievement and personal development. Goal-striving directed toward the fulfilment of self-concordant goals not only tends to be more persistent, vigorous, and determined (Sheldon & Elliot, 1999) but can engender feelings of *eudaimonic well-being*. The easiest way to understand the experience of eudaimonia is by considering it alongside *hedonic enjoyment*. Some experiences engender only the latter. Let us imagine a surfer, spending a day catching some waves at Bondi beach, Australia. There is strong potential for this to offer a large number of hedonic pleasures; laughing with friends on the beach, catching the first (and last!) wave of the day, heading off in the evening to light a barbecue and watch the sunset. All these activities lead to joyous, transient highs. Sometimes, however, intrinsically motivated experiences such as these can facilitate experiences of both hedonic enjoyment *and* eudaimonia. By way of an example let us now imagine someone in a similar costal environment, except this time on a beach further north up the Australian East coast and in the run up to a major surf competition, for example the Quiksilver Pro Gold Coast. While they may likewise experience periods of hedonia throughout the day, the opportunity to spend a day honing their craft in preparation for this "competition-of-a-lifetime," for them, also inspires another feeling, that of "being where one wants to be, doing what one wants to do" (Norton, 1976, p. 216): this feeling experienced in the pursuit of self-actualization is that of eudaimonic well-being (Waterman, 1993; Waterman, Schwartz & Conti, 2008). In the context of DMCs, with action aligned to facilitate the achievement of a self-concordant goal, the experience is often perceived as acute.

This strong positive emotionality is characteristic of both individual and group DMC experiences. The question therefore arises, "Can the goal of a group project in an instructed classroom environment be able to reach similar levels of self-concordance and identity-relevance for learners?" That is, do the similarly strong positive emotional responses of both individual and group DMCs emerge from the same genesis? In some instances, this may indeed be the case (or at least be partly the case), and certainly a teacher's role in the introduction of any group project in educational contexts is to help students connect with the goal on more than merely a superficial level (see Colombo, 2017, for a particularly good example of a L2 project goal being personalizable across a diverse student group). However, in the context of group DMCs, another factor has been argued to be of greater importance, and it is here that we again return to the importance of group dynamics.

The positive emotionality in group DMCs is also rooted in the feeling of being a member of a productive group, and the emotional and social well-being that this can generate (Dörnyei et al., 2016). The basic human need for relatedness is a core principle of self-determination theory (Deci & Ryan, 1985; see also Oga-Baldwin & Hirosawa, this volume), and in educational contexts, when striving for mutual goals, what can emerge is "an emotional bonding with collaborators liking each other, wanting to help each other succeed, and being committed to each other's well-being" (Johnson, Johnson & Smith, 1998, p. 19). The emotional well-being that such experiences of group DMCs can generate can be powerfully experienced, encapsulated, for example, in the words of Hotaka, a Japanese student who experienced a group DMC during a charity fundraising project while studying on a five-week business English course in Australia: "this experience becomes, nutrition of my life, in the future … and this course made, made my life complete!" (Muir, 2020, p. 136).

Emotional Contagion and DMCs

How is it that individuals, in experiencing group DMCs, come to collectively experience this group-level emotional emergence so strongly? An explanation has been put forward foregrounding the notion of *emotional contagion* (see also Gregersen & Al Khateeb, this volume). As we might expect from this moniker, we can understand emotional contagion in simple terms as "the transfer of moods or emotions from one person to another" (Barsade et al., 2018, p. 137). Interestingly, this is thought to occur at both *conscious* and *unconscious* levels, the former through, for example, emotional social comparison processes, and the latter leading to participants reportedly not being aware that such an influence has occurred, nor the resulting effects on either their emotion or subsequent behavior (see Barsade et al., 2018). It is worth considering why emotional contagion does not take hold and escalate—for example as seen in the case of DMCs—more frequently. DMCs are understood as only emergent when a final puzzle piece finally falls into place: DMC emergence cannot reliably be predicted in advance, due to the unknowable set of initial conditions governing a system (in this case an intact class group), and with each condition itself also continually in a state of flux and continually affecting and being affected by those around it (Verspoor, 2015, see also Muir, 2021). Barsade et al. (2018, p. 142) stress the fact that "the importance of moderators in understanding the degree to which emotional contagion will occur" is "striking." Some moderators they highlight include group membership stability, group conflict, and task and social interdependence. However, in the context of group emotion research in personality psychology this, too, is foregrounded as an important area for further research (ibid.).

Group emotion

Parkinson, Fischer, and Manstead (2005, p. 113) rightly point out that "the notion of group emotion initially seems strange, because it conflicts with the commonsense assumption that the locus of emotional experience is the individual." Yet, even from the very brief nods to some related literatures that I have been able to offer throughout this chapter, we can see some evidence that the social and emotional influence from acting as a member of a group can be considerable, as can be the reciprocal influence of individuals on the group itself. It has even been suggested by some that "the development of group emotion is what defines a group and distinguishes it from merely a collection of individuals" (Barsade, 2002, p. 644; Barsade & Gibson, 2012). Since initial examination of this idea (see e.g. Bartel & Saavedra, 2000; George, 1990; Totterdell et al., 1998), it has been taken up by a number of other researchers, including Barsade and her colleagues (cf. Barsade & Gibson, 1998; Barsade et al., 2018; Barsade & Knight, 2015; Kelly & Barsade, 2001). The emergence of group affect (across much of this research the terms "emotion" and "affect" tend to be used somewhat interchangeably, even though at individual levels of understanding each have distinct definitions) is affected by both *top-down* and *bottom-up* processes. As Parkinson et al. (2005, p. 113) describe:

> the influence of a group on the emotional lives of its individual members is complemented by a reciprocal influence that individuals exert on the emotional character of the group. Indeed, the convergence of group affect is probably based on two complementary processes. The first involves group norms relating to emotion shaping each individual's feelings and expressions by a top-down process. The second involves the interpersonal influence of each group member on those with whom he or she interacts. The bottom-up coordination of emotion (working either by emotional contagion or the reciprocal negotiation of social appraisals [...]) consolidates lower-level interpretative, affective, or evaluative trends into shared group emotion.

Whichever factor is most influential in any instance is likely to vary by context (for example, where only limited communication is available, top-down processes are likely to be most influential; Parkinson et al., 2005). Further to the role of group norms in contributing to "the emotional character of the group" (for "the influence of these norms extends beyond the regulation of emotional expression and communication, and *can penetrate to the experience of emotion*," Parkinson et al., 2005, p. 114, emphasis added), Barsade et al. (2018, p. 141) have likewise suggested that not only can emotional contagion shed light on the creation of group emotion, "there is evidence that emotional contagion has a powerful impact on group dynamics through its influence on individual emotions and the affective convergence of the group toward particular emotions."

Looking to the Future

Developing understanding of group emotion may be important for several reasons, not only because of the practical acknowledgement that teaching groups of learners tends to be the normal classroom reality. Project-based learning is experiencing a resurgence of interest both across education as a whole and in the context of language learning, and this may be rooted in no small part in our developing understanding of many of the issues involved in facilitating productive and worthwhile educational projects (for two recent edited volumes in the context of language learning see Beckett & Slater, 2020 and Gras-Velazquez, 2020). Developing understanding in this regard also deserves to be brought to the fore owing to the positive effects that can be facilitated. For example, in research into group emotion and emotional contagion (outside of the context of education) positive effects have been documented to include increased cooperation and decreased conflict (Barsade, 2002) and perceived performance (Totterdell, 2000). In the context of group DMC research, there is initial evidence that such experiences may lead students to experience similar positive outcomes. These may include, for example, increased efforts with regard to not wanting to be absent from class, students working more productively together (e.g., actively seeking out peers outside of class time to offer help), reduced anxiety, and increased student confidence (see Muir, 2020, for initial investigation). It is important to note that in this study (Muir, 2020), students were explicit in their reports of the perceived importance of the social climate and positive group emotion that was facilitated via the emergence of the group DMC as being core to these positive evaluations.

Perhaps more significantly, some evidence also suggests that the experience of group DMCs may in fact have tangible *longer-term* positive effects for individuals. Muir (2020) argues that evidence pointing toward some enduring positive effects in the context of study abroad—including, for example, on students' motivation, invested effort and ideal selves, identifiable as long as six months after students return to their home countries (Fryer & Roger, 2018)—may actually be attributable to the experience of a *DMC* rather than these study abroad experiences themselves. While there are, at present, certainly many more questions in need of answering than those for which we already have research evidence to support, it is undoubtedly the case that pursuing them may lead to the emergence of highly productive lines of inquiry.

PART FIVE

Emerging Topics

CHAPTER 16

Complexity Theory: From Metaphors to Methodological Advances

Ali H. Al-Hoorie and Phil Hiver

Introduction

In recent years, scholarship in second language development (SLD) has pivoted toward a transdisciplinary conceptualization that positions the learner in context as central to the multifaceted, dynamic, and emergent process of learning and development (The Douglas Fir Group, 2016). This realization has increased momentum for a complexity turn (Dörnyei, MacIntyre, & Henry, 2015), one which challenges researchers to adopt a pragmatic transdisciplinary approach to research that is problem-oriented in nature. This reorientation of the field has strong roots in Zoltán Dörnyei's thinking (e.g., 2008, 2017). Many excellent volumes explore this topical area in some depth (de Bot, Lowie, & Verspoor, 2005; Larsen-Freeman & Cameron, 2008). These and other sources have introduced the new generation of SLD scholars to the promise of a conceptual reorientation around complex dynamic systems theory (CDST) in the field of SLD (see Larsen-Freeman, 2017, for one review). Yet, as with other disciplines' earliest experiences drawing on understandings from CDST, it is apparent that the empirical work in our field has yet to catch up with the rich conceptualizations found in theoretical discussions. Simultaneously investigating "the ongoing multiple influences between environmental and learner factors in all their componential complexity" (Dörnyei, 2009c, p. 229) remains an uphill challenge both at the individual level of development and across broader patterns or commonalities. One inhibitor to scholarship informed by complexity theory has been applied linguists' uncertainty regarding what conducting actual empirical research entails. This has resulted in a lack of consensus regarding which phenomena or questions merit examination, how systematic investigation should be structured and conducted (e.g., with regard to instrumentation and data collection), and how the results of this research should be analyzed and interpreted.

In response, SLD researchers have begun to expand the toolbox of methods available to conduct research in a dynamic vein (e.g., Dörnyei et al., 2015; Hiver & Al-Hoorie, 2020b; Verspoor, de Bot, & Lowie, 2011). Hiver and Al-Hoorie (2016) have also proposed a dynamic ensemble, which details ways in which CDST constrains methodological choices while at the same time encouraging innovation and diversification. Parallel to these advances, however, the field has developed the habit of drawing heavily from a short list of statistical methods. In her survey of major SLD journals, Lazaraton (2000) reported that the proportion of studies using Pearson product-moment correlations and t-tests (and ANOVAs) holds the lion's share, approaching 90 percent. Over a decade later, this situation has changed little (Plonsky, 2013), which raises the obvious question of whether these statistical methods are optimal.

If some of the methods that are in widespread use across the field are ill-suited to studying the complex and dynamic realities of SLD and situating these phenomena firmly in context, it would seem that an expansion of the available methods is needed. In this chapter, we provide an overview of some limitations of these methods, as well as alternative procedures for overcoming these limitations. We focus on common quantitative procedures, including correlation, multiple regression, t-test, and ANOVA. We conclude by highlighting reliability issues likely to arise from the type of methodological discussion we present here.

SLD research drawing from CDST is no stranger to these concerns (de Bot & Larsen-Freeman, 2011), in that there is a need to broaden the range of quantitative tools available to CDST research. Some work has already been done, especially at the descriptive level (e.g., Verspoor et al., 2011). In the words of David Byrne (2009), however, "the central project of any science is the elucidation of causes that extend beyond the unique specific instance" (p. 1). In this chapter, we adopt an inferential approach, which is equally important.

Correlation

There are at least two technical limitations affecting the substantive interpretation of (zero-order) correlations: one related to shared variance and the other to measurement error. These two points are both crucial to a more sophisticated understanding of complex phenomena.

Shared Variance

A correlation between two variables can be thought of as "raw," in that it does not distinguish between shared and unique variance. Unique variance is the proportion of variance that an independent variable uniquely explains in a dependent variable, that is, after statistically partialing out the contribution of the other independent variables in the model. On the other hand, shared variance includes redundantly explained variance. When investigating a theory, it is important to determine unique variance because including shared variance may spuriously inflate coefficients obtained, and this may have substantive consequences. "Indeed, redundancy among explanatory variables is the plague of our efforts to understand the causal structure that underlies observations in the behavioral and social sciences" (J. Cohen, Cohen, West, & Aiken, 2003, p. 76).

Using multiple regression, instead of correlation, can take shared variance into account. In fact, regression is the origin of correlation, not the other way around as some might assume, a misconception that probably arises because correlation—for pedagogical reasons—is typically taught first in introductory statistics courses. Correlation can be described as the relationship that does not regress (see Campbell & Kenny, 1999). In fact, even the *r* that is used as a symbol for correlation actually stands for regression (Campbell & Kenny, 1999; Miles & Banyard, 2007). The story does not end with correlation. Both *t*-test and ANOVA are considered special cases of regression (J. Cohen, 1968). That is, because there are only two groups in a *t*-test (or more than two in the case of ANOVA), the statistical formulae can be considerably simplified, but fundamentally they are still a regression formula.

As an illustration of the advantage of using multiple regression over correlation to account for shared variance, we simulated three variables using R (R Core Team, 2014). The correlation matrix of the variables is in Table 16.1. Imagine that the two independent variables (IV1 and IV2) are *motivation* and *attention in class*, respectively, while the dependent variable (DV) is final *achievement*. As shown in Table 16.1, each variable predicts achievement reasonably well according to conventional standards. Notice, however, that the two IVs are also correlated with each other at .27 (which is not uncommon in the social sciences). This suggests that individuals with higher motivation also tend to pay more attention in class. This overlap (see the dashed area in Figure 16.1A) is not adjusted for in the correlation of each IV with the DV in Table 16.1 (hence, we call them raw). As a rule of thumb, the variance of the DV explained by the two IVs would be expected

Table 16.1 Simulated correlations among three variables (*N* = 300).

	IV1	IV2
IV1	–	
IV2	.27	–
DV	.46	.32

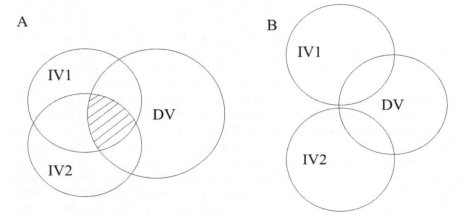

FIGURE 16.1 *Overlap between two independent variables (A) versus no overlap (B).*

to decrease by .27² (or .14 in total, depending on the internal structure of the variables). The .46 and .32 coefficients are valid only when the correlation between the two IVs is zero, as in Figure 16.1B.

In order to find out the exact magnitude of this expected decrease, we ran multiple regression on this simulated dataset. Figure 16.2 compares the results with those from Table 16.1, which assumes that the two IVs are correlated at zero. When the correlation between the two IVs is .27, the coefficients are the same as those in Table 16.1 (.46 and .32). However, when this correlation is zero, the coefficients shrink. IV2 shows a marked drop, which could have considerable substantive consequences. These coefficients are called first-order correlations because one variable is partialed out in each case, while those in Table 16.1 are zero-order correlations. Thus, because of the insensitivity of correlation to shared variance, researchers are at risk of obtaining inflated correlation coefficients and losing precision.

Although regression is most commonly used to model linear relationships, nonlinear regression offers more flexibility in many situations, especially for CDST researchers. Statistician Simon Jackman makes this point clearly:

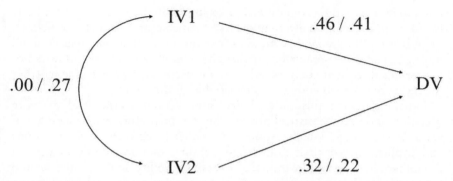

FIGURE 16.2 *Comparison of the regression coefficients when the independent variables are correlated at .00 versus at .27.*

if there is one statistical model that we expect Ph.D. students to understand, it is the regression model ... No class on the linear regression model is complete without showing students how logarithmic transformations, polynomials, taking reciprocals or square roots, or interactions can be used to estimate non-linear relationships between y and predictors of interest.

(Jackman, 2009, pp. 100–2)

With application to modeling dynamic change and development, Seber and Wild (1989) explain that the decision to select a linear or nonlinear model is based on theoretical considerations or observation of nonlinear behavior, such as visual inspection or formal tests. Especially for extended timescales, nonlinear modeling tends to be more appropriate (e.g., Miles & Shevlin, 2001, p. 136). Rodgers, Rowe, and Buster (1998) also argue that linear models may be appropriate in the exploratory stages of research when little is known about the specific mechanism involved. This is not a cure-all data analysis technique, however, and as the authors point out: "We emphasize that nonlinear dynamic models should not generally substitute for traditional linear analysis. They have different goals, fit different types of data, and result in different interpretations" (Rodgers et al., 1998, p. 1097).

Measurement Error

The second limitation of correlation is that it does not account for measurement error. This limitation also applies to regression analysis. Both of these procedures assume that the variables in the model were measured perfectly. This rarely happens, except perhaps in clear-cut variables such as gender. In most cases, isomorphic parallels between a reality and a measurement of that reality are limited, which introduces a level of unreliability into the estimation. For example, if the reliability of a scale is .70, which is commonly thought to be satisfactory (though see below), there is still .30 unreliability (or .51 error variance)[1] that goes unaccounted for. In conventional practice, whether the reliability is .80 or .60 does not matter in subsequent analyses; reliability is used only to determine whether the measure is "good enough" to proceed with the analysis.

However, taking this unreliability into account would lead to more precision and more statistical power. This can be performed through latent variable modeling, which requires specialized software such as Amos and Mplus, but which is nonetheless gaining traction rapidly in various disciplines. In order to illustrate the effect of reliability on the results, we ran the simulated data generated above in Amos three times, each time setting the reliability at a different level: .95, .80, or .65. This allows examining how the results are influenced by the different levels of reliability. Reliabilities were set by fixing the error variance of the latent variable using the formula: $SD^2_{scale} \times (1 - rho)$ (Brown, 2015).

The results are shown in Figure 16.3. When reliability is very high (.95), the results are very similar to those from multiple regression (see Figure

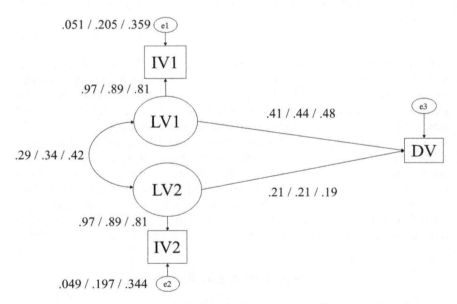

FIGURE 16.3 *Comparison of standardized structural coefficients at three levels of reliability: .95/.80/.65. Squares and ovals denote observed and unobserved variables, respectively. Note that this convention was not used in Figure 16.2 in order to avoid suggesting that latent variable modeling was performed there (see J. Cohen et al., 2003, p. 66, for a similar approach). DV = dependent variable, IV = independent variable, LV = latent variable.*

16.2, correlation at .27), again demonstrating that multiple regression assumes that the variables are measured with perfect reliability. However, as the reliability decreases, the two sets of results diverge. The coefficient increases in the case of LV1, but decreases in the case of LV2. Bollen (1989) has demonstrated that in the case of correlation (or simple regression), measurement error attenuates (or underestimates) the relationship, but in the case of multiple regression the bias may be upward or downward (as in Figure 16.3). With a reliability of .65, the coefficient for LV2 drops to .19 (recall that Table 16.1 reports a coefficient of .32!). A drop of this magnitude would most likely have significant substantive consequences.

This example illustrates that reliability is more than merely a sign to telling the researcher whether the measure is good enough to proceed with further analyses. Incorporating reliability can increase the precision of the estimate, which sometimes leads to a dramatic change in the results. This strategy works best when the measures are already reasonably reliable, and so researchers should still aim to obtain measures with good reliability and then adjust for the remaining unreliability. On the other hand, since they do not account for reliability, correlation and regression risk obtaining inaccurate results. In very early phases of a line of research, correlation may be informative. As knowledge advances, greater use of latent variable modeling would be more appropriate.

ANOVA and *t*-test

The same problem described above applies to ANOVA and *t*-test, in that these procedures also assume that the variables are measured without error. Again, measurement error can be accounted for through latent variable modeling. The latent equivalent of *t*-test and ANOVA is multi-group confirmatory factor analysis (MG-CFA, e.g. Brown, 2015). In this case, instead of using the observed means for comparing groups, the latent means are used after adjusting for measurement error. In the case of multi-item scales, using the observed mean is justified only when each item contributes equally to the latent mean, which again requires perfect reliability.

A second problem with *t*-test and ANOVA is that, unlike MG-CFA, they do not allow testing for measurement invariance, that is, whether the two (or more) groups interpret the items in a conceptually similar manner (Hiver & Al-Hoorie, 2020a). For example, when comparing two groups, a mean difference might be because one group actually has a higher latent score, but it might also be because the two groups simply understand the items differently. That the groups understand the items in a similar way is "a logical prerequisite" (Vandenberg & Lance, 2000, p. 9) to any meaningful interpretation of this difference. Items could be interpreted differently in cross-cultural and cross-age comparisons. When measurement invariance does not hold, it means that the measure needs refinement (see, e.g., Davidov,

Meuleman, Cieciuch, Schmidt, & Billiet, 2014). The same is true in cross-time comparisons, as understanding of abstract notions might change over time. The measurement invariance assumption can be investigated both in classical test theory and in modern test theory (for accessible applications, see Davidov, 2008; Engelhard, 2013; Sass, 2011; Steinmetz, Schmidt, Tina-Booh, Wieczorek, & Schwartz, 2009).

Reliability

Last but not least, the increasing interest in CDST may encourage innovations in instruments of measurement, which leads to a greater need to examine the validity of scores derived from those new instruments. There is no reason to assume that validity issues are irrelevant to CDST-inspired instruments, or that issues of complexity and dynamic change nullify conventional notions of validity (Hiver & Al-Hoorie, 2020b). Indeed, "the ability to use scores for an intended research purpose is *only* justifiable if sufficient evidence exists for the valid interpretation of the test scores" (Purpura, Brown, & Schoonen, 2015, p. 41, original emphasis).

In the discussion above, we mentioned that many researchers use reliability to determine whether their measures are good enough to proceed with the analysis. One widespread rule of thumb is to recommend a reliability of .70. The origin of this rule of thumb is that .70 accounts for 50 percent of the variance (or more exactly $.70^2 = .49$). Clearly, accounting for only about 50 percent of the variance is not a remarkable feat. In fact, Lance, Butts, and Michels (2006) describe this cutoff recommendation as an "urban legend," a myth that has persisted over the decades. According to psychometricians Nunnally and Bernstein (1994, p. 265) a reliability of .70 is considered as "only modest" (p. 265). Instead, acceptable reliability "should not be below .80 for widely used scales" (Carmines & Zeller, 1979, p. 51).

Another important consideration is that even a reliability as high as .80 is suitable only for group-level analysis. However, CDST researchers are typically interested in individual-level applications. A reliability of .80 would introduce a high margin of error for individual-level applications. As Nunnally and Bernstein explain,

> We have noted that the standard error of measurement is almost one-third as large as the overall standard deviation of test scores even when the reliability is .90. If important decisions are made with respect to specific test scores, a reliability of .90 is the bare minimum, and a reliability of .95 should be considered the desirable standard.
>
> (Nunnally & Bernstein, 1994, p. 265)

Another advantage of higher levels of reliability is the ability to split samples into subgroups. It is not uncommon that researchers need to create

Table 16.2 Reliability levels and number of distinct subgroups

Reliability	Subgroups
.50	1
.70	2
.80	3
.90	4
.94	5
.96	7
.97	8
.98	9

subgroups of their participants. The reliability of the instrument can decide how many subgroups can be created. Table 16.2 presents a breakdown of the relationship between reliability level and district subgroups (Fisher, 1992).

Based on the level of reliability, therefore, the researcher can make an informed and more accurate decision about how many subgroups (or strata) can be meaningfully created. This, in turn, highlights the need for more attention and effort to be focused on instrument construction and validation in our field. Apparently, the myth that .70 reliability (or just below it) is satisfactory has led to a sense of complacency and lack of interest in refining instruments in our field.

Conclusion

Throughout this chapter, our message has been that quantitative methodology should play a vital role in CDST research. It is high time we put to rest the persistent myth that quantitative data elicitation and analyses are poorly suited to of CDST research: This is categorically not true, although there are quantitative designs that are much more suited to investigating dynamic change and interconnectedness than others (e.g., Molenaar, Lerner, & Newell, 2014; Valsiner, Molenaar, Lyra, & Chaudhary, 2009). Furthermore, it would be misleading to claim that qualitative designs are inherently more compatible with CDST: They are not. From the perspective of CDST's philosophy of science, advocating a qualitative-only approach is neither defensible nor pragmatic for the range of phenomena that necessitate investigation (Hiver & Al-Hoorie, 2016, 2020b). Qualitative research designs do not by themselves guarantee a more complex and dynamic perspective for research, particularly if the research design is not inherently connected to or informed by the conceptual framework of complexity (Dörnyei et al., 2015). As others have noted, the selection of methods for complexity-based inquiry in SLD does not suggest an either/or choice, and we do not, of course, wish to understate the value of qualitative methods that allow finely grained observations, having both reviewed and used some of these methods ourselves firsthand.

Importantly, the potential of quantitative analyses for CDST research extends past the mundane comparisons of groups and measurements of linear relationships into the more compelling areas of identifying underlying structure, accounting for variation at different levels, discerning temporal processes and events, quantifying trends, predicting group membership, applying spatial analysis, and studying networked phenomena nested in contexts. We have written on these and other methods in book-length form elsewhere (Hiver & Al-Hoorie, 2020b) and encourage interested readers to explore these to the extent they feel comfortable with such innovative methods. Provided that research applying a dynamic perspective ensures that, from the earliest stages of design, there is no disconnect between the conceptual framework of CDST and the statistical analyses used, there is every reason to believe that quantitative methods will serve to advance and accelerate our understanding of SLD.

CHAPTER 17

"OH, HI. HELLO": Desire for English in the Semiotics of an Indonesian Product Leaflet

Martin Lamb

Introduction

Motha and Lin have argued that "at the centre of every English language learning moment lies desire ... for what is believed to lie beyond the doors that English unlocks" (2014, p. 331). In this chapter I will draw on data from a longitudinal study of the motivation of nine Indonesian learners of English (Lamb, 2007) to explore the desires that English can arouse in one particular part of the Global South, as well as the identities and power that it affords to those who can appropriate it. The main data consists of a product leaflet written by one of the participants, Tahira, an elite school pupil at age 12 and already at age 22 the part-owner of three online accessories businesses while doing a part-time master's program. A critical discourse analysis (CDA) of this leaflet, alongside selected excerpts from interviews with Tahira and another participant from 2002 to the present day, uncovers the shared desires, tastes, and mutual recognition of a new metropolitan elite in Indonesia, and points toward one motivational strategy available to local teachers of English.

Critical Discourse Analysis
and Motivation to Learn

CDA encompasses a wide range of epistemological and methodological approaches to the analysis of texts (see Lin, 2014 for an overview) that have in common an interest in the "social, ideological and political dimension of discourse" (Cameron & Panović, 2014, p. 1) and an assumption that the linguistic choices made by a speaker or writer are as revealing of social/ideological/political beliefs and intentions as the ideas actually expressed. CDA practitioners therefore look for patterns of usages in texts—sometimes but not always using systemic functional linguistics as a descriptive framework (e.g., Fairclough, 2003)—including the lexical choices, phrase and sentence grammar, text structure, the way it references other texts (intertextuality), and how it incorporates other non-textual elements like sounds and images, in order to understand the stance being taken by the speaker/writer and the broader ideologies they reflect or represent. CDA practitioners often have an overt political agenda—they are concerned with exposing and countering social inequalities or political oppression—and would argue that objectivity is anyway impossible since all social analysts have their own agendas and perspectives; a researcher gains trust by being as open and reflexive as possible.

CDA has rarely been used in researching motivation to learn language, though its untapped potential has been noted by Ushioda (2020b). One core overlapping concept is "identity." Social theories of learning view motivation as a desire for a new identity, usually involving membership of a new community of practice, whether that be an MBA program, a company board, a sports club, or an imagined community of global English speakers (Lamb, 2013); poststructuralists (e.g. Motha & Lin, 2014) have emphasized the way that this desire is itself socially constructed and politically constrained. In Bourdieusian terms (see Pennycook, 2001 for an accessible description of Bourdieu's theory), community memberships are not usually open to anyone but have to be earned through the accumulation of appropriate social, cultural, or economic capital; membership is signaled through the display of such capital. Education is a field where highly valued cultural capital (including language) is reproduced, being passed on from one generation to another. Commerce is a field where such capital is traded in citizens' ongoing struggle to create and articulate their desired identities. A commercial text, such as an advertisement or (I will argue) a product leaflet, is potentially replete with verbal and visual messages about desired identities and, by logical extension, undesired identities, that is, the distinction from others. As Cameron and Panović (2014) put it, CDA can ask

> how the linguistic choices made in these texts do the work of constructing
> and addressing the various categories or types of consumer identified by

advertisers. A related 'critical' question is to what extent these textual constructions depend on and recycle dominant ideologies, so that in identifying with the positions on offer, consumers are also 'buying into' certain kinds of power and inequality.

(p. 10)

CDA of this English language product leaflet produced by Tahira and her colleagues may therefore tell us something about their motivations, that of their customers, and of the ideologies and power relations dominating contemporary urban society in Indonesia.

Context: Young Indonesians Learning English in the Early Twenty-First Century

This chapter builds on an ad hoc program of research in Indonesia that began with a doctoral project aimed at understanding the impact of schooling on young teenagers' motivation for learning English (Lamb, 2007). It was a mixed-method study that involved two questionnaires for the whole school cohort and three interviews and class observations with twelve individual cases, administered over a period of twenty months. Although the formal L2 learning experience was for many learners uninspiring, their motivation for English was not diminished, and I attributed this largely to identification processes, nurtured and developed through social interaction at home, in the local community and in the media, which encouraged many young Indonesians to view English as integral to their future lives. Five years later, interviews with nine of the case study learners revealed a growing divergence in English competence among the learners, which I explained in terms of the strong ideal L2 selves which drove some individuals to make considerable efforts to learn, compared to motivationally weaker ought-to L2 selves in those who were making less progress (Lamb, 2011). Another five years on, when the case study participants were in their early 20s, a further round of interviews revealed that some were now using English confidently in work and/or study, while others expressed deep frustration that they had not been able to realize their hopes of learning the language (Lamb, 2018).

Although the study primarily drew on constructs and methods from motivational psychology, a parallel study utilizing the sociological construct of "investment" (Norton, 2000) would have drawn attention to the way the participants' identities and learning practices were being shaped by global and local power relations, with their own efforts (differentially supported) aimed at not just mastering a new linguistic code but at appropriating new material and symbolic resources, the better to position themselves within those relations of power. Such a study would also have noted how, by the time the participants were leaving full-time education, they were living in "a new world order transformed by advancements in technology and new forms of mobility" (Darvin, 2020, p. 252). The range of multilingual communities to which they could belong, or imagine belonging, had multiplied; with advancing globalization, the value of English as cultural capital in various fields of work and play had risen significantly; and so had young people's "desire for the language, for the identities represented by particular accents and varieties of English, and images that are associated with English" (Motha & Lin, 2014, p. 332).

This can be illustrated by my interactions with two of the participants, Ridwan and Tahira, who from the beginning appeared to be at opposite ends of the academic achievement spectrum. To deal with Ridwan first, he was the fourth of five children in a provincial middle-class family (father a civil servant, mother a high school teacher), and, though designated by his teacher as a "low motivation" student in my original study, he was always cognizant of the potential value of English in his life: "important, important, the thing is, if you want to become a businessman, you have to know English, if not you're going to be deceived by people who do have English" [Interview #3, age 12—translated]. At age 17, he was encountering English on a daily basis ("as soon as you open a website, the explanations are in English" [interview #4]), and aware that in the internet cafés he frequented, if one had some specialist knowledge of English computer terminology "we could teach it to someone else and get a profit." Soon after that encounter, he dropped out of high school, and when I met him at age 22, he was living in Jakarta and eking out a living on the fringes of the fashion industry (two siblings were successful models) by, among other things, trading in textiles, designing T-shirts, and helping to make promotional videos. English was "so important" to him, he said, because there were many foreigners among his firm's clients and he needed to be able to communicate with them; he also made English language slogans for printing on T-shirts.

Our own meeting, which he had arranged to take place in a fashionable shopping mall café with a couple of his friends in attendance, was also an opportunity to perform an English-speaking identity and he sprinkled the conversation with English words and phrases wherever he could, as in this exchange:

I: What's your job then?
R: Working *itu* … entertainment … entertainment … *perubahan-perubahan naik nah sekarang sudah pingin belajar bahasa inggris banget, sekarang* my friend and my manager … *Inggris is eh penting. Bahasa inggris itu penting*[1]

Ridwan's desire for English was undiminished, yet his frustration was evident. A poor schooling experience, not helped by his propensity for alienating teachers, had left him only with the highly truncated repertoires (Blommaert, 2010) that he had appropriated from regular computer usage and occasional commercial encounters.

Turning now to Tahira, at age 12 she was admitted to the elite "accelerated learning" class of her school year, and was among the top performers in that class. Her father was a civil servant while her mother did not work— she consistently mentioned her parents as "my motivation to succeed in life" [interview #6, age 28]. From an early age her heart was set upon leaving the Sumatran town to study at an Islamic boarding school in Java, and then moving on to a top university. By the age of 17 she was indeed studying Industrial Design at Indonesia's best technological university, in one of the country's most cosmopolitan cities. English had never been her favorite school subject but she had consistently invested effort in learning the language:

> I think mastering English is a must if we want to compete in globalization era which is already in front of us. In that era it seems like there's no limit among the country. I means, after I graduate from my study in Institute _ _ _, there'll be opportunity for me to work with peoples from around the world in a multinational company. *[language learning journal, written at age 17; all quotations in original English]*

Five years later, at age 22, Tahira had already graduated and was an entrepreneur with her own start-up company designing, making, and selling a range of high-end products, including bags, notebooks, and various leather items. She was also studying for a part-time MBA that involved a two-month sojourn in New York. At the time I spoke to her she described herself as "a person that's driven by passion and things, and now I see English as my ... as my media or, an aid to understand and to engage to my field of passion" [interview #5, age 22].

Just as with Ridwan, my interview with Tahira took place in one of the city's trendiest shopping malls, and as we sat down she presented me with the gift of a leather notebook, which was for sale on one of her company websites. After expressing my thanks, I opened the wrapping and found a product leaflet inside which—like the notebook itself—had been designed by Tahira and her two colleagues and featured, in large capitalized, italicized letters, the message "*OH, HI. HELLO.*" This was certainly eye-catching but it was only much later that I read the document in full, in its quirky yet sophisticated English, and puzzled about what it was "doing," inside the wrapping of a notebook made and sold in west Java.

Critical Discourse Analysis of the Product Leaflet

The remainder of the chapter presents an analysis of the document, first considering its basic form and function, then asking why it was written exclusively in English, before examining the rhetorical and linguistic choices made by Tahira and colleagues in the main message.

Form and Function

A folded-out greyscale image of the whole document is presented in the Appendix (Figure 17.1). In the actual product, the paper was folded twice so that there were four separate "pages," with the capitalized headings CONTENTS; OH, HI. HELLO; COMPOSITION AND CARE; CONTACTS.

On the front "CONTENTS" page there were three lines in much smaller font, "an anseris premium leather notebook" over a sketch of the notebook itself, "a replacement lace" inside a sketch of a lace, and below, "and this mini guide card (obviously)." The ambiguous term "guide card" suggests that the producers (Tahira and colleagues) were not sure what genre it belonged to, for while it did function as a "care guide," with advice, for example, on keeping it away from water and direct sunlight, it also detailed the product's composition (e.g., "NATURAL PAPER (that's 90% recycled, yay us!))," while the "CONTACTS" page, with the sub-line "there's a lot more where this came from" gave information about the company webpage, Twitter account, and contact email address. The page headed "OH, HI. HELLO" consisted only of a personal message directed at purchasers—not, we should note, directed at customers, since they would only have been able to read it once they had actually bought the product.

The leaflet is therefore a hybrid genre, blending features from different types of text (care guide, contents list, ingredients, advertisement) and having no single essential function. Like the leather notebook itself, it is a luxury, but one that makes both the producers and consumers feel better about themselves. The parchment-style paper is attractive and suggests rarity, something not mass-produced, and the image of the goose that underlays the text on three of the pages both references the brand name "Anseris"—*Anser* is the Latinate term for the genus waterfowl—and also travel, as geese are well known for their seasonal migration. As Tahira said to me in interview, "when we compose we like to make it as subtle and as ... so we can deliver our soul in the product. So that it becomes [a] product and not just a commodity" [interview #5]. In other words, she is trying to position purchasers not as customers but as peers who share their good tastes and leisured lifestyles; and who, of course, also share their comfortable familiarity with colloquial and commercial English.

The Choice of English

There is an extensive literature on the use of English in advertising and commerce in non-Anglophone contexts; Kuppens (2010) identifies four rationales:

- To expand the market for a product beyond the mother tongue (MT) population

- Because English is better able than the MT to convey the qualities of the product, for instance, due to relative brevity or because there are no equivalent words in the MT

- For its cultural connotations, for instance to index "freedom" (associated with the United States), or "class and tradition" (associated with the UK), or as a global language to index worldliness and cosmopolitanism

- As a cue to subtle transcultural intertextuality within the discourse itself, that is, references to other (English language) texts that readers might recognize

The latter two reasons are relevant here. It is significant that there is no Indonesian at all in the document—this is not a bilingual text. Normally this might be meant to signal that the product is made in the West and thus of high quality, but the leaflet makes clear that it is actually made in Indonesia: "your notebook's leather cover was taken from local cow, hence minimizing the carbon footprint released from overseas distribution, because we love the earth too."

This statement also strongly suggests that the targeted customers were Indonesian ("locals"). Tahira confirmed this, saying that the product was placed in local galleries and "arts events," as well as being offered on her company website. When I queried her on whether her customers would understand the leaflet's English, she replied:

I think when I analyse those who bought our product, I think they have almost the same background or English knowledge with us, the three of us. They might understand it because not …. I don't mean to be rude but I think the ordinary people don't interest with this product, you know … ? [interview #5]

The choice of English for the leaflet, like for the product descriptions on her company websites, was very deliberate then, to attract a certain sort of clientele while excluding others; "the market is very niche. Well, the one who want to write in a leather journal is not very much …." What is more, the use of English was not merely emblematic (Hyde, 2002) as it might have been on Ridwan's T-shirt designs; the text of the leaflet was meant to be read and understood, crafted to appeal to that target clientele: the cosmopolitan middle-class English-speaking elite to which Tahira and her colleagues themselves aspired.

While the product itself was not Western, the leaflet assumes that purchasers are familiar with Western consumer goods labeled in English, as there is evidence of transcultural intertextuality here, cued by the use of English. For example, the care guide section mimics the standard instructions that might be found on Western products, but subverts them in the sublines, as here:

KEEP AWAY FROM WATER

altough your notebook is so natural it almost felt hippie, it's not waterproof ...

KEEP AWAY FROM DIRECT SUNLIGHT

please be a sweetheart and keep the leather away from direct sunlight and oils of any kind ....

Tahira and her colleagues thus assume her clients easily recognize these English language phrases and appreciate the added explanation, written in a jokey personalized way at odds with the usual technical phrasing. This is similar to what Kuppens (2010, p. 119) terms "ego enhancement" in postmodern advertising, where intertextuality is used (often by subtle reference to other well-known advertisements or media products) to amuse viewers/readers and credit them with being able to see through classic advertising strategies.[2] "By positioning the viewers [or readers] as the holder of the necessary cultural capital, the advertiser appears to speak to the viewer [or reader] as a peer" (ibid.). The leaflet is cementing a bond between the producers and consumers of the notebook as cosmopolitan English speakers of uncommon refinement.

The Message

In this section I analyze the page containing the main message to purchasers, with the eye-catching heading "OH, HI. HELLO." The punctuation indicates how it is intended to be "heard," with a short pause between the first two words, and a longer pause between the second and third. Said in this way, the phrase takes on a slightly flirtatious note: the speaker is surprised (the small case words inserted after HI—"we didn't see you there"—are hardly noticed on first reading), but then there is recognition; if not of the actual person, but of the type of person who is "there." The "HELLO" is not just a greeting but conveys interest, the promise even of future intimacy. Bourdieu (1991) argues that cultural capital only has value when *recognized* as legitimate by the other. The verbal exchange here symbolizes this act of recognition, as the seller (Tahira and colleagues) recruits the buyer as a peer, a person with distinctive knowledge and tastes.

The next sentence is slightly jarring. It contains two formal speech acts: thanking and then congratulating—as if the speaker is aware of the need to draw back slightly from their enthusiastic greeting. The direct exclamation "congratulations!" on the following line re-establishes the conversational tone of the beginning, and the next utterance, "*yay*," enclosed by unconventional asterisks, takes the discourse to another level of informality, invoking American youth street slang. To an Anglophone reader there is an obvious contradiction here—the kind of youth who uses this language would be unlikely to have much use for a leather notebook. But as I have already stressed, this product is not intended for an Anglophone customer-base but for young Indonesians similar to those who created the product and wrote the leaflet, for whom "yay" might carry connotations of freedom and joy.

Now the "conversation" is put on this very informal footing, the writers can return to the more intimate tone of the opening with the coy "now, don't be shy …, " possibly a teasing reference to the renowned modesty of the Javanese, which they are suggesting should be cast aside now in celebrating their purchase. "Open it, this is all yours" emphasizes the pleasure of possession, assuring the purchaser that there is no need to be embarrassed about feelings of privilege or indulgence.

The following section opens with "we know you're kind of excited and all …, " again carrying the implication that the makers of the product already *know* the customer well. It continues "so please don't let us withhold you any much longer," non-standard forms that would be recognized as such only by a native-speaker, not by the target market. There is a coda: "and oh—we love you too," neatly echoing the earlier comment "we hope you'll love it," and finally cementing the relationship of one of mutual admiration. In fact, the way the text here has run to hyperbole manages to introduce a note of self-parody that the writers believe will be recognized by the readers, in turn signaling their respect for them by implying that they know they are not the type of customer easily seduced by marketing blurb, but instead discerning enough to treat the whole interaction as a game. In Bourdieu's terms, they are encouraging the *mis*recognition of the tawdry commercial exchange—the payment of money for goods—as something more like an exchange of gifts between friends.

Discussion and Implications

So what does this document analysis tell us about the English language learning motivation of young adult Indonesians? Having just examined one text, the analysis obviously shares the limitations of other "single-text, single-shot approaches" (Lin, 2014, p. 228) to CDA and I am not aware if Tahira's company had other products with similarly styled inserts. The document is a generic hybrid and so cannot be said to typify a particular discourse. What it does constitute is an instance of communicative practice among the emerging educated middle class of metropolitan Indonesia, which might be paraphrased along these lines:

we the makers of this product know who you purchasers are because you're like us—you speak our language, you share our tastes for retro personal accessories, you're wealthy enough to afford a quality leather notebook but also thoughtful enough to use one, you have the opportunity for travel though like us you care for the environment—and it's our pleasure to share this and our other products with you.

As such, this is an instance of "elite multilingualism," "a phenomenon that brings social and/or material capital, a sense of belonging, prestige, excellence, privilege, and access through the use of specific linguistic resources for certain social groups and individuals" (Barakos & Selleck, 2019, p. 362). Eliteness is not a straightforward concept—there may be said to be multiple elites in any country, Indonesia included, and Tahira, her colleagues and customers may well not consider themselves to be part of an elite. In the neighboring country of the Philippines, for example, Reyes (2017) discusses "elite bifurcation" where an educated, culturally sophisticated middle-class elite distinguish themselves partly through their use of Standard English from a pretentious, wealthy, consumerist Taglish-speaking middle-class elite. In political and economic terms, there is another elite—sometimes dubbed the 1 percent, though in Indonesia more like the 0.01 percent—with wealth and power beyond the imaginings of Tahira and friends. As Thurlow and Jaworksi (2017) suggest, eliteness is something that people do, through language or other semiotic resources, to assert privilege and superiority, and include or exclude others.

What we see in this product leaflet is English being used to "do eliteness," to establish distinction, and to co-construct specific elite identities. Rather like the Saab owners studied by Dong and Blommaert (2016) who "set themselves off against 'ordinary' Chinese citizens by means of elaborate discourses and semiotic enactments, organized around specific luxury commodities" (p 34), Tahira and colleagues are highly educated and well qualified, but the kind of English deployed in the leaflet is not "school English"—as we have seen it borrows creatively from genres of commerce, youth culture, and environmentalism amongst others. Only someone with a cosmopolitan outlook and more worldly experiences could have appropriated such discoursal repertoires, the leaflet is saying; producers and consumers alike are members of a youthful cultural elite. It is not only in consumerist contexts that English performs this function in Indonesia. Politicians pepper their speeches with English phrases, expensive private hospitals cover their walls with notices in English, elite educators employ English as a medium of instruction (Coleman, 2016). In all cases, the practice is designed to include some people—those who have the right kind of capital to invest—and exclude others. There is an assumption that people like Ridwan would lack both the symbolic (English) and the material (money) capital to buy the work, as well as the refined taste and reflective disposition to appreciate it.

Although the product leaflet therefore fits into a pattern of elitist practices, I must acknowledge ambivalent feelings about it. Having observed Tahira's development from the age of 11 and been witness to her own considerable investment of effort into learning English, I find her linguistic achievements admirable, and her self-advancement in English as well as in other academic/vocational fields will no doubt bring her rewards. But it also provides employment for others, satisfies consumer demand, and inspires other young people. As stated at the beginning, her social background was not particularly privileged and not dissimilar to that of Ridwan, but a mix of small structural advantages (e.g., parents with a distinct interest in education) and her own personal talents and predispositions has enabled her to achieve a cosmopolitan English-mediated identity, while Ridwan, who shared many of her aspirations, remains marginalized and frustrated.

For both, the learning of English was an emotional enterprise and a form of "linguistic entrepreneurship," which reflected the neoliberal ideologies pervasive within twenty-first-century Indonesian education (in urban centers at least) to "strategically exploit language-related resources for enhancing one's worth in the world" (De Costa, Park & Wee, 2016, p. 695). The product leaflet epitomizes the desired learning outcomes of such a language education. Readers committed to resisting the advance of neoliberalism may view their starkly diverging trajectories as evidence of structural iniquities; readers of a less critical bent may regret Ridwan's frustrations but celebrate Tahira's success. De Costa (2019, p. 456) argues that "elite multilingualism can impact learning and teaching negatively," yet the emotional allure of joining an elite—whether economic, academic, sporting or cultural—helps to fuel the motivation of learners and galvanize the work of teachers and institutions. Mastery of a high-status language enables a playful act of "self-actualization," as Tahira described the product leaflet, but it also enables many acts of enterprise or benevolence that would otherwise be impossible, as she pointed out in her most recent communication: "As a Muslim," she reminded me, "my responsibilities in this world are to be an as beneficial person as I can" [interview #6].

In fact, whatever their position on the advance of neoliberalism, local teachers could usefully exploit real world texts like this in their school English lessons (cf. Gorter, 2018). On the one hand, the collection (easily done these days with a mobile phone camera) and analysis of English signage and notices in the environment can itself be a motivational learning activity for pupils; such texts would certainly have been more appealing to Ridwan than the bland coursebooks which deterred him from investing in school English, and could have taught him personally meaningful words and phrases. On the other hand, teachers could also exploit such texts to develop critical thinking; not just about the machinations of corporate advertisers and public authorities, but about the place of English in their physical environment, the doors it opens and closes in their society, and the desires or enmities it invokes in themselves.

APPENDIX

FIGURE 17.1 *Copy of the leaflet (grayscale version).*

CHAPTER 18

Migration, Plurilingualism, and Motivation: Extending the Research Agenda

Vera Busse

Introduction

European language education in the second decade of the twenty-first century faces new challenges that do not only call into question traditional approaches to language teaching but also demand a radical shift in the second language (L2) motivational research agenda. First and foremost, current migratory movements, mobility across countries, and globalization processes have made schools all over Europe more diverse than ever. This diversity cannot be ignored; all teaching must be planned accordingly and then operate on the basis that diversity and multilingualism are the norm rather than the exception (Busse, 2019). Stimulating relevant attitudes—in both teachers and students—and finding different ways to address this rich linguistic and cultural diversity in a productive way have become mandatory for all subjects and is particularly relevant in the field of language education due to the very nature of learning content.

A major European achievement was reached through formulating common European guidelines and policies (Council of Europe, 2008) that specify normative demands and provide a future vision of European education, serving as a road map for policy makers, schools, practitioners, and researchers alike. These educational guidelines do refer not only to relevant content knowledge and skills but also to the attitudinal dimension of learning. One may highlight the European educational commitment to combat racism, xenophobia, and intolerance in general (Council of Europe, 2008, p. 32), and the need to stimulate intercultural learning, to foster mutual respect, open-mindedness, as well as an appreciation of and interest in linguistic and cultural diversity in the language classroom in particular (Council of Europe, 2007, p. 105). The latter objectives are undoubtedly vital if democratic culture, cooperation, and lasting peace are to be achieved in a region that has historically been a hotbed of war and ever-lasting conflicts.

Foreign language education, regardless of the specific language(s) being taught, is responsible for stimulating interest in learning further languages and for motivating students to broaden their language horizon (Council of Europe, 2007). It should be highlighted that European guidelines specify the learning of two languages in addition to the national language (p. 24) as to combat language hegemony (p. 29). In short, language education is to lay the adequate educational groundwork for plurilingual language development of future European citizens.

Starting from the normative demands outlined above, the present chapter shows that there is a considerable need to extend the current research landscape if students are to be prepared according to European educational standards. The chapter then summarizes findings from a recent research project conducted in a multiethnic school setting, which points to the potential of merging insights from multilingual education and L2 motivational research.

Extending the Research Landscape

The divide between language policies, current development in language education, and practices at schools has been the subject of much recent debate. One may highlight the imbalance between the value schools and language education place on languages that are associated with a high social prestige (traditional foreign languages) and the value placed on migratory and minority languages (see also Busse, 2017a, 2017b). One may also highlight the increasingly narrow focus in contemporary language education, as efforts to promote language learning in most European educational systems are increasingly directed toward learning English only (see also the recent MLJ special issue *Beyond Global English*, specifically Dörnyei & Al-Hoorie, 2017).

Studies in Germany further show that migratory languages (e.g., Turkish and Arabic), but also languages of neighboring countries like French or Dutch, are often seen negatively and frequently judged as disagreeable (Eichinger et al., 2009; Plewnia & Rothe, 2011). At the same time, there is a rise of xenophobic attitudes and right-wing rhetoric within many

European countries (see also Wodak, KhosraviNik & Mral, 2013). While the latter underlines the need for stimulating appreciation of and interest in linguistic and cultural diversity as envisioned by European guidelines, language education appears to have undergone few changes over the last decades. Little time is usually afforded to stimulating interest and curiosity in Europe's linguistic and cultural diversity. In fact, the linguistic diversity as presented in the classroom is often ignored (e.g., Bailey & Marsden, 2017; Hall & Cook, 2012).

In Germany, for instance, educational scientists have long criticized the "monolingual habitus" of schools (Gogolin, 2008) which presupposes that the majority of students are monolingual (German), although this is no longer the case in most areas. Multilingual education suggests that an approach that normalizes the existence of linguistic (and cultural) diversity in the classroom and includes it in teaching can empower students (Cummins, 2000). Creating an opportunity for students to make use of their linguistic resources in the classroom is also beneficial to their learning and for their developing multilingual competencies (Cenoz & Gorter, 2014). However, plurilingual practices that enable students to make use of their linguistic repertoires are seldom applied in EFL teaching in Germany (Göbel & Helmke, 2010; Göbel & Vieluf, 2017).

How can L2 motivational research address the divides and challenges outlined above? In the past, L2 motivational research—similarly to most research on foreign language teaching—has also shown a considerable monolingual bias in that (a) the "normal" language learner is conceptualized as monolingual and (b) research either examines or seeks to stimulate students' motivation for learning one other language (either second or foreign) with the bulk of research focusing on learning English (for the latter, see also Boo, Dörnyei, & Ryan, 2015). This monolingual bias is no longer viable in migration societies and particularly problematic in light of the European language education aims outlined above. The research landscape needs to be extended through research that provides language educators with insights on (a) how to draw on linguistic and cultural diversity in the classroom, (b) how to foster students' curiosity in and motivation for learning several languages, and (c) how to stimulate relevant appreciative attitudes.

The prolific research that has been conducted on the motivational force of the ideal L2 self for English in recent years may provide a starting point (see González-Mujico, this volume; Papi, this volume). Although the concept has yet to be made applicable to the understanding of the motivation to learn other or various languages (Dörnyei & Al-Hoorie, 2017), first attempts have already been made. There is some research to suggest that leaners with ideal selves of a cosmopolitan nature may be particularly interested in learning foreign languages (FLs) and gaining intercultural experiences (Busse, 2013, 2017b; Lanvers, 2012). These plurilingual aspirations have been described as a plurilingual ideal *Bildungs-Selbst* (Busse, 2017b) because being fluent in different FLs can be perceived as a way of becoming an educated person and a way to broaden one's horizon. As such, it may also relate to what has been termed an *international posture* (Yashima, 2002). Though the latter concept has been applied to describe English as a foreign language (EFL) learners in Japan, the underlying tenets—an openness to and interest in relating oneself to the world beyond national borders and a willingness to interact with different cultural groups—may well play a role in a young European's plurilingual *Bildungs-Selbst*.

The term *plurilingual* is used to distinguish the ideal *Bildungs-Selbst* conceptually from a bilingual or multilingual self (e.g., Pavlenko, 2006), which usually refers to speakers who already use two or more languages in their daily lives as, for instance, in the case of students with a migration background or speakers of minority languages. In contrast, a plurilingual ideal *Bildungs-Selbst* refers to a wish to learn new languages beside or in addition to the national language(s) and/or family language(s). It is thus applicable to all students, irrespective of language background, and is seen as indicating an openness and appreciation of other languages and cultures that are not already part of students' daily lives. Little is known, however, about what kind of educational groundwork needs to be provided in order to foster such plurilingual ideal selves.

Promoting Positive Attitudes and Plurilingual Ideal Selves in Students

In a recent study (Busse, Cenoz, Dalmann & Rogge, 2020), we conducted an intervention in a multiethnic primary school where we combined insights from multilingual education and L2 motivational research. The sample comprised 42 EFL learners (18 girls, 24 boys). Each group was randomly assigned to either the experimental approach or regular teaching (*n* = 21). An equal number (10) in each group used languages other than German at home.

Following a multilingual perspective on language teaching, students in the intervention group were encouraged to draw on their linguistic resources; that is, they were given the opportunity to translate target words in all languages they were familiar with through different activities, and sound and similarities between words were explored. In addition, two affective-experiential activities were conducted. Affective-experiential learning in general draws on students' emotions and has been shown to be beneficial for student motivation and for addressing the attitudinal dimensions of learning (e.g. Busse & Krause, 2016; Busse, Riedesel, & Krause, 2017). In our particular study, a treasure chest was presented to students that contained pictures of the many languages present in the class. Students were asked to reflect together on why their languages could be considered a treasure and to share moments with their peers where speaking different languages may have felt particularly enriching. In addition, students participated in a dream journey during which different languages could be heard; the latter aimed at stimulating students' visions of themselves as users of multiple languages. It was modeled on didactic material developed for promoting an ideal English self (Hadfield & Dörnyei, 2013), and adapted to the plurilingual focus of our study.

It was assumed that both activities would be perceived as motivating by students and would help foster positive affect for three reasons. First, affective-experiential activities in general generate emotional participation and are therefore often perceived as motivating by students (see also Busse & Krause, 2016; Busse, Riedesel, & Krause, 2017). Second, by conveying the value of plurilingualism through a treasure chest activity and by creating space for reflection upon the value of speaking different languages, monolingual and multilingual students alike are incentivized to broaden their language repertoire. At the same time, the negative social positioning of migrant students is tackled, which may enhance positive affect among these students. Third, dream journeys can help students conjure up the image of a future self speaking another language, which can be a powerful motivator (see Dörnyei, 2009a). It can be assumed that the same holds true with regard to imagining speaking various languages (e.g., Henry, 2017).

We gathered relevant learning prerequisites (prior language knowledge, cognitive ability) and investigated intervention effects through pre-, post-, and follow-up tests. In addition, we measured affect after each of the five 45-minute lessons (for methodological details, see Busse et al., 2020; research instruments can also be found at https://www.iris-database.org).

The results indicate that the approach was successful. Students in the intervention group showed significant gains in plurilingual ideal self aspirations. In answering open-ended questions, they also reported more interest in linguistic diversity compared to the control group, listing a wider range of languages they would like to learn including the languages present in the classroom and other migrant languages. Importantly, students in the experimental group showed larger positive affect throughout all lessons and made much larger learning progress, performing significantly better on productive and receptive vocabulary tests than the control group. This result is worth highlighting, given that the students in the intervention group had less time on task and less time to engage with the textbook exercises due to the two affective-experiential activities and the time provided for inclusion of family languages in the class activities. It was particularly surprising that the advantage of the intervention group over the control group was also present when words were counted as memorized only when spelled correctly, given that the intervention group had spent less time reading and writing the new words. Our approach thus appears promising.

As the study was conducted with EFL beginners, language progress was measured only in terms of expansion of vocabulary and focused mainly on concrete nouns. Future studies should thus also look at other areas of language development, for example, the impact of multilingual practices on other aspects of lexical development (abstract nouns and other parts of speech) and grammar development when working with more advanced learners. Importantly, future studies should further investigate the effect of individual components of the intervention to explore the extent to which they contribute to, on the one hand, stimulating students' interest in and motivation for learning various languages, and, on the other hand, fostering relevant attitudes and appreciation of linguistic diversity and migrant languages in the classroom.

Conclusion

Current migratory movements as well as European plurilingual and intercultural learning aims call into question traditional approaches to language teaching. Addressing linguistic and cultural diversity in the classroom in a productive way as well as stimulating relevant attitudes and motivation for learning several languages needs to be at the forefront of contemporary language education. This demands a radical shift in the L2 motivational research agenda. Merging insights from multilingual education and L2 motivational research seems promising in order to adequately address diversity and to promote foreign language learning at school beyond EFL learning.

CHAPTER 19

English as a Lingua Franca and Second Language Motivation

Zana Ibrahim

Second language (L2) motivation research has long been concerned with the importance of goals in directing learners' focus and energy toward a future end point (e.g., Oxford & Shearin, 1994; Tremblay & Gardner, 1995). Most of the L2 motivation theories and models thus far have incorporated some form of future goals as an essential part (see Al-Hoorie, 2017 for a review). Yet, rarely did any inclusion and conceptualization of goals in the literature touch upon specifying what a common goal would be like for most L2 learners. Mostly a goal has been defined as "success in L2 learning," which could mean different things to different learners, from obtaining working L2 knowledge, functioning in an environment for which limited L2 is needed, to acquiring native-like proficiency or even higher such as mastering the L2 grammar beyond the average native speaker's knowledge. The term that has also frequently been used as an indication of what an L2 goal might be has been "L2 success" (e.g., Dörnyei, & Skehan, 2003). The problem with this general conceptualization is that the goal is not specifically described, an element which is necessary for a goal to be effective (Locke, 1996; Locke & Latham, 2005), and leaving it to learners to discover or decide what their learning goal is can be misleading as they will not be empowered to set concrete learning goals. L2 teachers might therefore face the challenge of setting learning goals for their students, and they may nonetheless not be in a much better position to do so, perhaps because of lack of training to play that role or because not all learners have a common goal shared with other classmates.

Whereas a second language learning goal can be easier to define for most learners of other languages, it is certainly not as such for the hundreds of millions of learners of English worldwide, perhaps not anymore (Seidlhofer, 2005; Widdowson, 1994). Due to its newly established status in the world, English is now studied by more learners than any other language, now and in history. As is seen as a vehicle for and a manifestation of globalization, English is being learned for purposes different from learning other languages, and that is to compete and operate in a globalized world where contact with other nationalities is the new reality of everyday life (Crystal, 2012). English is used to access resources, do business and trade, travel, study abroad, and engage in cross-cultural and international communication. For the majority of learners of English today, the goal of integrating into an English-speaking country, associating with an English-speaking country's culture, or even interacting with native English speakers is increasingly not essential. To most learners today, successful communication with non-native users of English is the primary instrumental goal of English learning (Lamb, 2004).

Despite this new status of English as a language of international communication, English learning learners, teachers, and institutions have not adapted to this new reality; achieving native-like proficiency, adhering to instruction goals set by textbooks that promote native-speakerism, and glorifying native-speaker ideals and standards still consume much of the dominant thinking in the global English language teaching (ELT) industry (Cogo & Jenkins, 2010; Cook, 1999; Seidlhofer, 2004). This is problematic in at least two major ways. First, setting the goal of reaching native-like proficiency is not in line with what the vast majority of current learners of English aim for since they want to learn the language to expand their employment opportunities and communicative repertoire in an increasingly globalized economy (Lamb, 2004). Second, by expecting from all learners to achieve a native-speaker proficiency, both learners and teachers of English are faced with an almost inevitable failure due to age and other factors (Skutnabb-Kangas, Phillipson, Panda & Mohanty, 2009). In this chapter, I argue for utilizing an alternative L2 goal for learners of English that would not only be more realistic and reasonable but also make a paramount difference in increasing their motivation as well as that of English teachers.

English as a Lingua Franca Concept

A lingua franca is a language which is used as a "lingual medium of communication between people of different mother tongues, for whom it is a second language" (Samarin, 1987, p. 371). In the case of English as a lingua franca, it has been defined as a "contact language" between persons who share neither a common native tongue nor a common (national) culture, and for whom English is the chosen foreign language of communication (Firth, 1996, p. 240). When used by non-native speakers in international communication settings, English as a lingua franca does not involve a native English speaker (Seidlhofer, 2004) although more recent conceptualizations of English as a lingua franca (ELF) include interactions between natives with non-natives as well long as they take place in an international setting (Mauranen, 2018). Not only do interlocutors have a different mother tongue, they also do not share a common culture (Jenkins, 2009). McKay (2011) instead uses the term English as an international lingual franca (EILF) "as an umbrella term to characterize the use of English between any two L2 speakers of English, whether sharing the same culture or not, as well as between L2 and L1 speakers of English" (McKay, 2011, p. 127). The current perspective of ELF mostly includes native and non-native speakers of English (Jenkins, 2007; Mauranen, 2012). This is mainly because in many international settings where English is used as the language of interaction, both native and non-native speakers might be involved (Mauranen, 2018).

Today, there are more non-native speakers of English than native speakers. By some estimates, over 80 percent of exchanges in the world today involve non-native speakers of English (Beneke, 1991) especially those in the *expanding circle* (Kachru, 1992; Seidlhofer, 2005). Therefore, besides the English spoken by native speakers, and the world Englishes spoken by former colonial nations (Kachru, 1992), the English used by users in international settings such as in most countries around the world has been dubbed another variety, which is English as an international lingua franca. Moreover, since the majority of its users are outside the sphere of English-speaking countries, ELF variety constitutes the largest number of speakers of English, whose interactions can be described as *sui generis* (House, 1999, p. 74), or "a linguistic phenomenon in its own right" (Seidlhofer, 2004, p. 213). The language today has "reached truly global dimensions," and is therefore being "shaped, in its international uses, at least as much by its nonnative speakers as its native speakers," and has "taken a life of its own" (Seidlhofer, 2004, pp. 211–12). Therefore, as proponents of the concept of ELF propose, norms of the language should no longer be defined as what is acceptable by native speakers, but equally by those who use it as an international lingua franca.

In addition to providing justification for a solid conceptual framework for ELF, in the last two decades, a number of researchers have attempted to define what this variety of English looks like (Seidlhofer, 2001). This has been done primarily through collecting and analyzing corpora of conversation and written accounts of English used by proficient users in international settings. Those attempts started with describing phonological (Jenkins, 2000), and then lexicogrammar features (Dewey, 2003; Kordon, 2003; Seidlhofer, 2004), and more recently there has been a number of systematic studies on pragmatic aspects of English as a lingua franca (Cogo, 2007; House, 2002). The core of the findings of this research program has been the following: ELF features a number of phonological, lexical, and grammatical irregularities and, by native speakers' standards, language errors, which do not generally pose a threat to intelligibility and communication (Seidlhofer, 2004). Moreover, despite differences in cultural backgrounds, non-native users usually manage to communicate successfully mainly through the use of effective communicative strategies (Mauranen, 2018; Murray, 2012). Indeed, some research findings have suggested that the presence of native speakers might be seen as greater risk to intelligibility than L2–L2 interactions (Matsumoto, 2011).

English as a Lingua Franca and Learners' Motivation

The concept of English as a lingua franca offers the potential to take both English learners and teachers into new territories in regard to their language learning goals and their appraisal of their competencies. Through a number of changes in perceptions, learners of English are expected to overcome a range of obstacles and find prospects that can create a positive impact on their overall motivation. As rarely has the L2 motivation field touched upon the issue of demotivation due to matters inherent to second language acquisition itself, ELF is of particular relevance to the realities of what it means to want to learn a second language as an adult. In other words, the process of learning a second language is a tedious job not only because of internal and external factors related to the individual learner but primarily because success in L2 learning is so relative that when it is used to refer to "ultimate attainment," it will naturally mean failure for the vast majority of learners.

Regardless of how motivated and committed an L2 learner might be, the goal of reaching ultimate attainment is nonetheless not feasible mainly because of biological reasons. According to the critical period hypothesis (Lenneberg, 1967) backed by much empirical evidence, the window to achieve native-like proficiency especially for phonology seems to close by as early as around age nine (see Hummel, 2014; Moyer, 2004; Ortega, 2013 for reviews). Based on most of the available empirical evidence, beyond the age of puberty and especially for phonological aspects of an L2, the goal of sounding similar to a native speaker is believed to be biologically predetermined to fail—except in few exceptional cases. As such, setting this goal is both unrealistic and demotivating. However, research into ELF phonological features (Jerkins, 2000) has shown that while many proficient users of English might "mispronounce" certain English sounds primarily due to the effect of their mother tongue, they usually do not cause unintelligibility or pose a threat to communication in interactions between non-native users of English. From a motivational perspective, this finding may be encouraging to English learners who aim to learn the language for international communication, mostly with non-native users in today's globalized world. Therefore, this warrants English teachers to reconsider the traditional goal of sounding as native-like as possible so they are effortlessly understood by native speakers of English. For language learners, this means an end to this unrealizable goal and a shift to what they can achieve and where they ought to be to function successfully as proficient English users. Though this might need more work from the part of English teachers, they were thought to make English learning classes "more motivating and enjoyable" (Jenkins, Cogo, & Dewey, 2011, p. 288).

Additionally, ELF can offer the potential for changing the image of who a successful and competent user of English is. Rather than setting a native-like L2 speaker who probably falls under the category of around 5 percent of individuals who can biologically pass for being native or native-like, learners of English can now form a more realistic future of themselves as a proficient user of the language regardless of whether they sound native or native-like. The ELF literature provides alternative conceptualizations to what L2 learners should set as an example of who they would like to be, which can motivate learners (Björkman, 2010; Cook, 1999; Ur, 2010).

Traditionally, L2 motivation has been conceptualized around the goal of integrating into the native speaker community (Gardner, 1985). While this is no longer the motive for millions of English learners around the world who are primarily concerned with becoming global citizens or employable in their own countries where English is gaining a higher status in the public domain (Lamb, 2004), neither should the new ideal of a successful English learner. Rather than sounding native-like, being a competent English user can give hope to learners for whom reaching native-like proficiency is neither possible nor necessary. That model can be a non-native teacher, successful entrepreneur, an actor, and so on.

ELF can also have a positive motivational impact on overcoming the anxiety related to fossilization (Han, 2004; Han & Odlin, 2006). Most L2 learners ultimately reach a plateau beyond which progress becomes difficult and time-consuming (Selinker, 1972). Fossilization is thought to occur especially with learners who manage to utilize effective communicative strategies because further linguistic progress will be perceived as unnecessary (Thornbury, 2005). However, fossilized learners are considered, including by English learners themselves, to have developed a linguistic repertoire that is insufficient, incomplete, and erroneous (Kuo, 2006; Ur, 2010). They are therefore encouraged to study more (which could mean years) and improve their grammatical and lexical accuracy. In most cases, this improvement is measured against standardized tests that are based on how close test takers' knowledge and performance are to native-speaker standards (Lowenberg, 1989). Whereas most of these learners are already totally capable and perhaps fluent communicators, this sense of incompetence can be demotivating, debilitating, and even detrimental to their already-occurring and efficient engagement with others. Despite creating a feeling of inefficacy, the fossilization effect generates an urge in them to picture themselves as deficient language learners rather than successful language users, which warrants a practically endless process of learning. Hence, their self-image will change from achievers to flawed attempters, and, rather than focusing on developing skills paramount to their life and careers, they will be preoccupied with reducing linguistic errors, which can cause further stress and anxiety. This can ultimately decrease their motivation to the extent of giving up altogether (Zheng, 2013).

Implications for Teaching

Once adopted as an acceptable form of English and the dominant one in international communication settings, ELF has the potential to have an influential motivational impact on learners. ELF can make learners to think about English and English learning differently in regard to what their realistic goal should be, how likely they can achieve it within a reasonable period of time, and how they perceive their performance in real-life situations. I briefly propose a few ways which English teachers can use to translate the positive impact of ELF into practical effect.

L2–L2 Interactions

Given that over 80 percent of interactions in English today involve no native speakers, more inclusion of L2–L2 interactions constitutes a safe and authentic material for English teaching. Teachers have always been eager to incorporate as much native-speaker conversation and language use samples as possible so they make their language teaching more authentic, which has been defined as language produced by native speakers (Little, Devitt, & Singleton, 1989). Yet, authenticity might now mean more L2–L2 or at least L1–L2 interactions especially because even in English-speaking countries, a sizable minority are L2 community users (McKay, 2011). This change in material selection can be motivating to English learners who see how language produced by competent L2 users is seen as natural, authentic, and realistic as by native English speakers. Additionally, they now perceive their class environment as a natural setting for language learning and use, and their L2 teacher as a legitimate source of instruction of English (Sifakis, 2007). A higher level of trust and association with their immediate learning environment such as the course, teacher, and learning materials can be a source of motivation (Masgoret & Gardner, 2003).

Modeling Successful English Users

ELF ideals will be fulfilled through adopting successful ELF users to replace the image of a native speaker as the model for most learners of English.

This will be achieved by depicting English users as the role model of who learners need to be in the future, and this could be motivating because their positive future image of themselves as successful English users will replace their dream of becoming someone they will never become. As such, the ultimate goal of a competent English user, regardless of to what extent they resemble native speakers, is now feasible and dependent on the amount of effort they exert rather than being from the few lucky ones who are biologically capable of reaching native-like proficiency. The likelihood of failing to achieve this goal is therefore minimized because it is relatively easy to identify L2 users who exemplify success rather than a failed learner with a fossilized or "deficient" proficiency (McKay, 2011, p. 130; Seidlhofer, 2005). Additionally, the unsuccessful learner is one who does not put in the required effort rather than an English speaker with a broken accent who needs to identify as a learner for life as their learning is incomplete (Jenkins et al., 2011). English learners now can assume a new identity that is linked to a positive perception of their future possibilities (Jenkins et al., 2011). To feature competent non-native English users, decisions about instruction materials selection have to be made that might be beyond the authority of individual teachers. Therefore, accompanying policy changes is required in regard to textbooks and instruction materials (Modiano, 2009). However, since ELF has not yet been widely adopted by teaching institutions, teachers of English can have a role in choosing and developing materials that include L1–L2 and L2–L2 interactions and language produced by proficient L2 users.

Focusing on Communicative Strategies

Although the dominant current second language teaching methodologies emphasize fluency over accuracy—as in the communicative language teaching approach (Richards, 2006)—or at least consider both of equal importance, English learners' progress is still largely assessed against a number of criteria set both by native speakers and in relation to native-speaker standards. This is evident in the universal descriptors of different proficiency levels of English users such as categorizing them against their approximation to native speaker norms (Jenkins, 2005). This suggests that despite reaching a level to engage in successful interactions with native speakers, these users need to continue learning to reach the upper scale of a "proficient user." Research on EFL users has shown that L2–L2 communication can be smoother than expected as ELF users seem to be capable of overcoming much of the misunderstanding that arises through negotiating meaning and overlooking cultural differences (Kaur, 2011). Hence, to help ELF learners to achieve the goal of successful engagement with other ELF users, teachers of English might focus on teaching pragmatic and communicative skills and strategies (McKay, 2003). This shift of emphasis on gaining structural knowledge to communicative competence can "free up resources for focusing on capabilities that are likely to be crucial in ELF talk" (Seidlhofer, 2004, p. 226). In regard to assessing learners' competence, successful engagement in communication with others including the degree of intelligible pronunciation can be considered as more paramount than whether they resemble native-like speakers (Jenkins, 2000).

Policy Implications

When we accept the notion that most interactions in English occur among non-native speakers, the educational goal of English instruction has to meet this expectation. To motivate learners to reach this goal, we can no longer define for them native-speaker-like learning goals (see also Ushioda, this volume, on social control). To do so, in addition to rectifying unrealistic perspectives of English learners and teachers, language learning institutions need to make changes that correspond to the new reality of English as an international lingua franca. The most important of such policies is the recruitment criteria to abandon native speaker requirement (Holliday, 2006). To set the goal of reaching proficiency rather than native-like command, competent non-native teachers of English can be as authoritative and inspiring as native-speaker teachers. They should therefore be viewed as "successful multilingual practitioners rather than second-rate users of English" who "bring to the classroom vital knowledge of local languages and cultures, which often renders them more effective than those from a monolingual background" (Sowden, 2012, p. 95).

Non-native teachers of English also represent cultures other than of the English-speaking countries. Users of English today do not come from an English-speaking country's culture, nor do they necessarily adopt these countries' cultural norms when they engage in communication with other users (Seidlhofer, Breiteneder, & Pitzl, 2006). Therefore, rather than benefiting from materials and textbooks developed by native-speaker countries' publishers, other resources can be used in the classroom such as textbooks that include contents from different cultures or those that link English use with users of multiple cultural, national, and ethnic backgrounds.

Moreover, private schools' promotion of creating an environment where only native English is used will need to revisit the notion of unrealistic imagined communities (McKay, 2011). To prepare learners to a brighter future, learners of English need to be able to successfully engage with native as well as non-native speakers. Given the recent demographic changes of the western societies, this ability is also essential in English-speaking countries.

Finally, the goal of teaching English for most learners today is to function in a globalized world, and, to this end, more appropriate assessment tools need to be developed. Rather than being compared against the idealized native speaker model that has little relevance to them, ELF users' proficiency can be assessed in reference to successful ELF users in their context such as in comparison to "the 'norms' of successful Asian multilinguals" (Kirkpatrick,

2012, p. 131). This could mean that different testing mechanisms need to be developed depending on what learners and users need the language for; whereas current standardized Western tests can be appropriate for admission to universities in English-speaking countries, it is probably fairer and more adequate to rely on alternative assessment schemes developed specifically for English for ELF context needs.

Conclusion

More work needs to be done at the larger societal level to recognize the new reality of what it means to be a successful user of English. For example, discriminatory practices against proficient but not native-like users of English in appointment, promotion, and recognition need to end. A culture of focusing on proper communication and successful interactions in the workplace and even in the public domain will intensify the principles of English as a lingua franca and the notion that being proficient in ELF settings can be sufficient. For English language learners, this means that the path to success is clear and possible, and effort alone is the passport to reach there.

CHAPTER 20

Using neuroELT Maxims to Raise Student Motivation in the EFL Classroom

Robert S. Murphy

Introduction

The effectiveness of this chapter will likely be judged by how motivated I can get you (the reader) to take interest in our *Maxims of neuroELT*. Over the years, my colleagues have noticed that if you put the word *neuro* in front of just about anything, it becomes quite the attention-grabber. For example, you could put *neuro* in front of everyday candy (making it *neuro-candy*), and it will somehow transform the candy into a magical brain-enhancing item. Such nonsense is fashionably brushed off as "neuro-bunk," and similarly, misguided/misinterpreted beliefs in *neuro-Education* are categorized as "neuro-myths"—the situation became so bleak that we now have entire books debunking neuromyths (Tokuhama-Espinosa, 2018). To help in the mission to counter the nonsense, what I have assembled in this chapter is a list of tried-and-true maxims that have stood up to scientific prodding while displaying significant pedagogical value in the EFL classroom; you will find no neuro-nonsense here.

If you learn how to implement these maxims, your classroom teaching should become less of a chore for you, your students should gain more motivation, and in many cases, that extra boost in motivation will lead to deeper learning of the teaching content. Everyone will likely become a bit happier and everyone will be likely be able to learn a bit more than before—*even the teachers*.

Neuro *What? neuroELT!*

For the past fifteen years or so, I've led a double life: one of a researcher/ teacher of *Applied Linguistics* (TESOL), and the other of a researcher/teacher of *Mind, Brain, and Education* studies. It is interesting to note that not all applied linguistics researchers are motivated to learn about how the brain *really* works. That may sound odd because the brain is what produces language and it is where learning occurs, but it is true; this "black box" treatment has been a long-standing norm (Dörnyei & Murphy, 2010). Accordingly, I have had to separate these two areas of my work. However, due to robust efforts of my colleagues over the past decade, *Mind, Brain, and Education* content has been gaining more credibility in other fields—especially within Asian ELT contexts. As we witnessed the growth in popularity of this area of research in Asia, it became necessary to find a suitable name—a name that would be both intuitive and memorable for busy teachers to latch onto. And so, upon deliberation, the intersect between English Language Teaching and neuroscience-based education was coined *neuroELT*. The name seems to have caught on relatively well. Research indicates that the term *neuroELT* has being in use in academic publications (including dissertations) and on the internet since as early as 2008; see fab-efl.com for a more complete history.

How does the *neuroELT* movement benefit teachers? A very common query is, "How can we expect busy language teachers to gain an interest in and master neuro-biology?" Can we presume language teachers will be motivated to keep up with neuroscientific findings? Moreover, there is a more impeding issue—that is, neuroscientific research seldomly readily translates over to usable content for language teaching contexts. What can be done about this dilemma? As you may have guessed by now, this is the raison d'être of the *Maxims of neuroELT*. With the help of a team of interns spanning over a decade of work, the arduous deciphering tasks and context testing projects have already been taken care of. The resulting list of *Maxims* are bite-sized, easy-to-remember phrases that embody "neuroscience for teachers" without requiring firsthand knowledge of the science to deploy them successfully—this should help sustain the motivation to use them in real life. The fact that they are bite-sized and worded to be easily memorable, while being scientifically backed, is what makes them stand out in the language teaching profession.

Seven Out of 52 Maxims

When our *neuroELT* Lab started out at the University of Kitakyushu, we had ten maxims; that number seemed fine at the time. But as we gained interns and more papers were getting published, the list of maxims naturally began to expand past the initial list of ten. That was a good thing. We take pride in the fact that our list grows/shrinks dynamically with changes in scientific discovery—as it should. In short, these maxims are not dogma. The list is an ever-changing culmination of our current understanding of these topics, based on science.

For this chapter, I have chosen to discuss seven of the current fifty-two maxims. Why is that? My doctoral research at the University of Nottingham with Zoltán Dörnyei (Murphy, 2019) was a lengthy process of testing the efficacy of progressive pedagogical designs. By the end of the multiyear project, seven of the best practices that emerged from that lengthy study happened to pair well with seven of the already established neuroELT maxims; in other words, regarding these seven findings, the outcomes were practically verbatim. This commonality raises the credibility of both of these research projects; both studies were formed under entirely different circumstances—yet they produced parallel results in this area. In short, what eventually emerged as a list of best practices for language teachers within an applied linguistics research context matched a separately established best-practice list from a neuro perspective. So, it became a no-brainer (pardon the pun) that these seven fully compatible "cross-over" practices were meant to be the soul of this chapter.

NeuroELT maxims: "The Chosen 7"

1. Choices fuel learner motivation
2. Real-time feedback is at the core of cognitive development
3. Aha moments enhance neural networks
4. Happy students learn better
5. Performances of understanding are essential for good assessment
6. Assess in three ways
7. Encourage mistakes; celebrate mistakes

The Maxims in Practice

In this section, we will look at each of the seven maxims in depth. I will provide the rationales for classroom inclusion, example usage from real classroom testing, and a further reading section (from pedagogical and from neuroscientific perspectives).

Maxim 1: Choices fuel learner motivation

Depending on your academic background, you may be for or against giving students choices in the classroom. For example, old-school Japanese classrooms in the Confucianism tradition honor the teacher in a way that demands the students to sit obediently and listen to the lecture. Most language teachers can probably guess that a lecture is not optimal for an

EFL conversation course. With that extreme case out of the way, let's look at what else this maxim stands for.

(a) When given a choice—even mundane ones—students often do realize and appreciate the autonomy that they are being provided. But even if they don't, this pressure-release context produces dopamine and other pleasurable chemicals in the brain while the task is taking place.

(b) Our brains are designed to remember pleasurable (and horrible) experiences. This is literally at the core of all learning, so allowing Joey to choose which passage he wants to read, or Sarah which activity she'd prefer to join in on, goes a long way toward positivity toward the content while it significantly raises the potential for remembering the content.

(c) When a teacher gives a student autonomy as a part of the pedagogical process, it provides "low confidence students" a chance to regain lost confidence with comfortable baby steps choice making. This can be therapeutic at just the right time for these students. Not all students may need this, but I often see this working well for a handful of students each year; the fear of choice slowly becomes a more pleasurable experience.

(d) This can also be used as a "dirty trick" to get students motivated for work. You can ask the students, "Ok, so I will be giving you a choice for this writing task: (1) You can choose to write a 500-word essay on xxx, or (2) you can choose to write an 800-word essay on yyy." In your mind, initially the task was literally only to get the students to write a 500-word essay (which they would have dreaded had you commanded them to "write 500 words"), but with a decision process involved, they are now suddenly happy with themselves for making the "clever" choice of 500 words instead of 800 words. Small tricks like this can quickly change the mood and motivation in students. There is nothing unethical about this—you will be surprised to see that often enough some students will choose the more difficult task! Either way, it's a win-win for you and for the students.

Immordino-Yang and French (2010) elaborates more on how involving students in the selection process of topics to be studied fosters emotional connection to that very material.

Maxim 2: Real-time feedback is at the core of cognitive development

Through evolution, humans crave "prediction-outcome" situations—such as with video games. As an experiment, right now try to imagine that you are at a carnival stand and you are about to throw a blueberry pie into the face of a person that you have always hated ... Now, you throw the pie!— but can you immediately turn around and walk away without looking at or at least listening to the outcome? Try it. Even as an imaginary story, I know you have a weirdly strong impulse right now to imagine the conclusion—at least the sound. How well did your throw the pie? Where did it hit? It is hard not to imagine these things now. (Go ahead and enjoy imagining the story conclusion ... then come back here). Isn't it interesting that we have this strange impulse to realize an outcome—even if it is imaginary?

This has strong implications for teaching. Why? Foremost, the classroom is an artificial context, so it is indeed much like that imaginary story above. That's a good thing because we know it will work in the classroom context. What are the main interesting points about this maxim?

(a) We receive a dopamine rush when we attempt do something that requires a skill set—like bungee jumping. The dopa rush hones our skills and focus—so there is a very important biological reason for this rush occurrence. We also get a rush if we hit a goal—in the classroom this would be akin to getting the correct answer *and being notified in real-time*. This allows us to better remember the skills necessary to complete the task again. (Important side note: This helps explain why a rise in a learner's test-taking skills, as a neurobiological skill set, may create a usable test-taking skill set in time for a particular school test—but this particular set of skills may have no effect on their real-world language usage/competence. From the opposite perspective but with similar logic to the neurobiology of skill-building, the development of real-world language competence may have no effect on the development of test-taking skills, nor the test outcomes. For example, it is reasonable for a competent native English speaker to test poorly on a standardized English language test if they happen to not understand *how* to take that particular test. So, "real-world competence as a skill set" and "test-taking as a skill set" are separate skill sets. It sounds obvious when explained in this way, but many classrooms do not explicitly bridge their assessment policies with real-world usage/competence so this dissonance can be highly problematic.)

(b) Babies learn their L1 via real-time feedback. As babies babble along, some of the babbles/noises receive more compliments and encouragement than other babbles/noises. So, the baby "learns" to focus their efforts on the sounds that produce the best results due to this disposition produced by real-time feedback. This is how we start off appreciating L1 usage.

(c) For younger L2 students in an ESL context, the mechanism works the same way as mentioned just above, so it is relatively easy for the ESL teacher of younger ages to be successful in raising competence.

However, let's consider an *EFL* context with an older student. The older student may not appreciate the "motherese" and cheerful clapping that a baby receives for encouragement, so that tactic may not be a good choice. In such a case, the older student will more likely appreciate real-time feedback in more concrete terms. They may also show a preference for feedback in their native tongue—at least at the beginner stages.

(d) The negative side of this is the potential for very long feedback delays that tests may sustain. For example, if George was told that the idiom is, "put your foot in your mouth" and not "put your shoe in your mouth" during class time—he may very well remember this correction. However, if he receives test results two weeks after taking the test and is then given a score sheet that simply says response number 15 was wrong—he would have no way of learning from his mistake. This is a lost opportunity, and it goes against all "formative assessment" principles that are now in vogue. Unfortunately, this "lost-opportunity" style of assessment still happens across the globe.

Sailer et al. (2007) note that "Subjects showed a distinct pattern of learning starting with an initial exploratory phase in which hypotheses about the correct strategy were generated and tested, followed by a phase of rapid strategy acquisition before reaching a final phase of proficiency" (1474). Therefore, when students are motivated and are in their *rapid strategy acquisition* phase, it would be a mistake to delay feedback because it would disrupt their nature flow of inspired learning.

Maxim 3: Aha moments enhance neural networks

There is a strong relationship between this maxim and the one just above regarding real-time feedback. An aha ("eureka!") moment is when we make a sudden realization regarding something that may have been puzzling us consciously or even often with a conundrum that may be lingering subconsciously. The realization of a solution is characteristically a "feel-good" moment. We tend to feel clever(er) when realizing a novel solution to a lingering problem. In connection with the above maxim, this helps explain why real-time feedback can be so pleasurable for students. Of course, sudden realizations can be regarding something negative, too ("Oh, no! Today is the 25th. I forgot to pay my credit card bill!"). Either way, these aha moments are there to help up remember important personal discoveries in daily life so that we can learn how to better navigate our lives.

How does this work out biologically? Each individual neuronal network in our brain is not built equally; they are all unique and grow/die dynamically. Through life's ups and downs (guided by aha moments), the networks that produce the most appropriate responses for our life's problems become *biased*. What does that mean? We end up using those better-solution-producing networks more often than the not-as-good networks. Via the process of neuronal myelination (giving a thicker coat of insulation to neurons), the more often used biased networks begin processing *much* faster than before, making them even more biased and more useful in real-time situations due to the much speedier processing. This is also why so-called outside-of-the-box thinking does not come as quickly as falling back on our regularly used (biased) ideas; for "outside of the box" thinking, we force ourselves to *not* use our speedily responding highly biased networks, but force the minor and weaker networks to come into play. We also force-create new networks to develop in this way. Interestingly, the more often we force ourselves to work with our "outside of the box" thinking skills, the faster and better those "outside of the box" thinking skills become, too. This is where this story goes full circle. The results of our "outside of the box" thinking literally causes aha moments, which is why those neural networks become enhanced. The "outside of the box" solution can eventually become the new norm—which means the prior norm network will slowly begin to atrophy (unless it is regularly called back into action).

Here are some classroom tactics based on this maxim:

(a) Utilize solvable mysteries; this means to find level-appropriate puzzles and questions for your students—not too easy, nor frustratingly hard.

(b) Make sure the textbook allows for these aha moments to occur frequently. If the textbook is not designed that way, it becomes the teacher's duty to design multiple aha moments into the course to compensate. You can no longer blame the textbook's design because you now know better—it is now in your hands.

(c) The teacher should also be comfortable with bringing small story nuggets that enhance the learning while including aha moments for the students. These short nuggets keep attention high and invariably make the teacher look good when implemented well. Some simple examples:

- Discuss the relationship between the dessert called "pie" and math's "pi."

- Discuss relationships across words and word families. For example: dome, domestic, and domain—with the Italian *duomo* and Greek *doma*.

- Explain why in English we have crude animal names like "cow," "deer," and "pig," but when we cook them into meals, we switch to *esprit* French naming conventions like *venison*.

(d) When students get used to aha moment nuggets, ask students to find their own and share them with the class; one or two students per day is fine. This will likely raise autonomous skills along with confidence levels.

Nauert (2018) succinctly explains the mechanics of how aha moments become memorable. This is Taylor (2006) regarding negative aha moments: "the brain is on alert in a positive, receptive way. But if hormones are pumping because of a perceived or potential threat ('The instructor is going to call on me and won't know the answer'), the brain is *less* available for learning" (p. 81). In this way, research shows that both positive and negative experiences are the most memorable; emotionless experiences fall through the cracks.

Maxim 4: Happy students learn better

There are still teachers who believe in militant teaching practices. For them, play is strictly for after the test. The most extreme case that I have personal knowledge of is a cram school camp that prohibited students to talk for an entire study week. To make matters worse, after passively listening to lectures all day long, the students had daily mastery exams. Each night, students who failed were put in "the punishment room." Their teachers' jobs were to scold the students until they *literally* broke out into tears. I would say this is tantamount to child abuse/torture. It is hoped that this maxim will help abolish such ridiculous practices.

I would like to discuss the positive side of this maxim as well. Studies (see below) show that happiness allows students to keep curiosity high—so, students tend to achieve higher academic performance and, more importantly, their motivation to keep high-achieving results lasts longer. This maxim will likely give teachers the extra nudge to keep "positivity" in mind—and to allow for a discussion of tactics that worked well and kept them positively motivated.

Tactics for the classroom based on this maxim:

(a) With a strong connection to the first maxim, allow for student autonomy. A dopamine rush from a "correct choice" made by the student is more favorable than negativity from an assignment that is perceived as punishment.

(b) Schedule weekly focus group sessions after class (three or four students, rotating schedule). Prepare a list of questions that commit students to deep discussions regarding the progress and the growth "they see in their classmates." Do not force the students to talk about their own growth (some may enjoy offering this anyway). Ask how the classroom teaching can be enhanced so that "we can help *those other students*" progress better. This focus group approach works amazingly well (Murphy, 2019). Two uncovered reasons:

- The students truly feel like a part of the learning/teaching process, as they should. This is important for their happiness and for their personal growth.

- The qualitative data received can be amazingly valuable because the students have insights into "other students' growth" that teachers are oblivious of. Weekly tactful pedagogical adjustments based the focus groups' output helps improve learning and greatly raises motivation of the focus group members as the see their work with you making a real difference.

(c) The teacher should also be comfortable with bringing small story nuggets that enhance the learning while including aha moments for the students. These short nuggets keep attention high and invariably make the teacher look good when implemented well.

According to Willis (2010), "In experiments using fMRI (Pawlak et al., 2003), subjects were shown photographs of people with happy or grumpy expressions. After viewing the faces, the subjects were shown a list of words ... The results revealed better recall by subjects who recalled the happy faces, and their scans during recall had higher activity in the prefrontal cortex" (p. 53). When subjects viewed grumpy faces, there was higher activity in the amygdala, but lower activity in the prefrontal cortex. When subjects viewed happy faces, it was the other way around, "suggesting the non-threatening condition favors conduction of information through the amygdala networks to the prefrontal cortex" (p. 54). Johnson (2006) noted that

When a mentor is supportive, caring, and encouraging, and offers enthusiasm balanced with an optimal learning environment, learners are assisted in moving there thinking activity into the higher brain regions (the frontal cortex), where reflective activity and abstract thinking take place ... during this process, the learner's neurotransmitters that power the frontal cortex (dopamine, serotonin, and norepinephrine) are stimulated, leading to greater brain plasticity and hence more neuronal networking and meaningful learning.

(p. 64)

Maxim 5: Performances of Understanding are essential for good assessment

How can we make learning/understanding visible? More importantly, how can we assess learning/understanding if it is *not* visible? As teachers, we must realize that while we cannot watch the learning networks fire up in the brain in real-time (unless we have the apparatus for it in our classrooms), we *can* do the next best thing. We can get our students to demonstrate their understanding of the concepts. This is called a Performance of Understanding (PoU) (Blythe & Associates, 1998).

A PoU is not a simplistic test; it is an opportunity given to students to synthesize their learning on their own terms and take it to the next level in the form of a real-time performance for the teacher (and the class) to assess in real time. An example of an effective PoU is the ability to conduct an interactive presentation on the subject covered. A PoU is not only fairer than the average paper-based test, but it also allows students to follow their passions, helps sustain motivation, and inspires further learning.

A well-designed PoU session should keep pressure minimized (possibly even fun), while making the performance as close to a real-world context as possible. Real-time assessment is straightforward—how much of their own learning/understanding are the students making visible thought their PoU session in real-time? Make sure the students realize that they are being assessed on content that is not based on simplistic rote memory of passages.

Sprenger (2013) explains, "Have students put information into their own words. This process, which I call 'recoding', is necessary to make sure students understand the word. This is a vital step in the memory process. Skipping this step can be disastrous as students may have a misconception that will be placed in long-term memory through incorrect rehearsals" (p. 13). Nevills and Wolfe (2009) noted that "Children are not held accountable for what they read (such as having to write a book report), but time is set aside to share reading experiences and recommend books" (p. 170). The interaction regarding experiences, thoughts, and recommendations is central to establishing a virtuous PoU session.

Maxim 6: Assess in three ways: The Trinity of Assessment

Trinity of what? Roughly a decade ago, based on research in neuro-education and classroom practice, this is what I coined the "Trinity of Assessment" (see Murphy, 2019):

(1) Self-Assessment

(2) Peer-to-peer Assessment

(3) Teacher-student Assessment

Most teachers employ at least *one* of the above assessments per course but rarely are all three employed within a single module of learning and used as a trinity set. Why is a *trinity* of assessment important? Self-assessment forces students to self-reflect; it causes meta-cognition to happen. Although some students may be conscious of their actions, not all students actually do this, and certainly not all do it in a uniform or predictable way. Simply allowing students to rate their work on a 1–5 scale after each completed section will do wonders for motivation and alignment.

The next step is to also allow for peer-to-peer assessment. When students are given time for a PoU, other students should have self-designed criteria to assess the performances. With each successive PoU, students *learn to want to do better* at designing assessment criteria and with their own performances.

With all this good assessment going on (while teachers are facilitating more than teaching), it may seem that teacher assessment may not even be needed. Indeed, in some cases, teacher assessment can be minimalized—but professional assessment is necessary as a sort of rudder for course correction when students require professional-level correction, and also as an anchor so that students don't go too far off the intended course. In more specific terms, students will need the occasional professional-level scoring from the teacher to keep them aligned and also to build confidence that they are (collectively) on the right path.

Learning to give students the right about of space and correction is not an easy balance to master. However, feedback from teachers whom I have directly trained shows that rather than teaching with overlong lectures, minimized teacher-talk can be more affective in the long term—this is because the other two forms of assessment within the trinity are being allowed to grow instead. Ambrose et al. (2010, pp. 27–31) suggested a set of strategies (relationship to trinity in parentheses):

- Talk to colleagues (peer-to-peer)

- Administer a diagnostic assessment (teacher)

- Have students assess their own prior knowledge (solo)

- Use brainstorming to reveal prior knowledge (teacher/solo/peer)

- Assign a concept map activity (teacher/solo)

- Looks for patterns of error in student work (teacher/solo)

Maxim 7: Encourage mistakes; celebrate mistakes

Yes—*encourage* mistakes. Logic mandates that students who are afraid of making mistakes and then shy away from usage opportunities literally have no potential to learn from making those mistakes—nor can they learn to become "good risk-takers." This second point is far more important than it may initially seem. Deep personalized learning and optimal growth of creativeness stem from being a so-called good risk-taker. Therefore, it is imperative for teachers to coach their students to *expect* to learn something interesting and worthwhile from their personal mistakes—not only from teacher talk.

You can go so far as to encourage them to make mistakes on purpose; they can stage mistakes for each other in the classroom and then discuss what they picked up and what can be learned from this experience (of performing and witnessing mistakes being made). In this way, the stigma about mistake-making can be effectively neutralized and/or turned into something much more positive. Therefore, you can direct student mistake occurrences to become a central part of your students' formative learning with you.

Schwartz and Fischer (2004) discuss a study that challenged scholars to light a bulb with only *one* length of wire and a battery. Naturally, they balked and then went through trail an error stages, trying to figure it out. "Once students have created their own sensorimotor understanding (via trial and error), they are usually ready to accept the resulting representations as *their own*. This is an important point for educators who believe that representational knowledge can be transferred to students by simply telling it to them—a process that forces them to 'borrow' representations instead of 'building' their own" (p. 177). The substance of the matter is that deep knowledge needs to be *built* via trial and error and then they *gain ownership* of the learning. Good teaching is not about "being told something" because this often leads to superficial learning and little to no *feelings of ownership*. Also, Cozolino (2013) notes that "It has been known for decades that enriched, stimulating environments have positive impacts on neural growth and learning. Rats raised in complex and stimulating environments show an array on neuroanatomical changes reflective of increased plasticity and brain growth" (p. 161). So, creating "owned" learning experiences from trial and error in positive contexts seems to be an optimal approach.

Conclusion

To make this a teacher-friendly chapter, I have minimized jargon usage. I hope the main points were clear and thought-provoking. My goal has been to get you hooked on using the *neuroELT* maxims to the degree that my colleagues and I have become hooked on them—and to elucidate how the maxims can be used to sustain student motivation through improved pedagogical approaches that are based on science.

CHAPTER 21

How Good Class Group Dynamics Socialize Well-Being into Cultures, Biologies, and Brains

Yoshifumi Fukada, Tim Murphey, Tetsuya Fukuda, and Joseph Falout

Other people form our most important environment and the stimuli that shape our brains, minds, and behaviour throughout the lifespan

(HARI, SAMS, AND NUMMENMAA, 2016, P. 1)

In light of current research and discussion, it may not be inappropriate to rephrase Descartes' philosophical statement as "I think about and with others, therefore I am."

(YBARRA ET AL., 2008, P. 257)

Introduction

This chapter explores how group dynamics contribute to psychological and physical well-being and to motivation in learning foreign languages. The **first** part covers anthropological developments from small groups to cultures. The **second** part describes how human connection or sense of belongingness affects people's health as well as their learning from the perspectives of biology, psychology, and neuroscience. The **third** part covers understandings from the recent social turn in SLA (Block, 2003) and discusses the positive impact of collaborative language learning within positive group dynamics on target language development. Then the **fourth** part provides a glimpse of recent research into how helping others learn may trigger social motivation within the self. Three basic types of class activities are highlighted, with explanations as to how they might promote positive group dynamics within the classroom. The evolutionary adaptive advantages of social learning lie deep within human ancestry and the motivational potentials of cooperative group dynamics.

Anthropology: Small Groups to Collaborative Cultures

Today's highly complex tasks for the widely diverse daily operations undertaken by humanity require advanced teaching and learning, which is not something that any species could develop just overnight. Recent anthropological theory proposes that before becoming modern *Homo sapiens*, meaning *wise humans*, humans progressed immensely during a stage called *Homo docens*, meaning *teaching humans* (Gärdenfors & Högberg, 2017). This anthropological stage was marked by social and cultural adaptation and sophistication that could be sustainable only through highly developed skills of teaching and learning. This theory has been somewhat corroborated by Ramachandran's (2011) theory that between 75,000 and 100,000 years ago the frontal cortex's motor neurons developed mirror neuron capacities so that humans could emulate and imitate each other better. Somewhere within this period came language, tool use, shelter, and the use of fire, all of which seem to have spread quickly and broadly across the species.

People now benefit from this earlier human developmental stage, particularly if they are given opportunities to assist in each other's learning. Current language learning theory has picked up on this inherent human capacity, with one proposal stressing that students' teaching their peers is also an effective way to help students enjoy learning more, as they receive positive altruistic teaching rushes (Murphey, 2017).

Results from one experimental study (Derex, Beugin, Godelle, & Raymond, 2013) give support to the idea that our species is naturally social and benefits from being so when trying to innovate and cope with the surrounding environment. The researchers asked university students to collaboratively design arrowheads and fishnets on computers, comparing groupings of two, four, eight, and sixteen participants. It was found that the larger groups innovated much better and faster—or in other words, cooperatively engineered more efficiently through learning together—which suggests that larger group sizes may have been the reason why forerunners to modern humans outlasted the Neanderthals. Although those who eventually became today's *Homo sapiens* may not have initially been smarter than the Neanderthals, their sociality helped improve not only their collective situations but also their individual intelligences, helping them survive while the Neanderthals died out.

The Fundamental Sociobiological Need for Humans to Connect, Bond, and Belong

Not long ago, teachers and administrators in school districts across the United States were targeted by a brochure entitled "Fostering School Connectedness" (Centers for Disease Control and Prevention, 2009), which contained specific ways to get students, families, and others within their communities to engage with each other and build meaningful relationships, trust, and positive social climates. The reason for suggesting measures to improve social connections was to improve student health and academic achievement. Perhaps the surprising point was that the brochure was not from any board of education, but from an agency in the US Department of Health and Human Services. This is an example of national medical and biological concerns telling schools they need to have better social environments if they want healthier students; this is biology telling sociology and schools to be more social for biological reasons. It appears to be clear that not belonging, not connecting, and not identifying with healthy others can greatly imperil our health and learning.

Bonding to social groups can lead to positive outcomes for individuals, magnified when a group's members energize each other toward shared feelings, goals, and activities. One example is when a sports team magically operates as a single unit throughout a game or season—a social phenomenon known as emotional contagion (Gregersen & Al Khateeb, this volume; Hatfield, Cacioppo, & Rapson, 1994) and flow (Csikszentmihalyi, 1990; Muir, this volume). However, the negative side of peer or group influence appears in such things as bullying and the insidious social pressure utilized by street gangs and organized crime. "Social support is a peculiar force and can operate in two different ways. Plenty of research suggests that being alone in the world is stressful. Loners and lonely people tend to have more of just about every kind of mental and physical illness than people who live in rich social networks" (Baumeister & Tierney, 2011, p. 175). Bonding is a meaning-giving mechanism for our minds.

Since early in the modern field of psychology, psychologists understood that humans are social beings who cannot live without others. For example,

Adler (1929) contested that people's troubles most often stemmed from problems in their interpersonal relations. He reasoned that worries about social problems could cause hesitation to get involved with others, and thus people need courage to promote their own engagement in interpersonal relations. The key to having such courage is a sense of self-worth gained through social contribution. Adler explained that when people feel they are valuable through helping others, they are more likely to step into relationships, which then secures in them feelings of self-worth and status within the community (Stone & Drescher, 2004).

More recently, social psychologists have recognized the fundamental human need to belong, or belongingness (Baumeister & Leary, 1995; Oga-Baldwin, this volume). This need is met when an individual perceives to have close connection, mutual care, and frequent contact with certain special others. The minimum number of these special others needed to sustain one's feeling of belongingness varies by individual, but most people usually need just a few (Baumeister & Leary, 1995) and even a supportive group can fulfill this need (Baumeister & Finkel, 2010). Some people, usually males, can also fulfill this need by seeking out membership in large groups, such as a company or university (Baumeister, 2005). Membership in groups gives people a group identity, that is, collective identity, and at the same time it enhances personal self-concept, particularly by increasing the sense of self-worth (Baumeister & Finkel, 2010). This social well-becoming in groups simultaneously produces healthier biologies.

Meaning, practice, community, and identity have also been identified by Wenger (1998) as four critical components in learning, and one of the subcomponents of community is belonging. When a learner belongs to a community of practice, their degree of belonging influences their degree of learning. School belonging can happen when "students have established a social bond between themselves, the adults in the school, and the norms governing the institutions" (Wehlage, 1989, p. 10). Since 1989, research on the relationship between school belonging and academic achievements has been extensively conducted in educational psychology. In language education or SLA, however, little research has been connected to school belonging, which makes it even more difficult to investigate. Belonging is one of the most important factors to explain effective learning, and language learning research would do well in addressing this deficiency (Murphey, Prober, & Gonzáles, 2010).

An emerging line of research in SLA is on how social climate in the classroom is perceived by learners. For example, perceived mutual respect from peers and emotional support from teachers predicted the senses of autonomy and competency, according to one study on secondary students in South Korea (Joe, Hiver, & Al-Hoorie, 2017). This corresponds to a wider body of research into the effects of school belonging, the sense of which also relates to a plethora of other positive academic behaviors, such as increased participation in school activities, higher rates of interest in school and achievement, and resilience in the face of academic hardships (Osterman, 2000). It has been shown that the greater the number of friendships and the deeper the friendships that schoolchildren have with their peers, the greater their academic motivation and performance (e.g., Altermatt & Pomerantz, 2003; Ladd, 1990). Conversely, low rates of school friendship and social rejection at school, unfortunately, more likely lead to the opposite effects.

With regard to students' connectedness with others, the neuroscientist Cozolino (2014) has cautioned that students may go through the same attachment protocols with teachers and other important people in their lives, especially grandparents who may be cohabitating with them. Thus, for educators, the takeaway is that we are not dealing with a clean slate when students walk into our first classes. They have already attached well or not to a variety of people and groups and some may come with excited amygdalas, fearful of new people, and trying to decide whether to fight, freeze, or take flight. It goes without saying that teachers experience these same psychodynamics with others regularly encountered at school, specifically students, co-workers, and administrators.

Cozolino (2013) also introduces in another work the concept of the neuronal synapse, the space between two neurons, to explain that we also metaphorically have a social synapse between two people. We can overcome difficulty of belonging to or connecting with others with smiles, words, gestures, touch, and so on, similar to how neurons fire signals through neurotransmitters and across the space and make connections that are then myelinated, or strengthened, over time. The social synapse can become a useful metaphor for those wanting to understand how people might bond and perform better as a networked group (see Murphy, this volume).

The Social Turn in Education: Seeing Something in the Other That May Eventually Become Part of the Self

Researchers in SLA now recognize that language learning most often occurs not alone but within a dynamic social environment. Block's (2003) publication of *The Social Turn in Second Language Acquisition* takes us back to the special issue of the *Modern Language Journal* that led with an article by Firth and Wagner (1997) criticizing the standard view of SLA as "individualistic and mechanistic, and that it fails to account in a satisfactory way for interactional and sociolinguistic dimensions of language" (p. 285). They proposed a rejection of a narrowly framed SLA that "essentialized interlocutors, with essentialized identities, who speak essentialized language" (Block, 2003, p. 4). Block makes "a case for a broader, socially informed and more sociolinguistically oriented SLA that does not exclude the more mainstream psycholinguistic one, but instead takes on board the complexity of context, the multilayered nature of language and an expanded view of what acquisition entails" (Block, 2003, p. 4).

Socially oriented SLA had already begun with many other researchers who were also working mainly with social interaction as the driving force of language acquisition. Many books from the past few decades can readily be found to have "interaction" in their titles, implying that it is mainly through social interaction that we acquire our languages. Examples include Rivers' (1987) *Interactive Language Teaching*, Brown's (1994) *Teaching by Principles: An Interactive Approach to Language Pedagogy*, and van Lier's (1996) *Interaction in the Language Curriculum*.

The social wave in SLA expanded when Schumann and his graduate students published *The Interactional Instinct* (Lee, Mikesell, Joaquin, Mates, & Schumann, 2009), and in *Alternative Approaches to Second Language Acquisition*, Atkinson (2011) continued to contest purely cognitive explanations as the sole basis of SLA. *Meaningful Action: Earl Stevick's Influence on Language Teaching* (Arnold & Murphey, 2013) compiled chapters from a diverse group of researchers who were mainly looking at what was happening "inside and between the people in the classroom" (Stevick, 1980, p. 4), that is, their sociality.

Groups of people engaging in cooperative learning are often perceived as specifically situated communities. For example, communities of practice (CoPs; Lave & Wenger, 1991), mentioned briefly earlier, are described as groups of people with different backgrounds, skills, and knowledge who acquire various skills or knowledge through social interactions, occasionally receiving scaffolding or support from more competent others. This is identified as situated learning. Situated language learning (Gee, 2004) therefore suggests that SLA research focus not on the group memberships involved in the learning but on the qualities and dynamics of the social spaces themselves. So the educational focus shifts from the students to their affinity space—"a place or set of places where people can affiliate with others based primarily on shared activities, interests, and goals, not shared race, class, culture, ethnicity, or gender" (Gee, 2004, p. 73). This definition implies that learners or students with different backgrounds can engage in situated learning while bonding through their shared activities, interests, and goals. Thus, for designing courses, class activities, and learning materials, teaching becomes an endeavor of finding students' shared activities, interests, and goals.

Teachers also need to be aware of what might promote the likelihood that group members from disparate backgrounds get along and bond, or "click," with each other. This can be encouraged by introducing click accelerators (Brafman & Brafman, 2010): vulnerability—revealing one's own vulnerable feeling such as fear and weakness to others; proximity—physically situating oneself close to others, which facilitates both verbal and nonverbal communication; resonance—sharing each other's emotions; similarity—sharing preferences and common points of reference; and feeling safe—giving support and comfort in times of hardship or difficulty.

Class activities can be designed to directly address one or more of these five dimensions. Through personal mistake stories (Hirosawa & Murphey, 2017), for example, teachers first demonstrate by telling their own mistake stories, and then in pairs or small groups students tell their own to each other. This activity helps bring students physically closer, revealing their personal vulnerabilities and their interpersonal similarities, sympathies, and emotions, all within the safety of the classroom.

Such socially focused activities work well for learning because students model each other more easily than they do native speakers or teachers. The more students see themselves in others, the more they begin to identify with the behaviors, thoughts, and values portrayed by the others within the interactions. The act of bonding draws student identities psychologically closer, and the greater the perceived similarities, the more likely that students become each other's near peer role models (NPRMs, Murphey & Arao, 2001). Students' social networks can host a rich array of NPRMs, and the more diverse the networks become, the more likely students can be braver to model others who are increasingly more divergent from themselves. Teachers can highlight excellent attributes of certain students and in doing so encourage even more students to model these capacities.

Social networks of ideal distant others who are worth modelling can also function at the imaginary level and positively influence learning. These networks are known as imagined social capital (Quinn, 2010), and are created by inviting the famous, the dead, and the purely imagined into one's psychologically constructed affinity space. For example, children can be readily seen to engage in such imaginary social play when they are alone, pretending to be superheroes, anime characters, and rock stars. These imaginary affiliations and interactions with otherwise untouchable others form a basis upon which modelling and learning takes place. Imaginary social capital helps give learners persistence and resilience during difficult periods, and can be beneficial for learning at any time but is especially effective when real social resources are limited. Similarly, imagined L2 communities give learners "a sense of community with people we have not yet met, but perhaps hope to meet one day" (Norton, 2013, p. 8). These imagined communities have been shown to promote the psychological investments made by immigrants to learn an L2 when social and linguistic limitations keep them apart from the communities in which they live and wish to belong (Norton, 2000).

Tapping into the Power of Social Motivation and Classroom Group Dynamics

Although most SLA researchers and teacher-trainers have promoted social interaction as a necessity in language classrooms, many teachers may still be following conventional teacher-dominant practices. Even supposedly learner-centered classrooms have been found to be largely silent and mostly devoid of on-task learner engagement (King, 2013b). The following section suggests three ways of infusing social engagement into classroom pedagogy while cultivating well-being: students singing together, teaching each other (and others out of school), and imagining, describing, and sharing their ideal classmates.

Students Singing Together

Music has been with humanity since before the rise of *Homo sapiens*. Its evolutionary social functions include: selecting mates; promoting social cohesion; motivating and guiding group effort; building perceptual development and motor skills in both intrapersonal and interpersonal coordination; encouraging conflict resolution; passing time in positive pursuits; transmitting transgenerational communication and education; validating and reinforcing or rebelling against social, cultural, and religious norms; reducing social isolation; and integrating disparate and disconnected elements into societies for creating cultural harmonies (Hallam, 2006). Groups of students singing together have been springing up in schools and communities worldwide in part because of the scientific community's attention to the evidence that singing together increases social belonging, physical health, and psychological well-being (Kang, Scholp, & Jiang, 2018; Launay & Pearce, 2015). For example, Stewart and Lonsdale (2016) collected questionnaire data from 375 participants who did chorus singing, solo singing, and team sports. The results show that choral singers and team sports players reported significantly higher well-being than solo singers, and also that choral singers thought their choirs to be more meaningful to them than team sports players. Apparently, the more activities synchronize people, the more the members tend to bond closely with each other and feel personal well-being.

Students Teaching Students

Teaching others helps students not only to learn the content better but helping-tasks bring with them many social attributes, most remarkably a meaningful feeling of altruistic contribution to others (Murphey, 2017). This tutoring effect has a long history. In Allen and Feldman's (1973) classical study, ten fifth graders who were identified to be "low-achieving" by their school principals taught reading to ten randomly selected third graders. The results showed that tutoring led to significantly better learning than studying alone. The researchers concluded that "acting as a tutor for a younger child is a useful technique for enhancing the academic performance of low-achieving children" (p. 7). Recent research in socio-neuroscience supports the idea that instead of keeping students quiet in class, keeping students talking to each other results in greater motivation to learn (Lieberman, 2013). Homework can mean teaching others outside of class what was learned in class. Then reporting back to peers in class, such as a show and tell in small groups, validates not only the learning done in class but also the learning done outside in the students' diverse communities (Murphey, 2017). Even tests can be made more social by allowing an extension to the test in which students ask and teach each other, and do self-grading before and after peer assistance (Murphey, 2019).

Students Visualizing Ideal L2 Classmates

The recently popular pedagogical use of the L2 motivational self system theory (Dörnyei, 2009a) has been found to increase motivation to learn languages. By focusing on an imaginary ideal self fluently and successfully using the language in a future situation, learners in the present become more likely to take action to learn and grow into these selves they envision. However, if learners are not sharing their future self visions with each other, they may form blinders that prevent them from visualizing even better possible future selves that classmates and other role models could inspire, and thus cause their academic goals and motivations to become stunted (Lockwood & Kunda, 1999).

One social pedagogical adaptation of ideal self visioning is ideal classmates visioning. In this procedure, students are first asked to describe how their classmates could help them. Then when these visions are shared among classmates, the potential is set for all students within a classroom to engage with others' visions and act upon them in mutual learning assistance (Murphey, Falout, Fukuda, & Fukada, 2014). When students know how their classmates want to be helped, they are more apt to accommodate their classmates.

A quantitative study on ideal L2 classmates (Murphey et al., 2014) was done in two stages over one semester. First, 449 students taking English communication courses answered the open-ended question: *Please describe a group of classmates that you could learn English well with. What would you all do to help each other learn better and more enjoyably?* Some comments were short, such as "smile" and "enjoy," while others were longer: for example, "We should talk with not only teacher but also class friends"; "The group that has good atmosphere to speak English is. There, everybody don't hesitate to speak English." These comments were then coded and sorted into sixteen descriptors of ideal classmates for this set of students (see https://sites.google.com/view/englisheducationresearch/home/ideal-classmates-resources). These sixteen descriptors were looped back (Murphey & Falout, 2010) to the students near the end of the semester for the second stage. To each descriptor were attached three statements for the students to mark their level of agreement with a six-point Likert scale (1 = Not at all; 6 = Very much): (a) This is important for successful learning, (b) My classmates have done this so far this semester, (c) I have done this so far this semester.

Analysis of the responses showed that all the descriptors were deemed important characteristics, as ten of the descriptors had a mean score of over 5.00, while the other six descriptors had a mean score of 4.72 or above. Moreover, the correlations between these three groupings were strong, with (a) and (b) at .582, (a) and (c) at .485, and (b) and (c) at .829. This last correlation was the strongest, indicating that the more the students thought their actual classmates acted like ideal classmates, the more they themselves acted like ideal classmates (and vice versa). This phenomenon was termed "reciprocal idealizing" (Murphey et al., 2014). Ideal classmates interventions have been applied to other language learning settings, such as university conversation class (Peragine, 2019), elementary school in Indonesia (Murphey & Iswanti, 2014), and junior high school in Japan (Davis, 2018).

Conclusion

This chapter has covered four parts: (1) Anthropology has explained that larger groups of early humans were more likely to survive than smaller groups and individuals, and create sustainable cultures through teaching. (2) Biology, neuroscience, and psychology present evidence that being social improves cognitive processing, and having a sense of belonging to others is a fundamental human motivation which helps guide people away from self-destructive behaviors and psychosis, and cultivates well-being and better biologies. (3) The social turn in education substantiates our diverse ways to theoretically and practically use the power of being social in the classroom. (4) Applications of how L2 educators can stimulate positive socio-dynamics include students singing together, teaching each other, and visualizing their ideal classmates. These capacities to be social and learn go hand in hand, just as altruism, belonging, and meaningful contributions are shining the light on some of the most important motivational trajectories, currents, and callings in SLA. The most prominent torchbearer in the field, Zoltán Dörnyei, has established, usually in the social spirit of collaboration with colleagues, more expansive and general understandings of classroom group dynamics, which are highly recommended for further reading: Dörnyei (1997), Dörnyei and Malderez (1997, 1999), Ehrman and Dörnyei (1998), and Dörnyei and Murphey (2003).

Afterword

Research into motivation to learn a new language (L2) has grown into a vibrant tradition on its own. Standing on the shoulders of a 60-year-long history (Al-Hoorie & MacIntyre, 2020), it exhibits a remarkable present maturity, marked by the first handbook devoted to this research domain (Lamb, Csizér, Henry, & Ryan, 2019). Both the vibrancy and the maturity can be credited in a very large part to Zoltán Dörnyei, who ever since the 1990s has led the L2 motivation community with incessant, brilliant, and caring work—initially from Eötvös Loránd University in his native Hungary and since 2000 from Nottingham University in the UK. In this afterword, as a way to celebrate the seminal contributions and intellectual leadership of Zoltán Dörnyei, I offer a personal—and admittedly partial—commentary on profitable directions for future growth of the L2 motivation field.

I would be remiss if I did not start by making an earnest note of what Dörnyei (2020) himself has identified as three areas of L2 motivation research where researchers in search of untrodden territories or "frontiers" (as he calls them) should venture next. I cannot think of anyone I would rather trust with the crystal ball of L2 motivation research than him. I thus echo here what he has prognosticated as three exciting directions: unconscious motivation, roles for vision, and motivational endurance. Let me expand briefly on each.

Consumers of L2 motivation research may not be fully aware of the fact that the research has always concentrated on conscious motives, those that can be reported on surveys that ask learners to react to statements such as "Whenever I think of my future career, I imagine myself using English" (which taps into the ideal-self) or "Studying English is important to me in order to gain the approval of my peers/teachers/family/boss" (which taps into the ought-to-self) (both are questionnaire statements taken from Taguchi, Magid, & Papi, 2009). But implicit social cognition has been long of keen interest to psychologists. A good example in the United States is the

Implicit Association Test (IAT), first launched in 1998 based on the work on implicit bias conducted by Anthony Greenwald, Mahzarin Banaji, and Brian Nosek. The IAT is widely used to measure unconscious and automatic evaluations of people due to implicit prejudice associated to social categorizations of racial, gender, and so on. Another notable theory invoking implicit motives is that of David McClelland, who also in the United States in the 1960s proposed the following idea. During early childhood, people develop different implicitly held valorizations and prioritizations of basic human needs for achievement, power, and/or affiliation; and these implicit motives later guide their goal-setting behavior and thus their consciously rationalized motivation. In L2 learning, too, it is more than likely that implicitly held attitudes, biases, and motives shape (and at times contradict) the consciously expressed motivational dispositions to learn a new language that the field currently studies so well. Scholars interested in investing in this research frontier can begin with the two empirical studies by Al-Hoorie (2016a, 2016b) and his (2019) review of unconscious motivation concepts.

The second frontier Dörnyei (2020) identifies, the roles for vision, is elucidated well in Part 3 in the present collection by Papi (who links vision and emotions, as Dörnyei, 2020, recommended), Thompson (who focuses on the possibility of image vividness in rural contexts for L2 learning), and González-Mujico (who discusses technology support for better mental imagery for L2 motivation). Dörnyei's third frontier refers to the need to crack the mystery of motivational endurance. Obviously, learning a new language takes a long time, and without sustaining motivation people's commitment may wane and never reach the point of self-fulfilling competency. The research challenge is to figure out how to investigate motivational forces across nested time scales but also across varying degrees of time-defined intensity, as reflected in key terms like energy, currents, and momentum. It is for this reason that complexity and dynamic systems theories (Ortega & Han, 2017) logically would have the best odds at elucidating motivational endurance. Paradoxically, however, these theories have tended to concentrate thus far on on-the-fly, moment-by-moment motivational flows and processes, and they do not easily add up to long-term sustainability. A promising approach is offered by Papi and Hiver (2020), who offer a window into the long-term dynamic changes of L2 motivation from middle school all the way to graduate school. Their methodology for tracing processes of key motivational interactions over time may open the door to future studies that further engage with the sustainability of long-term motivation to learn a new language. More generally, longitudinal designs can also be invaluable to study motivational endurance (e.g., Ushioda, 2001).

To these three frontiers that Dörnyei (2020) has submitted to the field for future circumnavigation, I would like to add two more, made possible through new lenses into L2 motivation research: a multilingual lens, and a social justice lens.

The multilingual lens into L2 motivation is needed for many reasons. From a theoretical standpoint, the bulk of extant research is about motivation to learn English as a foreign language and, as Dörnyei and Al-Hoorie (2017) have poignantly noted, this makes researchers of languages other than English (LOTEs) reluctant to participate in knowledge production about L2 motivation as well as limits the generalizability of present insights. From a construct validity standpoint, motivation for multilingual and multiple-language learning needs to be understood because the majority of the world is multilingual. In fact, many people do not stop at learning one new language but will end up learning two or more, for a number of circumstantial and elective reasons; this is true of European countries (e.g., in Sweden, Henry, 2020a) but also of geographies that are imagined as monolingual and/or consumed by the desire to learn English only. For example, in China some college students may embark on the study of German for the competitive edge beyond English it can give them in the job market (Wang & Liu, 2020) and in Saudi Arabia some youth engage in leisure learning of Japanese for the imagined benefits of a more meaningful adult life (Al-Nofaie, 2018). Indeed, ever since the nudge given by Ushioda and Dörnyei (2017) with their special issue of the *Modern Language Journal* on the topic, we are already seeing a rapid growth of motivation studies that focus on multiple-language learning or on multilinguals.

The social justice lens into L2 motivation presents itself as a challenging, but equally urgent, frontier. I see two directions for it. One is investigating majority-language speakers' motivation to learn languages other than English. These learning contexts are often characterized by monolingual predispositions that can directly obstruct motivation to learn languages, and particularly minority and immigrant languages. How can these monolingual predispositions be destabilized and countered through the study of a non-English L2? A particularly challenging case is that of mother-tongue English speakers, who live surrounded by contradictory positive and negative language ideologies, pro- and anti-migration sentiments, and global neoliberal forces, as Thompson (2017a, this volume) has explored for the United States and Lanvers (2017) for the United Kingdom. The benefits of understanding motivation to learn LOTEs by majority-language speakers, including English-mother-tongue speakers, will spur sure social benefits if such efforts help us unlock the secret to convince monolinguals that they can invest in language learning and find success in their elective, late-timed bilingualism. More generally, L2 motivation researchers could investigate the possibility that tolerance of linguistic diversity is a side benefit of motivating majority-language speakers to learn other languages beyond the almighty English. Researchers interested in this direction can follow the lead of Busse (this volume) and Busse, Cenoz, Dalmann, and Rogge (2020), who report on efforts to stimulate—from a very young age—critical attitudes and transnational motivation toward multilingualism, in their case in Germany.

The other direction for the application of a social justice lens turns its gaze onto the intersection of L2 motivation with systemic forces in the social-historical spheres of life beyond individuals' psychology. The guiding question here is: What are the social, ideological, and geopolitical dimensions of L2 motivation, and how do long-standing world inequities shape motivational dynamics? The well-known construct of investment proposed by Bonny Norton (Norton Peirce, 1995) invited L2 motivation researchers to venture into this direction. Yet, it has not had much apparent traction within L2 motivation research proper. Openings toward this kind of social justice work can be found in the present volume in the chapters by Lamb and by García. Interestingly, Lamb is well known for his lifetime work on the motivation to learn English in Indonesia, a Global South context; and García has devoted her career to the study of bilingual learning by Latinx communities in the United States, that is, a Global South context within the Global North. Using critical discourse analysis, Lamb (this volume) reconceptualizes motivation to learn English as a desire to co-construct an English-speaking elite identity, and he sees this desire with ambivalence: as a catalyst for better English attainment with potentially exclusionary consequences. García (this volume) calls for an engagement with the realities of linguistically minoritized communities, whose motivations for learning the majority and minority languages and for maintaining their multilingualism are constantly eroded and under the siege of oppressive systemic forces. Can other researchers of L2 motivation become interested in addressing the social, ideological, and geopolitical dimensions of (implicit and conscious, fleeting, dynamic, and enduring) motives and motivations to learn a new language? García views the reliance on psychological constructs and theories as a muffler in the study of L2 motivation in contexts of linguistic minoritization. Critical epistemologies and knowledges from the Global South will also be needed, she admonishes. Indeed, it has for some time now been a source of puzzlement to me that L2 motivation researchers have not seen the interconnectedness between their preeminently psychological research and more critical lines of inquiry in applied linguistics. This is despite the obvious interest in social and qualitative dimensions of the relevant phenomena among many L2 motivation researchers—including Dörnyei himself. Lamb's chapter shows these types of epistemological amalgamation are possible and profitable. Perhaps experimenting with diverse epistemologies so as to squarely address social justice concerns in L2 motivation research is another needed frontier for those interested in contributing to Dörnyei and Al-Hoorie's (2017) call for much more study of L2 motivation as it relates to non-English target languages across diverse geographies.

The multilingual and the social justice lenses, and the new frontiers for L2 motivation research they might open, seem imminent and urgent. Imminent because, as I just discussed, the L2 motivation community has already begun to explore these new territories, including several contributors to this book. The lenses are also urgent because our times of pandemic unrest have transformed our understanding of the world and reset our priorities in ways that beg for deliberate, nontrivial responses to the many challenges of multilingual equity.

Everyone knows that motivation is one of the most central forces needed to explain human action and human activity. In the fields of language learning and teaching, everyone knows without motivation to learn a new language, nothing much would happen out of people's (compulsory or voluntary) engagement with formal or informal language study. It is therefore extremely fortunate that the field has had Zoltán Dörnyei as a major influence nurturing it and leading the way since the 1990s. The vibrant, collective work of the contributors gathered in this volume is a testament and homage to Dörnyei's indelible mark on the field of L2 motivation!

Lourdes Ortega, PhD
Professor
Georgetown University

NOTES

Foreword

1   Cognitive neuroscientists have conducted research on the four modes of mental imagery named above, as well as on the following mental imagery modes: motor and kinesthetic (movement), somesthetic (tactile), gustatory (taste), cross-modal, and synesthetic. For detailed research in each area, see Lacey and Lawson (2013). Such research greatly expands the possibilities for enhancing the mental imagery of L2 learners and teachers.

Chapter 12

1   For further discussion on the epistemological status of concepts such as emotion, see https://johnschumann.com.

Chapter 16

1   The logic behind this is that the reliability of a scale is equivalent to its inter-item correlation, and so squaring the reliability gives the proportion of variance shared among these items. Therefore, if the reliability is .70, then the error variance would be $1 - .70^2 = .51$, which is the proportion of variance *not* explained. This applies to group-level analysis. To apply it to individual scores, we can use the formula for the standard error of measurement: $SD_{scale} \sqrt{1 - .70}$ (see R. J. Cohen, Swerdlik, & Sturman, 2013).

Chapter 17

1   R's utterance might be translated as "Working, that's …. entertainment … entertainment … there are so many changes these days, now I really do want to learn English, now my friend and my manager [says] English is important … English, that's important."

2   A recent example in the UK is the Oasis drinks company billboard ads; one read, "It's summer. You're thirsty. We've got sales targets." The frank admission of commercial motives in the last statement, combined with the empathetic reference to the reader's thirst, is intended to create the effect of mates helping each other out.

REFERENCES

Adler, A. (1929). *The science of living*. Garden City, NY: Garden City Publishing Company.

Adolphs, S., Clark, L., Dörnyei, Z., Glover, T., Henry, A., Muir, C., ... Valstar, M. (2018). Digital innovations in L2 motivation: Harnessing the power of the Ideal L2 Self. *System*, 78, 173–85.

Agha, A. (2005). Voice, footing, enregisterment. *Journal of Linguistic Anthropology*, 15(1), 38–59.

Al-Hoorie, A. H. (2015). Human agency: Does the beach ball have free will? In Z. Dörnyei, P. MacIntyre, & A. Henry (Eds.), *Motivational dynamics in language learning* (pp. 55–72). Bristol, Blue Ridge Summit: Multilingual Matters.

Al-Hoorie, A. H. (2016a). Unconscious motivation. Part I: Implicit attitudes toward L2 speakers. *Studies in Second Language Learning and Teaching*, 6(3), 423–54.

Al-Hoorie, A. H. (2016b). Unconscious motivation. Part II: Implicit attitudes and L2 achievement. *Studies in Second Language Learning and Teaching*, 6(4), 619–49.

Al-Hoorie, A. H. (2017). Sixty years of language motivation research: Looking back and looking forward. *SAGE Open*, 7(1).

Al-Hoorie, A. H. (2018). The L2 motivational self system: A meta-analysis. *Studies in Second Language Learning and Teaching*, 8(4), 721–54.

Al-Hoorie, A. H. (2019). Motivation and the unconscious. In M. Lamb, K. Csizér, A. Henry, & S. Ryan (Eds.), *The Palgrave handbook of motivation for language learning* (pp. 561–78). Cham, Switzerland: Palgrave Macmillan.

Al-Hoorie, A. H., & Al Shlowiy, A. (2020). Vision theory vs. goal-setting theory: A critical analysis. *Porta Linguarum*, 33, 217–29.

Al-Hoorie, A. H., & MacIntyre, P. D. (Eds). (2020). *Contemporary language motivation theory: 60 years since Gardner and Lambert (1959)*. Bristol, UK: Multilingual Matters.

Al-Hoorie, A. H., Hiver, P., Kim, T.-Y., & De Costa, P. (2021). The identity crisis in language motivation research. *Journal of Language and Social Psychology*, 40(1), 136–53.

Allen, V. L., & Feldman, R. S. (1973). Learning through tutoring: Low-achieving children as tutors. *Journal of Experimental Education*, 42, 1–5.

Al-Nofaie, H. (2018). The attitudes and motivation of children towards learning rarely spoken foreign languages: A case study from Saudi Arabia. *International Journal of Bilingual Education and Bilingualism*, 21(4), 451–64.

Altermatt, E. R., & Pomerantz, E. M. (2003). The development of competence-related and motivational beliefs: An investigation of similarity and influence among friends. *Journal of Educational Psychology*, 95(1), 111–23.

Ambrose, S., Bridges, M. W., DiPietro, M., Lovett, M. C., & Norman, M. K. (2010). *How learning works: Seven research-based principles for smart teaching.* San Francisco, CA: Jossey-Bass.

Amoura, C., Berjot, S., Gillet, N., & Altintas, E. (2013). Desire for control, perception of control: Their impact on autonomous motivation and psychological adjustment. *Motivation and Emotion,* 38(3), 323–35.

Anzaldúa, G. (1987). *Borderlands/La Frontera. The New Mestiza.* San Francisco: Aunt Lute Books.

Anzaldúa, G. (2015). *Light in the dark/Luz en lo oscuro. Rewriting identity, spirituality, reality.* (A. L. Keating Ed.). Durham, NC.: Duke University Press.

Appleton, J., Christenson, S., & Furlong, M. (2008). Student engagement with school: Critical conceptual and methodological issues of the construct. *Psychology in the Schools,* 45(5), 369–86.

Arnold, J. (Ed.) (1999). *Affect in language learning.* Cambridge, UK: Cambridge University Press.

Arnold, J., & Murphey, T. (Eds.) (2013). *Meaningful action: Earl Stevick's influence on language teaching.* Cambridge, UK: Cambridge University Press.

Assor, A., Roth, G., & Deci, E. L. (2004). The emotional costs of parents' conditional regard: A Self-Determination Theory analysis. *Journal of Personality,* 72(1), 47–88.

Atkinson, D. (Ed.) (2011). *Alternative approaches to second language acquisition.* London, UK: Routledge.

Aubrey, S. (2017). Measuring flow in the EFL classroom: Learners' perceptions of inter- and intra-cultural task-based interactions. *TESOL Quarterly,* 51(3), 661–92.

Austin, J. T., & Vancouver, J. B. (1996). Goal constructs in psychology: Structure, process, and content. *Psychological Bulletin* 120, 338–75.

Bailey, E. G., & Marsden, E. (2017). Teachers' views on recognising and using home languages in predominantly monolingual primary schools. *Language and Education,* 31(4), 283–306.

Bailis, D. S., & Segall, A. (2004). Self-determination and social comparison in a health-promotion setting. *Basic and Applied Social Psychology,* 26, 25–33.

Bakker, A. B., Demerouti, E., & Burke, R. (2009). Workaholism and relationship quality: A spillover-crossover perspective. *Journal of Occupational Health Psychology,* 14(1), 23.

Ball, D. L., & Forzani, F. M. (2010). What does it take to make a teacher? *Phi Delta Kappan,* 92(2), 8–12.

Ball, D. L., & Forzani, F. M. (2011). Teaching skillful teaching. *The Effective Educator,* 68, 40–5.

Bandura, A. (1977). *Social learning theory.* Englewood Cliffs, NJ: Prentice Hall.

Bandura, A. (1997). *Self-efficacy: The exercise of control.* New York, NY: Freeman.

Banegas, D. (2013). The integration of content and language as a driving force in the EFL lesson. In E. Ushioda (Ed.), *International perspectives on motivation: Language learning and professional challenges* (pp. 82–97). Basingstoke, UK: Palgrave Macmillan.

Barakos, E., & Selleck, C. (2019) Elite multilingualism: Discourses, practices, and debates. *Journal of Multilingual and Multicultural Development,* 40(5), 361–74.

Bargh, J. A. (1990). Auto-motives: Preconscious determinants of social interaction. In E. T. Higgins, & R. M. Sorrentino (Eds.), *Handbook of motivation and cognition* (vol. 2, pp. 93–130). New York: Guilford Press.

Bargh, J. A. (2017). *Before you know it: The unconscious reasons we do what we do*. New York: Atria.

Bargh, J. A., & Chartrand, T. L. (1999). The unbearable automaticity of being. *American Psychologist*, 54, 462–79.

Barkley, E. F. (2010). *Student engagement techniques: A handbook for college faculty*. San Francisco, CA: Jossey-Bass.

Barsade, S. G. (2002). The ripple effect: Emotional contagion and its influence on group behavior. *Administrative Science Quarterly*, 47(4), 644–75.

Barsade, S. G., & Gibson, D. E. (1998). Group emotion: A view from top and bottom. *Research on Managing Groups and Teams*, 1, 81–102.

Barsade, S. G., & Gibson, D. E. (2012). Group affect: Its influence on individual and group outcomes. *Current Directions in Psychological Science*, 21(2), 119–23.

Barsade, S. G., & Knight, A. P. (2015). Group affect. *Annual Review of Organizational Psychology and Organizational Behavior*, 2, 21–46.

Barsade, S. G., Coutifaris, C. G. V., & Pillemer, J. (2018). Emotional contagion in organizational life. *Research in Organizational Behavior*, 38, 137–51.

Bartel, C. A., & Saavedra, R. (2000). The collective construction of work group moods. *Administrative Science Quarterly*, 45(2), 197–231.

Bauman, R., & Briggs, C. L. (2003). *Voices of modernity: Language ideologies and the politics of inequality*. Cambridge: Cambridge University Press.

Baumeister, R. F., & Leary, M. R. (1995). The need to belong: Desire for interpersonal attachments as a fundamental human motivation. *Psychological Bulletin*, 117, 497–529.

Baumeister, R.,. F., & Tierney, J. (2011). *Willpower: Rediscovering the greatest human strength*. New York, NY: Penguin Press.

Baumeister, R. F. (2005). *The cultural animal: Human nature, meaning, and social life*. Oxford, UK: Oxford University Press.

Baumeister, R. F., & Finkel, E. J. (2010). *Advanced social psychology: The state of the science*. Oxford, UK: Oxford University Press.

Becker, A. L. (1995). *Beyond translation: Essays toward a modern philosophy*. Ann Arbor, MI: University of Michigan Press.

Becker, E. S., Goetz, T., Morger, V., & Ranellucci, J. (2014). The importance of teachers' emotions and instructional behavior for their students' emotions–An experience sampling analysis. *Teaching and Teacher Education*, 43, 15–26.

Beckett, G. H., & Slater, T. (Eds.) (2020). *Global perspectives on project-based language learning, teaching, and assessment: Key approaches, technology tools, and frameworks*. New York & Abingdon, UK: Routledge.

Ben Malek, H., Berna, F., & D'Argembeau, A. (2018). Envisioning the times of future events: The role of personal goals. *Consciousness and Cognition*, 63, 198–205.

Beneke, J. (1991) Englisch als lingua franca oder als Medium interkultureller Kommunikation. In R. Grebing (ed.) *Grenzenloses Sprachenlernen. Festschrift für Richard Freudenstein* (pp. 54–66). Berlin: Cornelsen.

Bhavsar, N., Ntoumanis, N., Quested, E., Gucciardi, D. F., Thøgersen-Ntoumani, C., Ryan, R. M., et al. (2019). Conceptualizing and testing a new tripartite measure of coach interpersonal behaviors. *Psychology of Sport and Exercise*, 44, 107–120.

Björkman, B. (2010). So you think you can ELF: English as a lingua franca as the medium of instruction. *HERMES-Journal of Language and Communication in Business* (45), 77–96.

Block, D. (2003). *The social turn in second language acquisition.* Washington, DC: Georgetown University Press.

Blommaert, J. (2010). *The sociolinguistics of globalization.* Cambridge: Cambridge University Press.

Blythe, Tina, & Associates (1998). *The teaching for understanding guide.* San Francisco: Jossey-Bass Publishers.

Boekaerts, M. (1987). Individual differences in the appraisal of learning tasks: An integrative view on emotion and cognition in emotion and cognition. *Communication & Cognition,* 20(2–3), 207–23.

Bollen, K. A. (1989). *Structural equations with latent variables.* New York, NY: Wiley.

Boo, Z., Dörnyei, Z., & Ryan, S. (2015). L2 motivation research 2005–2014: Understanding a publication surge and a changing landscape. *System,* 55, 145–57.

Bourdieu, P. (1991). *Language and symbolic power.* (G. Raymond, & M. Adamson, trans). Cambridge: Polity Press.

Bozhovich, L. I. I. (2009). The social situation of child development. *Journal of Russian & East European Psychology,* 47(4), 59–86.

Brafman, O., & Brafman, R. (2010). *Click: The forces behind how we fully engage with people, work, and everything we do.* New York, NY: Crown Business.

Bronson, M. (2000). *Self-regulation in early childhood: Nature and nurture.* New York: Guildford Press.

Brophy, J. E. (2004). *Motivating students to learn* (2nd ed.). Mahwah, NJ: Erlbaum.

Brophy, J., & Good, T. L. (1986). Teacher behavior and student achievement. In M. L. Wittock (Ed.), *Handbook of research on teaching* (3rd ed., pp. 328–75). New York: Macmillan.

Brouwer, A. M. (2017). *Motivation for sustaining health behavior change: The self-as-doer identity.* New York: Routledge.

Brown, H. D. (1994). *Teaching by principles: An interactive approach to language pedagogy.* Englewood Cliffs, NJ: Prentice Hall Regents.

Brown, T. A. (2015). *Confirmatory factor analysis for applied research* (2nd ed.). New York, NY: Guilford.

Busse, V. (2009). Motivation, language identity and the L2 self. *System,* 37(4), 741–3.

Busse, V. (2013). An exploration of motivation and self-beliefs of first year students of German. *System,* 41(2), 379–98.

Busse, V. (2017a). Zur Förderung positiver Einstellungen gegenüber sprachlicher Diversität als europäisches Bildungsziel: Status quo und Desiderate [Promoting positive attitudes towards linguistic diversity as a European educational objective: status quo and desiderata]. *Zeitschrift für Fremdsprachenforschung,* 28(1), 53–75.

Busse, V. (2017b). Plurilingualism in Europe: Exploring attitudes towards English and other European languages among adolescents in Bulgaria, Germany, the Netherlands, and Spain. *The Modern Language Journal,* 101(3), 566–82.

Busse, V. (2019). *Umgang mit Mehrsprachigkeit und sprachsensibler Unterricht aus pädagogischer Sicht: Ein einführender Überblick [Addressing multilingualism and language-sensitive teaching from a pedagogical point of view: An introductory overview].* In J. Goschler, & M. Butler (Hrsg), *Sprachsensibel unterrichten in den Fächern* (1–34). Oldenburg: Germany.

Busse, V., & Göbel, K. (2017). Interkulturelle Kompetenz in der Lehrerinnen- und Lehrerbildung: Zum Stellenwert interkultureller Einstellungen als Grundlage relevanter Handlungskompetenzen. [Intercultural competence in teacher education: On the importance of intercultural attitudes for relevant practical skills]. *Beiträge zur Lehrerinnen- und Lehrerbildung*, 35(3), S, 427–39.

Busse, V., & Krause, U.-M. (2016). Instructional methods and languages in class: A comparison of two teaching approaches and two teaching languages in the field of intercultural learning. *Learning and Instruction*, 42, 83–94.

Busse, V., Cenoz, J., Dalmann, N., & Rogge, F. (2020). Addressing linguistic diversity in the language classroom in a resource-oriented way: An intervention study with primary school children. *Language Learning*, 70(2), 382–419.

Busse, V., Riedesel, L., & Krause, U.-M. (2017). Anregung von Reflexionsprozessen zur Förderung interkultureller Kompetenz: Ergebnisse einer Interventions- und einer Interviewstudie [Stimulating reflection processes to promote intercultural competence: Results from an intervention and an interview study]. *Zeitschrift für Pädagogik*, 63, 362–86.

Bygate, M., & Samuda, V. (2009). Creating pressure in task pedagogy: The joint roles of field, purpose, and engagement within the interaction approaches. In A. Mackey, & C. Polio (Eds.), *Multiple perspectives on interaction: Second language research in honour of Susan M. Gass* (pp. 90–116). New York: Routledge.

Byrne, D. (2009). Case-based methods: Why we need them; what they are; how to do them. In D. S. Byrne, & C. C. Ragin (Eds.), *The SAGE handbook of case-based methods* (pp. 1–10). London, UK: SAGE.

Cai, S., & Zhu, W. (2012). The impact of an online learning community project on university Chinese as a foreign language students' motivation. *Foreign Language Annals*, 45(3), 307–29.

Cameron, D., & Panović, I. (2014). *Working with written discourse*. London: Sage.

Campbell, D. T., & Kenny, D. A. (1999). *A primer on regression artifacts*. New York, NY: Guilford.

Carmines, E. G., & Zeller, R. A. (1979). *Reliability and validity assessment*. Beverly Hills, CA: SAGE.

Carson, R. L., Weiss, H. M., & Templin, T. J. (2010). Ecological momentary assessment: A research method for studying the daily lives of teachers. *International Journal of Research & Method in Education*, 33(2), 165–82.

Cenoz, J., & Gorter, D. (2014). Focus on multilingualism as an approach in educational contexts. In A. Creese, & A. Blackledge (Eds.), *Heteroglossia as practice and pedagogy* (pp. 239–54). Berlin, Germany: Springer.

Census Bureau, U. S. (n.d.). *State population totals: 2010–2019*. The United States Census Bureau. Retrieved February 1, 2020, from https://www.census.gov/data/tables/time-series/demo/popest/2010s-state-total.html

Centers for Disease Control and Prevention (2009). *School connectedness: Strategies for increasing protective factors among youth*. Atlanta, GA: Department of Health and Human Services.

Chan, L. (2014). Effects of an imagery intervention on Chinese university students' possible L2 selves and learning experiences. In K. Csizér, & M. Magid (Eds.), *The impact of self-concept on L2 learning* (pp. 357–76). Bristol, UK: Multilingual Matters.

Chen, B., Vansteenkiste, M., Beyers, W., Boone, L., Deci, E. L., Van Der Kaap-deeder, J., et al. (2015). Basic psychological need satisfaction, need frustration, and need strength across four cultures. *Motivation and Emotion*, 39, 216–36.

Chen, J. C., & Brown, K. L. (2011). The effects of authentic audience on English as a second language (ESL) writers: A task-based, computer-mediated approach. *Computer Assisted Language Learning*, 25(5), 1–20.

Chirkov, V. I. (2009). A cross-cultural analysis of autonomy in education: A self-determination theory perspective. *Theory and Research in Education*, 7(2), 253–62.

Chirkov, V., Ryan, R. M., Kim, Y., & Kaplan, U. (2003). Differentiating autonomy from individualism and independence: A self-determination theory perspective on internalization of cultural orientations and well-being. *Journal of Personality and Social Psychology*, 84(1), 97–110.

Cho, M. (2018). Task complexity and modality: Exploring learners' experience from the perspective of flow. *The Modern Language Journal*, 102(1), 162–80.

Clark, D. M., & Wells, A. (1995). A cognitive model of social phobia. In R. G. Heimberg, M. R. Liebowitz, D. A. Hope, & F. R. Schneier (Eds.), *Social phobia: Diagnosis, assessment and treatment* (pp. 69–93). New York: Guilford Press.

Claro, J. (2020). Identification with external and internal referents: Integrativeness and the Ideal L2 Self. In A. Al-Hoorie, & P. D. MacIntyre (Eds.), *Contemporary language motivation theory: 60 years since Gardner and Lambert (1959)* (pp. 233–61). Bristol: Multilingual Matters.

Cogo, A. (2007). *Intercultural communication in English as a lingua franca: A case study*. PhD thesis, King's College London.

Cogo, A., & Jenkins, J. (2010). English as a lingua franca in Europe: A mismatch between policy and practice. *European Journal of Language Policy*, 2(2), 271–93.

Cohen, J. (1968). Multiple regression as a general data-analytic system. *Psychological Bulletin*, 70(6, Pt.1), 426–43.

Cohen, J., Cohen, P., West, S. G., & Aiken, L. S. (2003). *Applied multiple regression/correlation analysis for the behavioral sciences* (3rd ed.). Mahwah, NJ: Lawrence Erlbaum.

Cohen, R. J., Swerdlik, M. E., & Sturman, E. D. (2013). *Psychological testing and assessment: An introduction to tests and measurement* (8th ed.). New York, NY: McGraw-Hill.

Cole, M., Levitin, K., & Luria, A. R. (2014). *The autobiography of Alexander Luria: A dialogue with the making of mind*. New York, NY: Psychology Press.

Coleman, H. (2016). The English Language as naga in Indonesia. In P. Bunce, V. Rapatahana, R. Phillipson, & T. Ruanni Tupas (Eds.), *Why English? Confronting the Hydra* (pp. 59–71). Bristol: Multilingual Matters.

Colombo, M. R. (2017). Understanding L2 motivation through selves and currents: Lessons from students in an innovative business Spanish course. Unpublished PhD dissertation. University of Iowa.

Cook, S. R., & J.-M. Dewaele (2021). The English language enables me to visit my pain. Exploring the healing role of a foreign language in survivors of sexuality persecution. *International Journal of Bilingualism*.

Cook, V. (1999). Going beyond the native speaker in language teaching. *TESOL Quarterly*, 33(2), 185–209.

Cooper, R. (1989). *Language planning and social change*. Cambridge: Cambridge University Press.

Costa, B., & Dewaele, J.-M. (2012). Psychotherapy across languages: Beliefs, attitudes and practices of monolingual and multilingual therapists with their multilingual patients. *Language and Psychoanalysis*, 1, 18–40.

Costa, B., & Dewaele, J.-M. (2019). The talking cure – building the core skills and the confidence of counsellors and psychotherapists to work effectively with multilingual patients through training and supervision. *Counselling and Psychotherapy Research*, 19, 231–40.

Council of Europe (2007). *From linguistic diversity to plurilingual education: Guide for the development of language education policies in Europe.* Prepared by the Council of Europe, Strasbourg. Retrieved April 7, 2019 from https://rm.coe.int/CoERMPublicCommonSearchServices/DisplayDCTMContent?documentId=09000016802fc1c4

Council of Europe (2008). *White paper on intercultural dialogue. Living together as equals in dignity.* Prepared by the Council of Europe Ministers of Foreign Affairs at their 118th Ministerial Session, Strasbourg. Retrieved April 7, 2019 from https://www.coe.int/t/dg4/intercultural/source/white%20paper_final_revised_en.pdf

Cozolino, L. (2013). *The social neuroscience of education.* New York, NY: W. W. Norton & Company.

Cozolino, L. (2014). *Attachment-based teaching: Creating the tribal classroom.* New York, NY: W. W. Norton & Company.

Crookes, G., & Schmidt, R. (1991). Motivation: Reopening the research agenda. *Language Learning*, 41, 469–512.

Crystal, D. (2012). *English as a global language.* Cambridge: Cambridge university press.

Csikszentmihalyi, M. (1990). *Flow: The psychology of optimal experience.* New York, NY: Harper Perennial.

Csizer, K. (2020). The L2 Motivation Self System. In M. Lamb, K. Csizér, A. Henry, & S. Ryan (Eds.), *The Palgrave handbook of motivation for language learning* (pp. 71–93). Basingstoke: Palgrave Macmillan.

Csizér, K. & Dörnyei, Z. (2005). Language learners' motivational profiles and their motivated learning behavior. *Language Learning*, 55, 613–59.

Csizér, K., & Kormos, J. (2009). Learning experiences, selves and motivated learning behavior: A comparative analysis of structural models for Hungarian secondary and university learners of English. In Z. Dörnyei, & E. Ushioda (Eds.), *Motivation, language identity and the L2 self* (pp. 98–119). Bristol: Multilingual Matters.

Csizer, K., & Lukacs, G. (2010). The comparative analysis of motivation, attitudes and selves: The case of English and German in Hungary. *System*, 38(1), 1–13.

Cummins, J. (2000). *Language, power and pedagogy: Bilingual children in the crossfire.* Clevedon, UK: Multilingual Matters.

D'Argembeau, A. (2016). The role of personal goals in future-oriented mental time travel. In K. Michaelian, S. B. Klein, & K. K. Szpunar (Eds.), *Seeing the future: Theoretical perspectives on future-oriented mental time travel* (pp. 199–214). Oxford: Oxford University Press.

D'Argembeau, A. (2020). Imagination and self-referential thinking. In A. Abraham (Ed.), *The Cambridge handbook of the imagination* (pp. 354–72). Cambridge: Cambridge University Press.

D'Argembeau, A., & Van Der Linden, M. (2012). Predicting the phenomenology of episodic future thoughts. *Consciousness and Cognition*, 21(3), 1198–206.

Damasio, A. (2010). *The self comes to mind.* New York: Vintage.

Danziger, K. (1997). *Naming the mind: How psychology found its language*. London, UK: Sage.

Darvin, R. (2020). L2 motivation and investment. In M. Lamb, K. Csizér, A. Henry, & S. Ryan (Eds.), *The Palgrave handbook of motivation for language learning* (pp. 245–64). Basingstoke: Palgrave Macmillan.

Darvin, R., & Norton, B. (2015). Identity and a model of investment in applied linguistics. *Annual Review of Applied Linguistics*, 35, 36–56.

Darvin, R., & Norton, B. (2016). Investment and language learning in the 21st century. *Langage et société* (3), 19–38.

Davidov, E. (2008). A cross-country and cross-time comparison of the human values measurements with the second round of the European Social Survey. *Survey Research Methods*, 2(1), 33–46.

Davidov, E., Meuleman, B., Cieciuch, J., Schmidt, P., & Billiet, J. (2014). Measurement equivalence in cross-national Research. *Annual Review of Sociology*, 40(1), 55–75.

Davis, W. (2018). Raising metacognitive awareness using ideal classmates. In J. Mynard, & I. Brady (Eds.), *Stretching boundaries. Papers from the third international Psychology of Language Learning conference, Tokyo, Japan, 7–10 June, 2018* (pp. 79–81). International Association of the Psychology of Language Learning (IAPLL).

De Bot, K., & Larsen-Freeman, D. (2011). Researching second language development from a dynamic systems theory perspective. In M. Verspoor, K. De Bot, & W. Lowie (Eds.), *A dynamic approach to second language development: Methods and techniques* (pp. 5–23). Amsterdam, The Netherlands: John Benjamins.

De Bot, K., Lowie, W., & Verspoor, M. (2005). *Second language acquisition: An advanced resource book*. London, UK: Routledge.

De Costa, P. (2019). Elite multilingualism, affect and neoliberalism. *Journal of Multilingual and Multicultural Development*, 40(5), 453–60.

De Costa, P., Park, J., & Wee, L. (2016). Language learning as linguistic entrepreneurship: Implications for language education. *Asia-Pacific Education Researcher*, 25(5–6), 695.

Deci, E. L., & Ryan, R. M. (2014). Autonomy and need satisfaction in close relationships: Relationships motivation theory. In N. Weinstein (Ed.), *Human motivation and interpersonal relationships* (pp. 53–73). Dordrecht: Springer.

Deci, E., & Ryan, R. (2000). The "what" and "why" of goal pursuit: Human needs and the self-determination of behaviour. *Psychological Inquiry*, 11, 227–68.

Deci, E., & Ryan, R. (2012). Motivation, personality, and development within embedded social contexts: An overview of self-determination theory. In E. Deci, & R. Ryan (Eds.), *The Oxford handbook of human motivation* (pp. 85–107). New York: Oxford University Press.

Deci, E. L., & Ryan, R. M. (1985). *Intrinsic motivation and self-determination in human behavior*. New York: Plenum Press.

Derex, M., Beugin, M., Godelle, B., & Raymond, M. (2013). Experimental evidence for the influence of group size on cultural complexity. *Nature*, 503, 389–91.

Dewaele, J.-M. (1993), Variation synchronique en interlangue française. Unpublished PhD dissertation. Vrije Universiteit Brussel.

Dewaele, J.-M. (2002). Psychological and sociodemographic correlates of communicative anxiety in L2 and L3 production. *International Journal of Bilingualism*, 6(1), 23–39.

Dewaele, J.-M. (2004). Slaying the dragon of fanaticism through enlightenment. Teaching languages and cultures in a post-9/11 world: An european perspective. *The Modern Language Journal*, 88(4), 663–6.

Dewaele, J.-M. (2005). Investigating the psychological and the emotional dimensions in instructed language learning: Obstacles and possibilities. *The Modern Language Journal*, 89(3), 367–80.

Dewaele, J.-M. (2010). *Emotions in multiple languages*. Basingstoke: Palgrave Macmillan.

Dewaele, J.-M. (2011). Reflections on the emotional and psychological aspects of foreign language learning and use. *Anglistik. International Journal of English Studies*, 22(1), 23–42.

Dewaele, J.-M. (2019a). When elephants fly: The lift-off of emotion research in applied linguistics. *The Modern Language Journal*, 103(2), 533–6.

Dewaele, J.-M. (2019b). The vital need for ontological, epistemological and methodological diversity in applied linguistics. In C. Wright, L. Harvey, & J. Simpson (Eds.), *Voices and practices in applied linguistics: Diversifying a discipline* (pp. 71–88). York: White Rose University Press.

Dewaele, J.-M., & Costa, B. (2013). Multilingual clients' experience of psychotherapy. *Language and Psychoanalysis*, 2(2), 31–50.

Dewaele, J.-M., & Li, C. (2018). Editorial of the special issue "Emotions in SLA." *Studies in Second Language Learning and Teaching*, 8(1), 15–19.

Dewaele, J.-M., & Li, C. (2020). Emotions in second language acquisition: A critical review and research agenda. *Foreign Language World [Chinese 外语界]*, 196(1), 34–49.

Dewaele, J.-M., & MacIntyre, P. D. (2014). The two faces of Janus? Anxiety and enjoyment in the foreign language classroom. *Studies in Second Language Learning and Teaching*, 4(2), 237–74.

Dewaele, J.-M., & MacIntyre, P. D. (2016). Foreign language enjoyment and foreign language classroom anxiety: The right and left feet of FL learning? In P. D. MacIntyre, T. Gregersen, & S. Mercer (Eds.), *Positive psychology in SLA* (pp. 215–36). Bristol, UK: Multilingual Matters.

Dewaele, J.-M., & MacIntyre, P. D. (2019). The predictive power of multicultural personality traits, learner and teacher variables on foreign language enjoyment and anxiety. In M. Sato, & S. Loewen (Eds.), *Evidence-based second language pedagogy: A collection of instructed second language acquisition studies* (pp. 263–86). London: Routledge.

Dewaele, J.-M., & Pavlenko, A. (2002). Emotion vocabulary in interlanguage. *Language Learning*, 52(2), 265–324.

Dewaele, J.-M., & Pavlenko, A. (Eds.) (2004). Bilingualism and emotion. *Estudios de Sociolingüística*, 5, 1.

Dewaele, J.-M., & Véronique, D. (2001). Gender assignment and gender agreement in advanced French interlanguage: A cross-sectional study. *Bilingualism: Language and Cognition*, 4(3), 275–97.

Dewaele, J.-M., Chen, X., Padilla, A. M., & Lake, J. (2019). The flowering of positive psychology in foreign language teaching and acquisition research. *Frontiers in Psychology. Language Sciences*, 10, 2128.

Dewaele, J.-M., Witney, J., Saito, K., & Dewaele, L. (2018). Foreign language enjoyment and anxiety in the FL classroom: The effect of teacher and learner variable. *Language Teaching Research*, 22(6), 676–97.

Dewey, M. (2003, April). *Codifying lingua franca English*. Paper presented at IATEFL Conference, Brighton.

Domakani, M. R., & Mohammadi, M. H. (2016). Iranian learners' L2 selves and their self-regulated learning strategies. *Mediterranean Journal of Social Sciences*, 7(3), 404–10.

Dong, J., & Blommaert, J. (2016). Global informal learning environments and the making of Chinese middle class. *Linguistics and Education*, 34, 33.

Dörnyei, Z. (1994a). Motivation and motivating in the foreign language classroom. *The Modern Language Journal*, 78(3), 273–84.

Dörnyei, Z. (1994b). Understanding L2 motivation: On with the challenge! *The Modern Language Journal*, 78(4), 515–23.

Dörnyei, Z. (1997). Psychological processes in cooperative language learning: Groups dynamics and motivation. *The Modern Language Journal*, 81(4), 482–93.

Dörnyei, Z. (1998). Motivation in second and foreign language learning. *Language Teaching*, 31(3), 117–35.

Dörnyei, Z. (2001). *Motivational strategies in the language classroom*. Cambridge, UK: Cambridge University Press.

Dörnyei, Z. (2002). The motivational basis of language learning tasks. In P. Robinson (Ed.), *Individual differences and instructed language learning* (pp. 137–58). Amsterdam: John Benjamins.

Dörnyei, Z. (2005). *The psychology of the language learner: Individual differences in second language acquisition*. Mahwah, NJ: Lawrence Erlbaum.

Dörnyei, Z. (2006). Individual differences in second language acquisition. *AILA review*, 19(1), 42–68.

Dörnyei, Z. (2008, March). *Are individual differences really individual?* Plenary presented at the American Association for Applied Linguistics (AAAL), Washington, DC.

Dörnyei, Z. (2009a). The L2 Motivational Self System. In Z. Dörnyei, & E. Ushioda (Eds.), *Motivation, language identity and the L2 self* (pp. 9–42). Bristol, UK: Multilingual Matters.

Dörnyei, Z. (2009b). *The psychology of second language acquisition*. Oxford: Oxford University Press.

Dörnyei, Z. (2009c). Motivation and the vision of knowing a second language. In B. Beaven (Ed.), *IATEFL 2008: Exeter conference selections* (pp. 16–22). Canterbury: IATEFL.

Dörnyei, Z. (2017). Conceptualizing learner characteristics in a complex, dynamic world. In L. Ortega, & Z. Han (Eds.), *Complexity theory and language development: In celebration of Diane Larsen-Freeman* (pp. 79–96). Amsterdam: John Benjamins.

Dörnyei, Z. (2019a). From integrative motivation to directed motivational currents: The evolution of the understanding of L2 motivation over three decades. In M. Lamb, K. Csizér, A. Henry, & S. Ryan (Eds.), *Palgrave Macmillan handbook of motivation for language learning* (pp. 39–69). Basingstoke: Palgrave.

Dörnyei, Z. (2019b). Task motivation: What makes an L2 task engaging? In Z. W. M. J. Ahmadian (Ed.), *Researching L2 task performance and pedagogy: In honour of Peter Skehan* (pp. 53–66). Amsterdam: John Benjamins.

Dörnyei, Z. (2019c). Psychology and language learning: The past, the present and the future. *Journal for the Psychology of Language Learning*, 1, 27–41.

Dörnyei, Z. (2019d). *Vision, mental imagery and the Christian life: Insights from science and scripture*. New York: Routledge.

Dörnyei, Z. (2020). *Innovations and challenges in language learning motivation*. London: Routledge.

Dörnyei, Z., & Al-Hoorie, A. H. (2017). The motivational foundation of learning languages other than global English: Theoretical issues and research directions. *The Modern Language Journal*, 101(3), 455–68.

Dörnyei, Z., & Chan, L. (2013). Motivation and vision: An analysis of future L2 self images, sensory styles, and imagery capacity across two target languages. *Language Learning*, 63(3), 437–62.

Dörnyei, Z., & Csizér, K. (1998). Ten commandments for motivating language learners: Results of an empirical study. *Language Teaching Research*, 2(3), 203–29.

Dörnyei, Z., & Kormos, J. (2000). The role of individual and social variables in oral task performance. *Language Teaching Research*, 4, 275–300.

Dörnyei, Z., & Kubanyiova, M. (2014). *Motivating learners, motivating teachers: Building vision in the language classroom*. Cambridge, UK: Cambridge University Press (Republished in China by the Beijing Language and Culture University Press, 2020).

Dörnyei, Z., & Malderez, A. (1997). Group dynamics and foreign language teaching. *System*, 25(1), 65–81.

Dörnyei, Z., & Malderez, A. (1999). The role of group dynamics in foreign language learning and teaching. In J. Arnold (Ed.), *Affective language learning* (pp. 155–69). Cambridge, UK: Cambridge University Press.

Dörnyei, Z., & Murphy, R. S. (2010). Where does psychology and second language acquisition research connect? An interview with Zoltán Dörnyei. *The Language Teacher*, 34(2), 19–23.

Dörnyei, Z., & Murphey, T. (2003). *Group dynamics in the language classroom*. Cambridge, UK: Cambridge University Press.

Dörnyei, Z., & Ottó, I. (1998). Motivation in action: A process model of L2 motivation. *Working Papers in Applied Linguistics (Thames Valley University, London)*, 4, 43–69.

Dörnyei, Z., & Ryan, S. (2015). *The psychology of the language learner revisited*. London: Routledge.

Dörnyei, Z., & Skehan, P. (2003). Individual differences in second language learning. In C. J. Doughty, & M. H. Long (Eds.), *The handbook of second language acquisition* (pp. 589–630). Oxford: Blackwell.

Dörnyei, Z., & Ushioda, E. (Eds.) (2009). *Motivation, language identity and the L2 self*. Bristol, UK: Multilingual Matters.

Dörnyei, Z., & Ushioda, E. (2011). *Teaching and researching motivation* (2nd ed.). Harlow, UK: Longman.

Dörnyei, Z., Henry, A., & Muir, C. (2016). *Motivational currents in language learning: Frameworks for focused interventions*. New York & Abingdon, UK: Routledge.

Dörnyei, Z., Ibrahim, Z., & Muir, C. (2015). 'Directed Motivational Currents': Regulating complex dynamic systems through motivational surges. In Z. Dörnyei, P. D. MacIntyre, & A. Henry (Eds.), *Motivational dynamics in language learning* (pp. 95–105). Bristol: Multilingual Matters.

Dörnyei, Z., MacIntyre, P. D., & Henry, A. (Eds.) (2015). *Motivational dynamics in language learning*. Bristol, UK: Multilingual Matters.

Dörnyei, Z., Muir, C., & Ibrahim, Z. (2014). Directed Motivational Currents: Energising language learning through creating intense motivational pathways. In D. Lasagabaster, A. Doiz, & J. M. Sierra (Eds.), *Motivation and foreign language learning: From theory to practice* (pp. 9–29). Amsterdam: John Benjamins.

Duffy, G. G., Miller, S., Parsons, S., & Meloth, M. (2009). Teachers as metacognitive professionals. In D.J. Hacker, J. Dunlosky, & A. C. Graesser (Eds.), *Handbook of metacognition in education* (pp. 240–56). New York: Routledge.

Duriez, B. (2011). The social costs of extrinsic relative to intrinsic goal pursuits revisited: The moderating role of general causality orientation. *Personality and Individual Differences*, 50(5), 684–7.

Egbert, J. (2003). A study of flow theory in the foreign language classroom. *The Modern Language Journal*, 87(4), 499–518.

Ehrman, M. E., & Dörnyei, Z. (1998). *Interpersonal dynamics in second language education: The visible and invisible classroom*. Thousand Oaks, CA: Sage Publications.

Eichinger, L. M., Gärtig, A.-K., Plewnia, A., Roessel, J., Rothe, A., Rudert, S., et al. (2009). *Aktuelle Spracheinstellungen in Deutschland. Erste Ergebnisse einer bundesweiten Repräsentativumfrage [Language attitudes in Germany: First results from a representative nation-wide survey]*. Mannheim: Institut für Deutsche Sprache.

Eitam, B., & Higgins, E. T. (2010). Motivation in mental accessibility: Relevance of a representation (ROAR) as a new framework. *Social and Personality Psychology Compass*, 4, 951–67.

Eitam, B., & Higgins, E. T. (2014). What's in a goal? The role of motivational relevance in cognition and action. *Behavioral and Brain Sciences*, 37, 141–2.

Ellis, N. C. (2019). Essentials of a theory of language cognition. *The Modern Language Journal*, 103(s), 39–60.

Ellis, R. (2003). *Task-based language learning and teaching*. Oxford: Oxford University Press.

Ellis, R. (2009). The differential effects of three types of task planning on the fluency, complexity, and accuracy in L2 oral production. *Applied Linguistics*, 30(4), 474–509.

Ellis, R., & Shintani, N. (2014). *Exploring language pedagogy through second language acquisition research*. New York: Routledge.

Engelhard, G. (2013). *Invariant measurement: Using Rasch models in the social, behavioral, and health sciences*. London, UK: Routledge.

Ernst, A., Philippe, F. L., & D'Argembeau, A. (2018). Wanting or having to: The influence of goal self-concordance on the representation of personal future events. *Consciousness and Cognition*, 66, 26–39.

Evans, P., McPherson, G. E., & Davidson, J. W. (2012). The role of psychological needs in ceasing music and music learning activities. *Psychology of Music*, 41(5), 600–19.

Fairclough, N. (2003). *Analysing Discourse: Text analysis for social research*. London: Routledge.

Firth, A., & Wagner, J. (1997). On discourse, communication, and (some) fundamental concepts in SLA research. *The Modern Language Journal*, 81(3), 285–300.

Firth, A. (1996). The discursive accomplishment of normality. On "lingua franca" English and conversation analysis. *Journal of Pragmatics*, 26, 237–59.

Fisher, W. P. (1992). Reliability, separation, strata statistics. *Rasch Measurement Transactions*, 6(3), 238.

Fishman, J. A. (1965). Who speaks what language to whom and when? *La Linguistique*, 2, 67–88.

Fishman, J. A. (1972). *Language in sociocultural change. Essays by Joshua A. Fishman*. Stanford, CA: Stanford University Press.

Fishman, J. A. (1989). *Language and ethnicity in minority sociolinguistic perspective*. Clevedon, England: Multilingual Matters.

Fishman, J. A. (Ed.) (1968). *Readings in the sociology of language*. Germany: De Gruyter Mouton.

Fitzgerald, M. S., & Palincsar, A. S. (2019). Teaching practices that support student sensemaking across grades and disciplines: A conceptual review. *Review of Research in Education*, 43, 227–48.

Flores, N. (2014). Let's not forget that translanguaging is a political act. [Online] *Educational Linguist*. Available at: https://educationallinguist.wordpress.com/2014/07/19/lets-not-forget-that-translanguaging-is-a-political-act/ [Accessed May 27, 2020].

Flores, N., & Rosa, J. (2015). Undoing appropriateness: Raciolinguistic ideologies and language diversity in education. *Harvard Educational Review*, 85(2), 149–72.

Forgas, J. P. (2008). Affect and cognition. *Perspectives on Psychological Science*, 3(2), 94–101.

Forzani, F. M. (2014). Understanding "core practices" and "practice-based" teacher education: Learning from the past. *Journal of Teacher Education*, 65, 1–12.

Foucault, M. (1980). *Power/knowledge: Selected interviews and other writings, 1972–1977* (1st American ed.). New York: Pantheon Books.

Fredricks, J., Blumenfeld, P., & Paris, A. (2004). School engagement: Potential of the concept, state of the evidence. *Review of Educational Research*, 74(1), 59–109.

Fredrickson, B. L. (2001). The role of positive emotions in positive psychology: The broaden and build theory of positive emotions. *American Psychologist*, 56(3), 218–26.

Frenzel, A. C., & Stephens, E. J. (2013). Emotions. In N.C. Hall, & T. Goetz (Eds.), *Emotion, motivation and self-regulation: A handbook for teachers* (pp. 1–56). Bingley, UK: Emerald.

Frenzel, A. C., Goetz, T., Lüdtke, O., Pekrun, R., & Sutton, R. (2009). Emotional transmission in the classroom: Exploring the relationship between teacher and student enjoyment. *Journal of Educational Psychology*, 101, 705–16.

Frenzel, A. C., Goetz, T., Stephens, E. J., & Jacob, B. (2009). Antecedents and effects of teachers' emotional experiences: An integrative perspective and empirical test. In P. A. Schutz, & M. Zembylas (Eds.), *Advances in teacher emotions research: The impact on teachers lives* (pp. 129–48). New York: Springer.

Froiland, J. M., & Worrell, F. C. (2016). Intrinsic motivation, learning goals, engagement, and achievement in a diverse high school. *Psychology in the Schools*, 53(3), 321–36.

Fryer, L. K., Bovee, H. N., & Nakao, K. (2014). E-learning: Reasons students in language learning courses don't want to. *Computers & Education*, 74, 26–36.

Fryer, M., & Roger, P. (2018). Transformations in the L2 self: Changing motivation in a study abroad context. *System*, 78, 159–72.

Funder, D. C. (2010). *The personality puzzle*. New York: Norton.

Furrer, C. J., & Skinner, E. A. (2003). Sense of relatedness as a factor in children's academic engagement and performance. *Journal of Educational Psychology*, 95(1), 148–62.

Gao, X. (2019). The Douglas Fir Group framework as a resource map for language teacher education. *The Modern Language Journal*, 103(s), 161–6.

Gao, X., & Xu, H. (2014). The dilemma of being English language teachers: Interpreting teachers' motivation to teach, and professional commitment in China's hinterland regions. *Language Teaching Research*, 18(2), 152–68.

García, O. (2009). *Bilingual education in the 21st century: A global perspective*. Malden, MA: Wiley-Blackwell.

García, O. (2020). Translanguaging and Latinx bilingual readers. *The Reading Teacher*, 73(5), 557–62.

García, O., & Kleifgen, J. A. (2019). Translanguaging and literacies. *Reading Research Quarterly*, 55(4), 553–71.

García, O., & Li, W. (2014). *Translanguaging: Language, bilingualism and education*. London: Palgrave Macmillan.

García, O., Flores, N., & Spotti, M. (Eds.) (2017). *The Oxford handbook of language and society*. Oxford: Oxford University Press.

García, O., Johnson, S., & Seltzer, K. (2017). *The Translanguaging classroom: Leveraging student bilingualism for learning*. Philadelphia, PA: Caslon.

Gärdenfors, P., & Högberg, A. (2017). The archaeology of teaching and the evolution of homo docens. *Current Anthropology*, 58(2), 188–208.

Gardner, R. C. (1985). *Social psychology and second language learning: The role of attitudes and motivation*. London, UK: Edward Arnold.

Gardner, R. C. (1988). The socio-educational model of second language learning: Assumptions, findings and issues. *Language Learning*, 38(1), 101–26.

Gardner, R. C. (2010). *Motivation and second language acquisition: The socio-educational model*. New York: Peter Lang.

Gardner, R. C. (2020). Looking back and looking forward. In A. Al-Hoorie, & P. D. MacIntyre (Eds.), *Contemporary language motivation theory: 60 years since Gardner and Lambert (1959)* (pp. 5–14). Bristol: Multilingual Matters.

Gardner, R. C., & Lambert, W. E. (1959). Motivational variables in second-language acquisition. *Canadian Journal of Psychology/Revue canadienne de psychologie*, 13(4), 266–72.

Gardner, R. C., & Lambert, W. E. (1972). *Attitudes and motivation in second-language learning*. Rowley, MA: Newbury House.

Garrett, N. (2009). Computer-assisted language learning trends and issues revisited: Integrating innovation. *The Modern Language Journal*, 93, 719–40.

Gee, J. P. (2004). *Situated language and learning*. New York, NY: Routledge.

George, J. M. (1990). Personality, affect and behavior in groups. *Journal of Applied Psychology*, 75(2), 107–16.

Gleason, J., & Suvorov, R. (2012). Learner perceptions of asynchronous oral computer-mediated communication: Proficiency and second language selves. *The Canadian Journal of Applied Linguistics*, 15(1), 100–21.

Göbel, K., & Helmke, A. (2010). Intercultural learning in English as a foreign language instruction: The importance of teachers' intercultural experience and the usefulness of precise instructional directives. *Teaching and Teacher Education*, 26(8), 1571–82.

Göbel, K., & Vieluf, S. (2017). Specific effects of language transfer promoting teaching and insights into the implementation in EFL-teaching. *Orbis scholae*, 11(3), 103–22.

Gogolin, I. (2008). *Der monolinguale Habitus der multilingualen Schule [The monolingual habitus of the multilingual school]*. Münster: Waxmann.

Gollwitzer, P. M., Fujita, K., & Oettingen, G. (2004). Planning and the implementation of goals. In R. F. Baumeister, & K. D. Vohs (Eds.), *Handbook of self-regulation: Research, theory, and applications* (pp. 211–28). New York: Guilford Press.

González Mujico, F., & Lasagabaster, D. (2019). Enhancing L2 motivation and English proficiency through technology. *Complutense Journal of English Studies*, 27, 59–78.

Gorter, D. (2018). Linguistic landscapes and trends in the study of schoolscapes. *Linguistics and Education*, 44, 80–5.

Gras-Velazquez, A. (Ed.) (2020). *Project-based learning in second language acquisition: Building communities of practice in higher education*. New York & Abingdon, UK: Routledge.

Gregersen, T., & Mercer, S. (Eds.) (2022). *Routledge handbook of the psychology of language learning*. New York: Routledge.

Grosjean, J. (1982). *Life with two languages*. Cambridge: Harvard University Press.

Guay, F., Ratelle, C., Larose, S., Vallerand, R. J., & Vitaro, F. (2013). The number of autonomy-supportive relationships: Are more relationships better for motivation, perceived competence, and achievement? *Contemporary Educational Psychology*, 38(4), 375–82.

Hadfield, J., & Dörnyei, Z. (2013). *Motivating learning*. Harlow, UK: Longman.

Hakanen, J. J., Bakker, A. B., & Schaufeli, W. B. (2006). Burnout and work engagement among teachers. *Journal of School Psychology*, 43, 495–513.

Hall, G., & Cook, G. (2012). Own-language use in language teaching and learning. *Language Teaching*, 45(3), 271–308.

Hallam, S. (2006). *Music psychology in education*. London, UK: Institute of Education, University of London.

Han, Z. (2004). *Fossilization in adult second language acquisition*. Clevedon, UK: Multilingual Matters.

Han, Z., & Odlin, T. (Eds.) (2006). *Studies of fossilization in second language acquisition* (Vol. 14). Clevedon: Multilingual Matters.

Hari, R., Sams, M., & Nummenmaa, L. (2016). Attending to and neglecting people: Bridging neuroscience, psychology and socially. *Philosophical Transactions Royal Society B*, 1–9.

Hartel, C. E. J., & Page, K. M. (2009). Discrete emotional crossover in the workplace: The role of affect intensity. *Journal of Managerial Psychology*, 24(3), 237–253.

Hatfield, E., Cacioppo, J., & Rapson, R. (1994). *Emotional contagion*. Cambridge, UK: Cambridge University Press.

Hattie, J. (2012). *Visible learning for teachers: Maximizing impact on learning*. New York: Routledge.

Hazen, K. (2018). Rural voices in appalachia: The shifting sociolinguistic reality of rural life. In E. Seale, & C. Mallinson (Eds.), *Rural voices: Language, identity, and social change across place*. Lanham, MD: Rowman & Littlefield.

Heller, M. (1999). *Linguistic minorities and modernity: A sociolinguistic ethnography.* New York: Longman.

Henrich, J., Heine, S. J., & Norenzayan, A. (2010). The weirdest people in the world? *Behavioral and Brain Sciences,* 33(2–3), 61–83.

Henry, A. (2017). L2 motivation and multilingual identities. *The Modern Language Journal,* 101, 548–65.

Henry, A. (2019). Online media creation and L2 motivation: A socially situated perspective. *TESOL Quarterly,* 53(2), 372–404.

Henry, A. (2020a). Learner–environment adaptations in multiple language learning: Casing the ideal multilingual self as a system functioning in context. *International Journal of Multilingualism.*

Henry, A. (2020b). Possible selves and personal goals: What can we learn from episodic future thinking? *Eurasian Journal of Applied Linguistics,* 6(3), 481–500.

Henry, A., & Davydenko, S. (2020). Thriving? Or Surviving? An approach–avoidance perspective on adult language learners' motivation. *The Modern Language Journal,* 104(2), 363–80.

Henry, A., Davydenko, S., & Dörnyei, Z. (2015). The anatomy of directed motivational currents: Exploring intense and enduring periods of L2 motivation. *The Modern Language Journal,* 99(2), 329–45.

Henry, A., Sundqvist, P., & Thorsen, C. (2019). *Motivational practice: Insights from the classroom.* Lund: Studentlitteratur.

Hessel, G. (2015). From vision to action: Inquiring into the conditions for the motivational capacity of ideal second language selves. *System,* 52, 103–14.

Higgins, E. T. (1987). Self-Discrepancy: A theory relating self and affect. *Psychological Review,* 94(3), 319–40.

Higgins, E. T. (1996). Knowledge activation: Accessibility, applicability, and salience. In E. T. Higgins, & A. W. Kruglanski (Eds.), *Social psychology: Handbook of basic principles* (pp. 133–68). New York: Guilford Press.

Higgins, E. T. (2012). *Beyond pleasure and pain: How motivation works.* Oxford: Oxford University Press.

Hill, P. W., & Rowe, K. J. (1998). Modelling student progress in studies of educational effectiveness. *School effectiveness and school improvement,* 9(3), 310–33.

Hirosawa, E., & Murphey, T. (2017). Self regulating beliefs about miss takes: Amygdala whispering to university students. *JALT CUE Circular,* 3, 3–5.

Hiver, P. (2017). Tracing the signature dynamics of language teacher immunity: A retrodictive qualitative modeling study. *The Modern Language Journal,* 101, 669–99.

Hiver, P., & Al-Hoorie, A. H. (2016). A dynamic ensemble for second language research: Putting complexity theory into practice. *The Modern Language Journal,* 100(4), 741–56.

Hiver, P., & Al-Hoorie, A. H. (2020a). Reexamining the role of vision in second language motivation: A preregistered conceptual replication of You, Dörnyei, and Csizér (2016). *Language Learning,* 70(1), 48–102.

Hiver, P., & Al-Hoorie, A. H. (2020b). *Research methods for complexity theory in applied linguistics.* Bristol, UK: Multilingual Matters.

Hiver, P., & Whitehead, G. E. K. (2018a). Teaching metacognitively: Adaptive inside-out thinking in the L2 classroom. In Å. Haukås, C. Bjørke, & M.

Dypedahl (Eds.), *Metacognition in language learning and teaching* (pp. 243–62). New York: Routledge.

Hiver, P., & Whitehead, G. E. K. (2018b). Sites of struggle: Classroom practice and the complex dynamic entanglement of language teacher agency and identity. *System*, 79, 70–80.

Hiver, P., Al-Hoorie, A. H., & Mercer, S. (Eds.) (2021). *Student engagement in the language classroom*. Bristol, UK: Multilingual Matters.

Hiver, P., Obando, G., Sang, Y., Tahmouresi, S., Zhou, A., & Zhou, Y. (2019). Reframing the L2 learning experience as narrative reconstructions of classroom learning. *Studies in Second Language Learning and Teaching*, 9, 85–118.

Hiver, P., Solarte, A. C., Whiteside, Z., & Kim, C. J. (2021). The role of language teacher metacognition and executive function in exemplary classroom practice. *The Modern Language Journal*.

Hiver, P., Zhou, S. A., Tahmouresi, S., Sang, Y., & Papi, M. (2020). Why stories matter: Exploring learner engagement and metacognition through narratives of the L2 learning experience. *System*, 91, 1–13.

Holliday, A. (2006). Native-speakerism. *ELT Journal*, 60(4), 385–87.

Horwitz, E. K. (1986). Preliminary evidence for the reliability and validity of a foreign language anxiety scale. *TESOL Quarterly*, 20(3), 559–62.

House, J. (1999). Misunderstanding in intercultural communication: Interactions in English as a lingua franca and the myth of mutual intelligibility. In C. Gnutzmann (Ed.), *Teaching and learning English as a global language* (pp. 73–89). Tübingen: Stauffenburg.

House, J. (2002). Pragmatic competence in lingua franca English. In K. Knapp, & C. Meierkord (Eds.), *Lingua franca communication* (pp. 245–67). Frankfurt: Peter Lang.

Houser-Marko, L., & Sheldon, K. M. (2006). Motivating behavioral persistence: The self-as-doer construct. *Personality and Social Psychology Bulletin*, 32, 1037–49.

Howarth, W. (1990). Oliver Sacks: The ecology of writing science. *The Modern Language Studies*, 20(4), 103–20.

Hua, Z., Li, W., & Jankowicz-Pytel, D. (2020). Translanguaging and embodied teaching and learning: Lessons from a multilingual karate club in London. *International Journal of Bilingual Education and Bilingualism*, 23(1), 65–80.

Huensch, A., & Thompson, A. S. (2017). Contextualizing attitudes toward pronunciation: Foreign language learners in the United States. *Foreign Language Annals*, 50(2), 410–32.

Hummel, K. M. (2014). *Introducing second language acquisition: Perspectives and practices*. New York: John Wiley & Sons.

Hyde, B. (2002). Japan's emblematic English. *English Today*, 18(3), 12–16.

Ibrahim, Z. (2016). Affect in directed motivational currents: Positive emotionality in long-term L2 engagement. In P. MacIntyre, T. Gregersen, & S. Mercer (Eds.) *Positive psychology in second language acquisition* (pp. 258–81). Bristol: Multilingual Matters.

Ibrahim, Z. (2017). Parameters inducing motivational surges in second language learning. *UKH Journal of Social Science*, 1(1), 24–33.

Ibrahim, Z., & Al-Hoorie, A. H. (2019). Shared, sustained flow: Triggering motivation with collaborative projects. *ELT Journal*, 73(1), 51–60.

Immordino-Yang, M. H., & French, M. (2010). The role of emotion and skilled intuition in learning. In David A. Sousa (Ed.), *Mind, brain, & education: Neuroscience implications for the classroom* (pp. 69–84). Bloomington, IN: Solution Tree Press.

Irvine, J. T., & Gal, S. (2000). Language ideology and linguistic differentiation. In P.V. Kroskrity (Ed.), *Regimes of language: Ideologies, politics and identities* (pp. 35–84). Santa Fe, New Mexico: School of American Research Press.

Ito, M., Baumer, S., Bittanti, M., Boyd, D., Cody, R., Herr, B., … Tripp, L. (2010). *Hanging out, messing around, geeking out: Kids living and learning with new media*. Cambridge, MA: MIT Press.

Iyengar, S. S., & Lepper, M. R. (1999). Rethinking the value of choice: A cultural perspective on intrinsic motivation. *Journal of Personality and Social Psychology*, 76(3), 349–66.

Izard, C. E. (2007). Basic emotions, natural kinds, emotion schemas, and a new paradigm. *Perspectives on Psychological Science*, 2, 260–80.

Jackman, S. (2009). *Bayesian analysis for the social sciences*. Chichester, UK: Wiley.

Jang, H., Reeve, J., & Deci, E. L. (2010). Engaging students in learning activities: It is not autonomy support or structure but autonomy support and structure. *Journal of Educational Psychology*, 103(2), 588–600.

Jang, H., Reeve, J., & Halusic, M. (2016). A new autonomy-supportive way of teaching that increases conceptual learning: Teaching in students' preferred ways. *The Journal of Experimental Education*, 84(4), 686–701.

Jang, H., Reeve, J., Ryan, R. M., & Kim, A. (2009). Can self-determination theory explain what underlies the productive, satisfying learning experiences of collectivistically oriented Korean students? *Journal of Educational Psychology*, 101(3), 644–61.

Järvelä, S., & Renninger, K. A. (2014). Designing for learning: Interest, motivation, and engagement. In K. Sawyer (Ed.), *The Cambridge handbook of the learning sciences* (pp. 668–85). Cambridge: Cambridge University Press.

Jenkins, J. (2000). *The phonology of English as an international language*. Oxford: Oxford University Press.

Jenkins, J. (2005). Teaching English pronunciation: A sociopolitical perspective. In C. Gnutzmann, & F. Intemann (Eds.), *The globalisation of English and the English language classroom* (pp. 145–58). Tübingen: Narr.

Jenkins, J. (2007). *English as a lingua franca: Attitudes and identity*. Oxford, UK: Oxford University Press.

Jenkins, J. (2009). English as a lingua franca: Interpretations and attitudes. *World Englishes*, 28(2), 200–7.

Jenkins, J., Cogo, A., & Dewey, M. (2011). Review of developments in research into English as a lingua franca. *Language Teaching*, 44(3), 281–315.

Jewitt, C. (2008). *The visual in learning and creativity: A review of the literature. A report for creative partnership*. London: Institute of Education.

Joe, H.-K., Hiver, P., & Al-Hoorie, A. H. (2017). Classroom social climate, self-determined motivation, willingness to communicate, and achievement: A study of structural relationships in instructed second language settings. *Learning and Individual Differences*, 53, 133–44.

Johnson, D. W., Johnson, R. T., & Smith, K. A. (1998). *Active learning: Cooperation in the college classroom* (2nd ed.). Edina, MN: Interaction Book Co.

Johnson, K. E. (2019). The relevance of a transdisciplinary framework for SLA in language teacher education. *The Modern Language Journal*, 103(S1), 167–74.

Johnson, S. (2006). The neuroscience of the mentor-learner relationship. *New Directions for Adult and Continuing Education* (110), 63–9.

Julkunen, K. (2001). Situation- and task-specific motivation in foreign language learning. In Z. Dörnyei, & R. Schmidt (Eds.), *Motivation and second language acquisition* (pp. 29–42). Honolulu: University of Hawai'i.

Kachru, B. (1992). *The other tongue* (2nd ed.). Urbana: University of Illinois Press.

Kang, J., Scholp, A., & Jiang, J. J. (2018). A review of the physiological effects and mechanisms of singing. *Journal of Voice*, 32(4), 390–5.

Kaplan, H. (2018). Teachers' autonomy support, autonomy suppression and conditional negative regard as predictors of optimal learning experience among high-achieving Bedouin students. *Social Psychology of Education*, 21(1), 223–55.

Katz, I., & Assor, A. (2006). When choice motivates and when it does not. *Educational Psychology Review*, 19(4), 429–42.

Kaur, J. (2011). Intercultural communication in English as a lingua franca: Some sources of misunderstanding. *Intercultural pragmatics*, 8(1), 93–116.

Kelly, J. R., & Barsade, S. G. (2001). Mood and emotions in small groups and work teams. *Organizational Behavior and Human Decision Processes*, 86(1), 99–130.

Kennerley, H., Kirk, J., & Westbrook, D. (2017). *An introduction to cognitive behaviour therapy: Skills and applications*. Singapore: Sage.

Khajavy, G. H., & Ghonsooly, B. (2017). Predictors of willingness to read in English: Testing a model based on possible selves and self-confidence. *Journal of Multilingual and Multicultural Development*, 38(10), 871–85.

Kim, T.-Y., & Kim, Y.-K. (2014). A structural model for perceptual learning styles, the ideal L2 self, motivated behavior, and English proficiency. *System*, 46, 14–27.

King, J. (2013a). *Silence in the second language classroom*. Basingstoke, UK: Palgrave Macmillan.

King, J. (2013b). Silence in the second language classrooms of Japanese universities. *Applied Linguistics*, 34(3), 325–43.

King, J. (2014). Fear of the true self: Social anxiety and the silent behaviour of Japanese learners of English. In K. Csizér, & M. Magid (Eds.), *The impact of self-concept on language learning* (pp. 232–49). Clevedon: Multilingual Matters.

King, J. (2016). Classroom silence and the dynamic interplay between context and the language learner: A stimulated recall study. In J. King (Ed.), *The dynamic interplay between context and the language learner* (pp. 127–50). Basingstoke, UK: Palgrave Macmillan.

King, J., & Smith, L. (2017). Social anxiety and silence in Japan's tertiary foreign language classrooms. In C. Gkonou, M. Daubney, & J. M. Dewaele (Eds.), *New insights into language anxiety: Theory, research and educational implications* (pp. 91–109). Bristol: Multilingual Matters.

King, J., Yashima, T., Humphries, S., Aubrey, S., & Ikeda, M. (2020). Silence and anxiety in the English-medium classroom of Japanese universities: A longitudinal intervention study. In J. King, & S. Harumi (Eds.), *East Asian perspectives on silence in English language education* (pp. 60–79). Bristol, UK: Multilingual Matters.

King, R. B., & McInerney, D. M. (2014). Culture's consequences on student motivation: Capturing cross-cultural universality and variability through personal investment theory. *Educational Psychologist*, 49(3), 175–98.

Kirkpatrick, A. (2012). English as an Asian Lingua Franca: the "Lingua Franca Approach" and implications for language education policy. *Journal of English as a Lingua franca*, 1(1), 121–39.

Koestner, R., Otis, N., Powers, T. A., Pelletier, L., & Gagnon, H. (2008). Autonomous motivation, controlled motivation, and goal progress. *Journal of Personality*, 76(5), 1201–30.

Kordon, K. (2003). Phatic communion in English as a lingua franca. Unpublished MA thesis. University of Vienna.

Kormos, J., & Csizér, K. (2014). The interaction of motivation, self-regulatory strategies, and autonomous learning behavior in different learner groups. *TESOL Quarterly*, 48(2), 275–99.

Kormos, J., & Wilby, J. (2020). Task motivation. In M. Lamb, K. Csizér, A. Henry, & S. Ryan (Eds.), *Palgrave Macmillan handbook of motivation for language learning* (pp. 267–86). Basingstoke: Palgrave Macmillan.

Kramsch, C. (2003). Metaphor and the subjective construction of beliefs. In P. Kalaja, & A. M. F. Barcelos (Eds.), *Beliefs about SLA: New research approaches* (pp. 109–28). Dordrecht: Springer.

Kubanyiova, M., & Crookes, G. (2016). Re-envisioning the roles, tasks, and contributions of language teachers in the multilingual era of language education research and practice. *The Modern Language Journal*, 100(S1), 117–32.

Kubanyiova, M., & Feryok, A. (2015). Language teacher cognition in applied linguistics research: Revisiting the territory, redrawing the boundaries, reclaiming the relevance. *The Modern Language Journal*, 99, 435–49.

Kuo, I. C. (2006). Addressing the issue of teaching English as a lingua franca. *ELT Journal*, 60(3), 213–21.

Kuppens, A. H. (2010). English in advertising: Generic intertextuality in a globalizing media environment. *Applied Linguistics*, 31(1), 115–35.

Kwan, B. M., Hooper, A. E. C., Magnan, R. E., & Bryan, A. D. (2011). A longitudinal diary study of the effects of causality orientations on exercise-related affect. *Self and Identity*, 10(3), 363–74.

Lacey, S., & Lawson, R. (2013). *Multisensory imagery*. New York: Springer.

Ladd, G. W. (1990). Having friends, keeping friends, making friends, and being liked by peers in the classroom: Predictors of children's early school adjustment? *Child Development*, 61, 1081–1100.

Lai, C. (2019). The influence of extramural access to mainstream culture social media on ethnic minority students' motivation for language learning. *British Journal of Educational Technology*, 50(4), 1929–41.

Lamb, M. (2004). Integrative motivation in a globalizing world. *System*, 32(1), 3–19.

Lamb, M. (2007). The impact of school on EFL learning motivation: An Indonesian case-study. *TESOL Quarterly*, 41(4), 757–80.

Lamb, M. (2011). Future selves, motivation and autonomy in long-term EFL learning trajectories. In G. Murray, T. Lamb, & X. Gao (Eds.), *Identity, motivation and autonomy: Exploring their links* (pp. 177–94). Bristol: Multilingual Matters.

Lamb, M. (2013). The struggle to belong: Individual language learners and teachers in Situated Learning Theory. In P. Benson, & L. Cooker (Eds.), *The applied linguistic individual: Sociocultural approaches to autonomy, agency and identity* (pp. 32–45). London: Equinox.

Lamb, M. (2017). The motivational dimension of language teaching. *Language Teaching*, 50(3), 301–46.

Lamb, M. (2018). When motivation research motivates: Issues in long-term empirical investigations. *Innovation in Language Learning and Teaching*, 12(4), 357–70.

Lamb, M., & Arisandy, F. E. (2019). The impact of online use of English on motivation to learn. *Computer Assisted Language Learning*, 33(1–2), 85–108.

Lamb, M., Csizér, K., Henry, A., & Ryan, S. (Eds.) (2019). *The Palgrave handbook of motivation for language learning*. Cham, Switzerland: Palgrave Macmillan.

Lambert, C., Philp, J., & Nakamura, S. (2017). Learner-generated content and engagement in second language task performance. *Language Teacher Research*, 21(6), 665–80.

Lambert, W. E. (1969). Psychological aspects of motivation in language learning. *Florida Foreign Language Report*, 7(1), 95–7.

Lambert, W. E. (1974). Culture and language as factors in learning and education. In F. E. Aboud, & R. D. Meade (Eds.), *Cultural factors in learning and education* (pp. 91–122). 5th Western Washington Symposium on Learning.

Lampert, M. (2010). Learning teaching in, from, and of practice: What do we mean? *Journal of Teacher Education*, 61, 21–34.

Lance, C. E., Butts, M. M., & Michels, L. C. (2006). The sources of four commonly reported cutoff criteria: What did they really say? *Organizational Research Methods*, 9(2), 202–20.

Lantolf, J. P., & Poehner, M. E. (2014). *Sociocultural theory and the pedagogical imperative in L2 education: Vygotskian praxis and the research/practice divide*. New York: Routledge.

Lantolf, J. P., Poehner, M. E., & Swain, M. (Eds.) (2018). *The Routledge handbook of sociocultural theory and second language development*. New York: Routledge.

Lantolf, J. P., & Swain, M. (2020). *Perezhivanie*: The cognitive-emotional dialectic within the social situation of development. In A. H. Al-Hoorie, & P. D. MacIntyre (Eds.), *Contemporary language motivation theory: 60 years since Gardner and Lambert (1959)* (pp. 80–108). Bristol, UK: Multilingual Matters.

Lanvers, U. (2012). "The Danish speak so many languages it's really embarrassing." The impact of L1 English on adult language students' motivation. *Innovation in Language Learning and Teaching*, 6(2), 157–75.

Lanvers, U. (2016). Lots of selves, some rebellious: Developing the self discrepancy model for language learners. *System*, 60, 79–92.

Lanvers, U. (2017). Contradictory others and the habitus of languages: Surveying the L2 motivation landscape in the United Kingdom. *The Modern Language Journal*, 101(3), 517–32.

Lanvers, U., Thompson, A. S., & East, M. (Eds.) (2021). *Language learning in anglophone countries: Challenges, practices, ways forward*. Basingstoke, UK: Palgrave MacMillan.

Larsen-Freeman, D. (2012). Complex, dynamic systems: A new transdisciplinary theme for applied linguistics? *Language Teaching*, 45, 202–14.

Larsen-Freeman, D. (2017). Complexity theory: The lessons continue. In L. Ortega, & Z. Han (Eds.), *Complexity theory and language development: In celebration of Diane Larsen–Freeman* (pp. 11–50). Philadelphia: John Benjamins.

Larsen-Freeman, D., & Anderson, M. (2013). *Techniques and principles in language teaching* (3rd ed.). Oxford: Oxford University Press.

Larsen-Freeman, D., & Cameron, L. (2008). *Complex systems and applied linguistics*. Oxford, UK: Oxford University Press.

Launay, J., & Pearce, E. (2015, December 4). The new science of signing together. *Greater Good Magazine*, https://greatergood.berkeley.edu/article/item/science_of_singing

Lave, J., & Wenger, E. (1991). *Situated learning: Legitimate peripheral participation*. New York, NY: Cambridge University Press.

Lawson, M. A., & Lawson, H. A. (2013). New conceptual frameworks for student engagement research, policy, and practice. *Review of Educational Research*, 83, 432–79.

Lazaraton, A. (2000). Current trends in research methodology and statistics in applied linguistics. *TESOL Quarterly*, 34(1), 175–81.

Lee, N., Mikesell, L., Joaquin, A., Mates, A., & Schumann, J. (2009). *The interactional instinct*. Oxford, UK: Oxford University Press.

Legault, L., Green-Demers, I., & Pelletier, L. G. (2006). Why do high school students lack motivation in the classroom? Toward an understanding of academic amotivation and the role of social support. *Journal of Educational Psychology*, 98(3), 567–82.

Lenneberg, E. H. (1967). The biological foundations of language. *Hospital Practice*, 2(12), 59–67.

Li, S., Hiver, P., & Papi, M. (Eds.) (2021). *The Routledge handbook of second language acquisition and individual differences*. New York: Routledge.

Li, W. (2011). Moment analysis and translanguaging space: Discursive construction of identities by multilingual Chinese youth in Britain. *Journal of Pragmatics*, 43(5), 1222–35.

Li, W. (2017). Translanguaging as a practical theory of language. *Applied Linguistics*, 39(1), 9–30.

Li, W., & Lin, A. M. Y. (2019). Translanguaging classroom discourse: Pushing limits, breaking boundaries. *Classroom Discourse*, 10(3–4), 209–15.

Lieberman, M. D. (2013). *Social: Why our brains are wired to connect*. New York, NY: Crown Publishers.

Lin, A. (2014). Critical discourse analysis in applied linguistics: A methodological review. *Annual Review of Applied Linguistics*, 34, 213–32.

Lin, A. M. Y. (2019). Theories of trans/languaging and trans-semiotizing: implications for content-based education classrooms. *International Journal of Bilingual Education and Bilingualism*, 22(1), 5–16.

Little, D., Devitt, S., & Singleton, D. (1989). *Learning foreign languages from authentic texts: Theory and practice*. Dublin: Authentik.

Little, S., & Al Wahaibi, S. (2017). "We are not as they think about us": Exploring Omani EFL learners' "selves" in digital social spaces. *Multicultural Education Review*, 9(3), 175–187.

Locke, E. A. (1996). Motivation through conscious goal setting. *Applied and Preventive Psychology*, 5(2), 117–24.

Locke, E. W., & Latham, G. P. (2005). Goal setting theory: Theory building by induction. In K. G. Smith, & M. A. Hitt (Eds.), *Great minds in management: The process of theory development* (pp. 128–50). Oxford: Oxford University Press.

Lockwood, P., & Kunda, Z. (1999). Increasing the salience of one's best selves can undermine inspiration by outstanding role models. *Journal of Personality and Social Psychology*, 76(2), 214–28.

Long, M. H. (2015). *Second language acquisition and task-based language teaching*. Malden, MA: Wiley-Blackwell.

Lowenberg, P. H. (1989). Testing English as a world language: Issues in assessing nonnative proficiency. In J. Alatis (Ed.), *Georgetown University Round Table on Languages and Linguistics* (pp. 216–27). Washington, DC: Georgetown University Press.

Lvovich, N. (2013). *The multilingual self: An inquiry into language learning*. New York: Routledge.

MacIntyre, P. D., & Doucette, J. (2010). Willingness to communicate and action control. *System*, 38(2), 161–71.

MacIntyre, P., & Gregersen, T. (2012). Emotions that facilitate language learning: The positive-broadening power of the imagination. *Studies in Second Language Learning and Teaching*, 2(2), 193–213.

MacIntyre, P. D., & Serroul, A. (2015). Motivation on a per-second timescale: Examining approach-avoidance motivation during L2 task performance. In Z. Dörnyei, P. D. MacIntyre, & A. Henry (Eds.), *Motivational dynamics in language learning*. Bristol: Multilingual Matters.

MacIntyre, P. D., Baker, S., & Sparling, H. (2017). Heritage passions, heritage convictions and the rooted L2 self: Music and Gaelic language learning in Cape Breton, Nova Scotia. *The Modern language journal*, 101, 501–16.

MacIntyre, P. D., MacKinnon, S. P., & Clément, R. (2009a). From integrative motivation to possible selves: The baby, the bathwater, and the future of language learning motivation research. In Z. Dörnyei, & E. Ushioda (Eds.), *Motivation, language identity and the L2 self* (pp. 43–65). Clevendon, UK: Multilingual Matters.

MacIntyre, P. D., MacKinnon, S. P., & Clément, R. (2009b). Toward the development of a scale to assess possible selves as a source of language learning motivation. In Z. Dörnyei, & E. Ushioda (Eds.), *Motivation, language identity and the L2 self* (pp. 193–214). Clevendon, UK: Multilingual Matters.

MacIntyre, P. D., Noels, K. A., & Clément, R. (1997). Biases in self-ratings of second language proficiency: The role of language anxiety. *Language Learning*, 47, 265–87.

MacIntyre, P. D., Dewaele, J.-M., Macmillan, N., & Li, C. (2020). The emotional underpinnings of Gardner's Attitudes and Motivation Test Battery. In A. Al-Hoorie, & P. D. MacIntyre (Eds.), *Contemporary language motivation theory: 60 years since Gardner and Lambert (1959)* (pp. 57–79). Bristol: Multilingual Matters.

Mackay, J. (2015). An ideal L2 self intervention: Implications for self-concept, motivation and engagement with the target language. Unpublished doctoral thesis. Universitat de Barcelona.

Magid, M. (2011, July). *A validation and application of the L2 motivational self system among Chinese learners of English*. Unpublished Doctoral Thesis. University of Nottingham.

Magid, M. (2014). A motivational programme for learners of English: An application of the L2 Motivational Self System. In K. Csizér, & M. Magid

(Eds.), *The impact of self-concept in language learning* (pp. 300–18). Bristol, UK: Multilingual Matters.

Magid, M., & Chan, L. (2012). Motivating English learners by helping them visualize their Ideal L2 Self: Lessons from two motivational programs. *Innovation in Language Learning and Teaching*, 6(2), 113–25.

Maher, K. (2020). A cognitive-behavioural theory-based approach to examining L2 learners' silent behaviour and anxiety in the classroom. In J. King, & S. Harumi (Eds.), *East Asian perspectives on silence in English language education* (pp. 80–104). Bristol, UK: Multilingual Matters.

Mahn, H., & John-Steiner, V. (2002). The gift of confidence: A Vygotskian view of emotions. In G. Wells, & C. Claxton (Eds.), *Learning for life in the 21st century* (pp. 46–58). New York: Wiley-Blackwell.

Makoni, S., & Pennycook, A. (2007). *Disinventing and reconstituting languages*. Bristol, UK: Multilingual Matters.

Markus, H. R., & Nurius, P. (1986). Possible selves. *American Psychologist*, 41, 954–69.

Markus, H., & Nurius, P. (1987). *Possible selves: The interface between motivation and the self-concept*. In K. Yardley & T. Honess (Eds.), *Self and identity: Psychosocial perspectives* (p. 157–72). New York: John Wiley & Sons.

Markus, H., & Wurf, E. (1987). The dynamic self-concept: A social psychological perspective. *Annual Review in Psychology*, 38, 299–37.

Masgoret, A. M., & Gardner, R. C. (2003). Attitudes, motivation, and second language learning: A meta-analysis of studies conducted by Gardner and associates. *Language learning*, 53(S1), 167–210.

Matsumoto, Y. (2011). Successful ELF communications and implications for ELT: Sequential analysis of ELF pronunciation negotiation strategies. *The Modern Language Journal*, 95(1), 97–114.

Maturana, H., & Varela, F. (1984). *El Árbol del conocimiento. Las bases biológicas del entendimiento humano*. Lumen: Editorial Universitaria.

Mauranen, A. (2012). *Exploring ELF: Academic English shaped by non-native speakers*. Cambridge: Cambridge University Press.

Mauranen, A. (2018). Second language acquisition, world Englishes, and English as a lingua franca (ELF). *World Englishes*, 37(1), 106–19.

McAdams, D. P., & Pals, J. L. (2006). A new Big Five: Fundamental principles for an integrative science of personality. *American Psychologist*, 61(3), 204–17.

McEown, M. S., Noels, K. A., & Saumure, K. D. (2014). Self-determined and integrative orientations and teachers. *System*, 45(C), 227–41.

McEwon, M. S., & Oga-Baldwin, W. L. Q. (2019). Self-determination for all language learners: New applications for formal language education. *System*, 86, 102–24.

McKay, S. L. (2003). Toward an appropriate EIL pedagogy: Re-examining common ELT assumptions. *International journal of applied linguistics*, 13(1), 1–22.

McKay, S. L. (2011). English as an international lingua franca pedagogy. In E. Hinkel (Ed.), *Handbook of research in second language teaching and learning* (pp. 140–57). New York: Routledge.

McKewan, J. (2009). Predeterminism. In H. J. Birx (Ed.), *Encyclopedia of time: Science, philosophy, theology, and culture* (pp. 1035–6). London: SAGE Publications.

Mercer, S. (2011). Understanding learner agency as a complex dynamic system. *System*, 39(4), 427–36.

Mercer, S. (2015). The dynamics of the self in SLA: A multilevel approach. In Z. Dörnyei, P. MacIntyre, & A. Henry (Eds.), *Motivational dynamics in language learning* (pp. 139–63). Bristol: Multilingual Matters.

Mercer, S. (2016). The contexts within me: L2 self as a complex dynamic system. In J. King (Ed.), *The dynamic interplay between context and the language learner* (pp. 11–28). Basingstoke: Palgrave Macmillan.

Mercer, S. (2018). Psychology for language learning: Spare a thought for the teacher. *Language Teaching*, 51, 504–25.

Mercer, S. (2019). Language learner engagement: Setting the scene. In X. Gao (Ed.), *Second handbook of English language teaching* (pp. 643–660). Basel: Springer.

Mercer, S., & Dörnyei, Z. (2020). *Engaging language learners in contemporary classrooms*. Cambridge, UK: Cambridge University Press.

Mercer, S., & Gregersen, T. (2020). *Teacher wellbeing*. Oxford: Oxford University Press.

Mercer, S., & Kostoulas, A. (Eds.) (2018). *Language teacher psychology*. Bristol, UK: Multilingual Matters.

Mercer, S., Talbot, K., & Wang, I. K.-H. (2021). Fake or real engagement – Looks can be deceiving. In P. Hiver, A. H. Al-Hoorie, & S. Mercer (Eds.), *Student engagement in the language classroom*. Bristol: Multilingual Matters.

Michaelian, K., Klein, S. B., & Szpunar, K. K. (Eds.) (2016). *Seeing the future: Theoretical perspectives on future-oriented mental time travel*. Oxford: Oxford University Press.

Mignolo, W. (2000). *Local histories/Global designs: Essays on the coloniality of power, subaltern knowledges and border thinking*. Princeton, NJ: Princeton University Press.

Mignolo, W. (2002). The geopolitics of knowledge and the colonial difference. *The South Atlantic Quarterly*, 101(1), 57–96.

Miles, J., & Banyard, P. (2007). *Understanding and using statistics in psychology: A practical introduction. Or, how I came to know and love the standard error*. London, UK: SAGE.

Miles, J., & Shevlin, M. (2001). *Applying regression & correlation: A guide for students and researchers*. London, UK: SAGE.

Milyavskaya, M., Inzlicht, M., Hope, N., & Koestner, R. (2015). Saying "no" to temptation: Want-to motivation improves self-regulation by reducing temptation rather than by increasing self-control. *Journal of Personality and Social Psychology*, 109(4), 677–93.

Modiano, M. (2009). Inclusive/exclusive? English as a lingua franca in the European Union. *World Englishes*, 28(2), 208–23.

Mok, N. (2015). Toward an understanding of perezhivanie for sociocultural SLA research. *Language and Sociocultural Theory*, 2(2), 139–59.

Molenaar, P. C. M., Lerner, R. M., & Newell, K. M. (2014). Developmental systems theory and methodology: A view of the issues. In P. C. M. Molenaar, R. M. Lerner, & K. M. Newell (Eds.), *Handbook of developmental systems theory and methodology* (pp. 3–15). New York, NY: Guilford.

Motha, S., & Lin, A. (2014). "Non-coercive rearrangements": Theorizing desire in TESOL. *TESOL Quarterly*, 48(2), 331–59.

Moyer, A. (2004). *Age, accent, and experience in second language acquisition: An integrated approach to critical period inquiry* (Vol. 7). Clevedon: Multilingual Matters.

Muir, C. (2019). Motivation and projects. In M. Lamb, K. Csizér, A. Henry, & S. Ryan (Eds.), *The Palgrave handbook of motivation for language learning* (pp. 327–46). Basingstoke: Palgrave.

Muir, C. (2020). *Directed motivational currents and language education: Exploring implications for pedagogy*. Bristol: Multilingual Matters.

Muir, C. (2021). Investigating group-DMCs and complexity in the L2 classroom. In R. Sampson, & R. Pinner (Eds.), *Complexity perspectives on researching language learner and teacher psychology* (pp. 189–207). Bristol: Multilingual Matters.

Muir, C., & Dörnyei, Z. (2013). Directed Motivational Currents: Using vision to create effective motivational pathways. *Studies in Second Language Learning and Teaching*, 3(3), 357–75.

Munezane, Y. (2015). Enhancing willingness to communicate: Relative effects of visualization and goal setting. *The Modern Language Journal*, 99(1), 175–91.

Murphey, T. (2017). Asking students to teach: Gardening in the jungle. In T. Gregersen, & P. MacIntyre (Eds.), *Exploring innovations in language teacher education* (pp. 251–68). Switzerland: Springer.

Murphey, T. (2019). Innovating with the "The Collaborative Social." In H. Reinders, S. Ryan, & S. Nakamura (Eds.), *Innovation in language learning and teaching: The case of Japan* (pp. 235–55). Cham, Switzerland: Palgrave Macmillan.

Murphey, T., & Arao, H. (2001). Changing reported beliefs through near peer role modeling. *TESL-EJ*, 5(3), 1–15.

Murphey, T., & Falout, J. (2010). Critical participatory looping: Dialogic member checking with whole classes. *TESOL Quarterly*, 44(4), 811–21.

Murphey, T., Falout, J., Fukada, Y., & Fukuda, T. (2012). Group dynamics: Collaborative agency in present communities of imagination. In S. Mercer, S. Ryan, & M. Williams (Eds.), *Psychology for language learning: Insights from research, theory and practice* (pp. 220–38). Basingstoke: Palgrave Macmillan.

Murphey, T., Falout, J., Fukuda, T., & Fukada, Y. (2014). Socio-dynamic motivating through idealizing classmates. *System*, 45, 242–53.

Murphey, T., & Iswanti, S. (2014). Surprising humanity! Comparing ideal classmates in two countries. *ETAS Journal*, 31(2), 33–5.

Murphey, T., Prober, J., & Gonzáles, K. (2010). Emotional belonging precedes learning. In A. M. F. Barcelos, & H. S. Coelho (Eds.), *Emotions, reflections, and (trans)formations of language teachers and teacher educators* [*Emoções, reflexões e (trans)formações de professores eformadores de línguas*] (pp. 43–56). Campinas, Sao Paulo: Pontes Publishers.

Murphy, R. S., Stubbings, C., & Uemura, T. (2017). NeuroELT perspectives: Directed motivational currents–theoretical, experimental, and pedagogical research–, University of Kitakyushu. *Kiban Center Kiyo Journal*, 29.

Murphy, R. S. (2019). *EFL coursebook innovation: The dynamics of L2 maturity, student engagement, and cognitive development*. Unpublished Dissertation. University of Nottingham.

Murray, N. (2012). English as a lingua franca and the development of pragmatic competence. *ELT Journal*, 66(3), 318–26.

Murray-Harvey, R. (2010). Relationship influences on students' academic achievement, psychological health and well-being at school. *Educational and Child Psychology*, 27(1), 104–13.

Nakai, Y. (2016). How do learners make use of a space for self-directed learning? Translating the past, understanding the present, and strategizing for the future. *Studies in Self-Access Learning Journal*, 7(2), 168–81.

Nauert, R. (2018). *How "Aha" moments are etched in memory.* Retrieved fromhttps://psychcentral.com/news/2011/03/11/how-aha-moments-are-etched-in-memory/24341.html

Nevills, P., & Wolfe, P. (2009). *Building the reading brain.* Thousand Oaks, CA: Corwin Press.

Nicholson, L. J., & Putwain, D. W. (2016). The importance of psychological need satisfaction in educational re-engagement. *Research Papers in Education*, 1–18.

Noels, K. A., Clément, R., & Pelletier, L. (1999). Perceptions of teachers' communicative style and students' intrinsic and extrinsic motivation. *The Modern Language Journal*, 83(1), 23–34.

Noels, K., Clément, R., & Pelletier, L. (2001). Intrinsic, extrinsic, and integrative orientations of French Canadian learners of English. *The Canadian Modern Language Review*, 57(3), 424–42.

Noels, K., Pelletier, L., Clément, R., & Vallerand, R. (2008). Why are you learning a second language? Motivational orientations and self-determination theory. *Language Learning*, 50(1), 57–85.

Norton, B. (2000). *Identity and language learning: Gender, ethnicity and educational change.* Harlow, UK: Longman/Pearson Education.

Norton, B. (2013). *Identity and language learning: Extending the conversation.* Bristol, UK: Multilingual Matters.

Norton, D. L. (1976). *Personal destinies: A philosophy of ethical individualism.* Princeton, NJ: Princeton University Press.

Norton Peirce, B. (1995). Social identity, investment, and language learning. *TESOL Quarterly*, 29(1), 9–31.

Ntoumanis, N., & Standage, M. (2009). Motivation in physical education classes: A self-determination theory perspective. *Theory and Research in Education*, 7(2), 194–202.

Nunan, D. (2004). *Task-based language teaching.* Cambridge: Cambridge University Press.

Nunnally, J. C., & Bernstein, I. H. (1994). *Psychometric theory* (3rd ed.). New York, NY: McGraw-Hill.

Nystrand, M., & Gamoran, A. (1991). Instructional discourse, student engagement, and literature achievement. *Research in the Teaching of English*, 25(3), 261–90.

Ockert, D. (2018). Using a tablet computer for EFL positive self-review: Increases in self-determination theory-based learning motives. *CALICO Journal*, 35(2), 1–18.

Oga-Baldwin, W. L. Q. (2019). Acting, thinking, feeling, making, collaborating: The engagement process in foreign language learning. *System*, 86, 102128.

Oga-Baldwin, W. L. Q., & Nakata, Y. (2015). Structure also supports autonomy: Measuring and defining autonomy-supportive teaching in Japanese elementary foreign language classes. *Japanese Psychological Research*, 57(3), 167–79.

Oga-Baldwin, W. L. Q., & Nakata, Y. (2017). Engagement, gender, and motivation: A predictive model for Japanese young language learners. *System*, 65, 151–63.

Oga-Baldwin, W. L. Q., Nakata, Y., Parker, P. D., & Ryan, R. M. (2017). Motivating young language learners: A longitudinal model of self-determined motivation in elementary school foreign language classes. *Contemporary Educational Psychology*, 49, 140–50.

Ortega, L. (2013). *Understanding second language acquisition*. Oxon: Routledge.

Ortega, L., & Han, Z. (Eds.) (2017). *Complexity Theory and language development: In celebration of Diane Larsen-Freeman*. Amsterdam: John Benjamins.

Osterman, K. F. (2000). Students' need for belonging in the school community. *Review of Educational Research*, 70(3), 323–67.

Otheguy, R., García, O., & Reid, W. (2015). Clarifying translanguaging and deconstructing named languages: A perspective from linguistics. *Applied Linguistics Review*, 6(3), 281–307.

Otheguy, R., García, O., & Reid, W. (2019). A translanguaging view of the linguistic system of bilinguals. *Applied Linguistics Review*, 10(4), 625–51.

Oxford, R., & Shearin, J. (1994). Language learning motivation: Expanding the theoretical framework. *The Modern Language Journal*, 78(1), 12–28.

Papi, M. (2010). The L2 motivational self-system, L2 anxiety, and motivated behavior: A structural equation modeling approach. *System*, 38(3), 467–79.

Papi, M. (2016). *Motivation and learning interface: How regulatory fit affects incidental vocabulary learning and task experience*. Unpublished doctoral dissertation. Michigan State University.

Papi, M. (2018). Motivation as quality: Regulatory fit effects on incidental vocabulary learning. *Studies in Second Language Acquisition*, 40(4), 707–30.

Papi, M., & Abdollahzadeh, E. (2012). Teacher motivational practice, student motivation, and possible L2 selves: An examination in the Iranian EFL context. *Language learning*, 62(2), 571–594.

Papi, M., Bondarenko, A., Mansouri, S., Feng, L., & Jiang, C. (2019). Rethinking L2 motivation research: The 2×2 model of L2 self-guides. *Studies in Second Language Acquisition*, 41(2), 337–61.

Papi, M., & Hiver, P. (2020). Language learning motivation as a complex dynamic system: A global perspective of truth, control, and value. *The Modern Language Journal*, 104(1), 209–32.

Papi, M., & Khajavi, G. H. (2021). Motivational mechanisms underlying second language achievement: A regulatory focus perspective. *Language Learning*, 71(2), 537–572.

Papi, M., & Teimouri, Y. (2012). Dynamics of selves and motivation: A cross-sectional study in the EFL context of Iran. *International Journal of Applied Linguistics*, 22(3), 287–309.

Papi, M., & Teimouri, Y. (2014). Language learner motivational types: A cluster analysis study. *Language Learning*, 64(3), 493–525.

Parkinson, B., Fischer, A., & Manstead, A. S. R. (2005). *Emotion in social relations: Cultural, group and interpersonal processes*. New York: Psychology Press.

Pavlenko, A. (1997), Bilingualism and cognition. Unpublished PhD dissertation. Cornell University.

Pavlenko, A. (2005). *Emotions and multilingualism*. Cambridge, MA: Cambridge University Press.

Pavlenko, A. (Ed.) (2006). *Bilingual minds: Emotional experience, expression, and representation*. Clevedon: Multilingual Matters.

Pavlenko, A. (2007). Autobiographic narratives as data in applied linguistics. *Applied Linguistics*, 28(2), 163–88.

Pavlenko, A., & Dewaele, J.-M. (Eds.) (2004). Languages and emotions: A crosslinguistic perspective. *Journal of Multilingual and Multicultural Development*, 25 (2–3), 93.

Pearson, J., & Kosslyn, S. M. (2015). The heterogeneity of mental representation: Ending the imagery debate. *Proceedings of the National Academy of Sciences*, 112(33), 10089–92.

Pekrun, R. (2000). A social-cognitive, control-value theory of achievement emotions. In J. Heckhausen (Ed.), *Motivational psychology of human development* (pp. 143–63). Oxford, UK: Elsevier.

Pekrun, R., & Linnenbrink-Garcia, L. (2012). Academic emotions and student engagement. In S. L. Christenson, A. L. Reschly, & C. Wylie (Eds.), *Handbook of research on student engagement* (pp. 259–82). New York, NY: Springer.

Pennycook, A. (2001). *Critical applied linguistics*. Mahwah, NJ: Lawrence Erlbaum.

Pennycook, A. (2017). Translanguaging and semiotic assemblages. *International Journal of Multilingualism*, 14(3), 269–82.

Peragine, M. (2019). Idealizing L2 classmates to combat amotivation, calculate motivational deviations, and foster group cohesiveness. *New Directions in Teaching and Learning English Discussion*, 7, 168–78.

Philp, J., & Duchesne, S. (2016). Exploring engagement in tasks in the language classroom. *Annual Review of Applied Linguistics*, 36, 50–72.

Pinner, R. S. (2019). *Authenticity and teacher-student motivational synergy: A narrative of language teaching*. London, UK: Routledge.

Pizzolato, J. E. (2007). Impossible selves: Investigating students' persistence decisions when their career-possible selves border on impossible. *Journal of Career Development*, 33(3), 201–23.

Plewnia, A., & Rothe, A. (2011). Spracheinstellungen und Mehrsprachigkeit. Wie Schüler über ihre und andere Sprachen denken [Language attitudes and multilingualism: How students think about their own and other languages]. In L. M. Eichinger, A. Plewnia, & S. Melanie (Eds.), *Sprache und Integration. Über Mehrsprachigkeit und Migration [Language and integration. About multilingualism and migration]* (pp. 215–53). Tübingen: Narr.

Plonsky, L. (2013). Study quality in SLA: An assessment of designs, analyses, and reporting practices in quantitative L2 research. *Studies in Second Language Acquisition*, 35(4), 655–87.

Potter, J. (2012). *Digital media and learner identity: The new curatorship*. New York, NY: Palgrave Macmillan.

Poupore, G. (2016). Measuring group work dynamics and its relation with L2 learners' task motivation and language production. *Language Teaching Research*, 20(6), 719–40.

Poupore, G. (2018). A complex systems investigation of group work dynamics in L2 interactive tasks. *The Modern Language Journal*, 102(2), 350–70.

Prior, M. T. (2019). Elephants in the room: An "affective turn," or just feeling our way? *The Modern Language Journal*, 103(2), 516–27.

Purpura, J. E., Brown, J. D., & Schoonen, R. (2015). Improving the validity of quantitative measures in applied linguistics research. *Language Learning*, 65(S1), 37–75.

Quijano, A. (2000). Coloniality of power, ethnocentrism, and Latin America. *NEPANTLA*, 1(3), 533–80.

Quinn, J. (2010). *Learning communities and imagined social capital: Learning to belong.* New York, NY: Continuum.

R Core Team (2014). *R: A language and environment for statistical computing.* Vienna: Austria. Retrieved from http://www.R-project.org/

Ramachandran, V. S. (2011). *The tell-tale brain: A neuroscientist's search for what makes us human.* New York, NY: W. W. Norton & Company.

Ratelle, C. F., Simard, K., & Guay, F. (2012). University students' subjective well-being: The role of autonomy support from parents, friends, and the romantic partner. *Journal of Happiness Studies*, 14(3), 893–910.

Ratner, C., & Silva, D. N. H. (Eds.) (2017). *Vygotsky and Marx: Toward a marxist psychology.* London: Taylor & Francis.

Rebuschat, P. (Ed.) (2015). *Implicit and explicit learning of languages.* Philadelphia: John Benjamins.

Reeve, J. (2012). A self-determination theory perspective on student engagement. In S. L. Christenson, A. L. Reschly, & C. Wylie (Eds.), *Handbook of research on student engagement* (pp. 149–72). New York: Springer.

Reeve, J. (2013). How students create motivationally supportive learning environments for themselves: The concept of agentic engagement. *Journal of Educational Psychology*, 105(3), 579–95.

Reeve, J., & Jang, H. (2006). What teachers say and do to support students' autonomy during a learning activity. *Journal of Educational Psychology*, 98(1), 209–18.

Reeve, J., & Lee, W. (2014). Students' classroom engagement produces longitudinal changes in classroom motivation. *Journal of Educational Psychology*, 106(2), 527–40.

Reeve, J., & Tseng, C.-M. (2011). Agency as a fourth aspect of students' engagement during learning activities. *Contemporary Educational Psychology*, 36(4), 257–67.

Reeve, J., Vansteenkiste, M., Assor, A., Ahmad, I., Cheon, S. H., Jang, H., et al. (2013). The beliefs that underlie autonomy-supportive and controlling teaching: A multinational investigation. *Motivation and Emotion*, 38, 93–110.

Reschly, A. L., & Christenson, S. L. (2012). Jingle, jangle, and conceptual haziness: Evolution and future directions of the engagement construct. In S. L. Christenson, A. L. Reschly, & C. Wylie (Eds.), *Handbook of research on student engagement* (pp. 3–20). New York: Springer.

Reyes, A. (2017). Inventing postcolonial elites: Race, language, mix, excess. *Journal of Linguistic Anthropology*, 27(2), 210–31.

Richards, J. C. (2006). *Communicative language teaching today.* Cambridge: Cambridge University Press.

Rivers, W. (1987). *Interactive language teaching.* Cambridge, UK: Cambridge University Press.

Robinson, M. D., & Clore, G. L. (2002). Episodic and semantic knowledge in emotional self-report: Evidence for two judgment processes. *Journal of personality and social psychology*, 83(1), 198.

Robinson, P. (2007). Task complexity, theory of mind, and intentional reasoning: Effects on L2 speech production, interaction, uptake and perceptions of task difficulty. *International Review of Applied Linguistics in Language Teaching*, 45(3), 193–213.

Robinson, P. (2011). Task-based language learning: A review of issues. *Language Learning*, 61(s1), 1–36.

Rodgers, J. L., Rowe, D. C., & Buster, M. (1998). Social contagion, adolescent sexual behavior, and pregnancy: A nonlinear dynamic EMOSA model. *Developmental Psychology*, 34(5), 1096–113.

Roffey, S. (2012). Pupil wellbeing – Teacher wellbeing: Two sides of the same coin? *Educational and Child Psychology*, 29(4), 8–17.

Rolland, L., Dewaele, J.-M., & Costa, B. (2017). Multilingualism and psychotherapy: Exploring multilingual clients' experiences of language practices in psychotherapy. *International Journal of Multilingualism*, 14(1), 69–85.

Ros i Solé, C., Calic, J., & Neijmann, D. (2010). A social and self-reflective approach to MALL. *ReCALL*, 22(1), 39–52.

Rosa, J., & Flores, N. (2017). Unsettling race and language: Toward a raciolinguistic perspective. *Language in Society*, 46(5), 621–47.

Rubin, J., & Jernudd, B. (Eds.) (1971). *Can language be planned? Sociolinguistic theory and practice for developing nations*. Honolulu: East West Center and University of Hawai'i Press.

Ryan, R. M., & Deci, E. L. (2017). *Self-determination theory: Basic psychological needs in motivation, development, and wellness*. New York: Guilford Press.

Ryan, R. M., & Deci, E. L. (2020). Intrinsic and extrinsic motivation from a self-determination theory perspective: Definitions, theory, practices, and future directions. *Contemporary Educational Psychology*, 61, 101860.

Ryan, R. M., Sheldon, K. M., Kasser, T., & Deci, E. L. (1996). All goals are not created equal: The relation of goal content and regulatory styles to mental health. In J. A. Bargh, & P. M. Gollwitzer (Eds.), *The psychology of action: Linking cognition and motivation to behavior* (pp. 7–26). New York: Guilford Press.

Sacks, O. (2014). Luria and "Romantic Science." In A. Yasnitsky, R. van der Veer, & M. Ferrari (Eds.), *The Cambridge handbook of cultural-historical psychology* (pp. 517–28). Cambridge: Cambridge University Press.

Safdari, S. (2021). Operationalizing L2 motivational self system: Improving EFL learners' motivation through a vision enhancement program. *Language Teaching Research*, 25(2), 282–305.

Sailer, U., Robinson, S., Fischmeister, F. P. S., Moser, E., Kryspin-Exner, I., & Bauer, H. (2007). Imaging the changing role of feedback during learning in decision-making. *Neuroimage*, 37(4), 1474–86.

Samarin, W. (1987). Lingua franca. In U. Ammon, N. Dittmar, & K. Mattheier (Eds.), *Sociolinguistics: An international handbook of the science of language and society* (pp. 371–4). Berlin: Walter de Gruyter.

Sampson, R. (2012). The language-learning self, self-enhancement activities, and self perceptual change. *Language Teaching Research*, 16(3), 317–35.

Sampson, R. (2016). *Complexity in classroom foreign language learning motivation. A practitioner perspective from Japan*. Bristol: Multilingual Matters.

Santos, B. D. S. (2007). Beyond abyssal thinking: From global lines to ecologies of knowledges. *Review (Fernand Braudel Center)*, 30(1), 45–89.

Santos, B. D. S. (2009). *Una Epistemologia del Sur. La reinvención del conocimiento y la emancipación social*. Buenos Aires: Siglo XXI Editores, CLACSO.

Santos, B. D. S. (2014). *Epistemologies of the South: Justice against epistemicide*. New York: Routledge.

Sass, D. A. (2011). Testing measurement invariance and comparing latent factor means within a confirmatory factor analysis framework. *Journal of Psychoeducational Assessment*, 29(4), 347–63.

Sato, M. (2020). Generating a roadmap for possible selves via a vision intervention: Alignment of second language motivation and classroom behavior. *TESOL Quarterly*, 55(2), 427–57.

Sato, M., & Lara, P. (2019). Interaction vision intervention to increase second language motivation: A classroom study. In M. Sato, & S. Loewen (Eds.), *Evidence-based second language pedagogy: A collection of Instructed Second Language Acquisition studies*. New York, NY: Routledge.

Sato, M., & Loewen, S. (Eds.) (2019). *Evidence-based second language pedagogy*. New York: Routledge.

Schumann, J. H. (1997). *The neurobiology of affect in language*. Malden: MA Blackwell Publishers.

Schunk, D. H., Pintrich, P. R., & Meece, J. R. (2014). *Motivation in education: Theory, research, and applications* (4th ed.). Harlow: Pearson Education.

Schwartz, M., & Fischer, K. W. (2004). Building general knowledge and skill: Cognition and microdevelopment in science learning. In A. Demetriou, & A. Raftopoulos (Eds.), *Cognitive developmental change* (pp. 157–85). Cambridge: Cambridge University Press.

Seale, E., & Mallinson, C. (Eds.) (2018). *Rural voices: Language, identity, and social change across place*. Lanham, MD: Rowman & Littlefield.

Seber, G. A. F., & Wild, C. J. (1989). *Nonlinear regression*. New York, NY: Wiley.

Seidlhofer, B. (2001). Closing a conceptual gap: The case for a description of English as a lingua franca. *International Journal of Applied Linguistics*, 11(2), 133–58.

Seidlhofer, B. (2004). 10. Research perspectives on teaching English as a lingua franca. *Annual Review of Applied Linguistics*, 24, 209–39.

Seidlhofer, B. (2005). English as a lingua franca. *ELT Journal*, 59(4), 339–41.

Seidlhofer, B., Breiteneder, A., & Pitzl, M. L. (2006). English as a lingua franca in Europe: Challenges for applied linguistics. *Annual Review of Applied Linguistics*, 26, 3–34.

Selinker, L. (1972). Interlanguage. *IRAL-International Review of Applied Linguistics in Language Teaching*, 10(1–4), 209–32.

Serafini, E. J. (2020). Further exploring the dynamicity, situatedness, and emergence of the self: The key role of context. *Studies in Second Language Learning and Teaching*, 10(1), 133–57.

Sheldon, K. M. (2014). Becoming oneself: The central role of self-concordant goal selection. *Personality and Social Psychology Review*, 18, 349–65.

Sheldon, K. M. (2015). Kennon M. Sheldon: A pioneer in social indicators. *Applied Research Quality Life*, 10, 197–9.

Sheldon, K. M., & Cooper, M. L. (2008). Goal striving within agentic and communal roles: Functionally independent pathways to enhanced well-being. *Journal of Personality*, 76, 415–47.

Sheldon, K. M., & Elliot, A. J. (1998). Not all personal goals are personal: Comparing autonomous and controlled reasons as predictors of effort and attainment. *Personality and Social Psychology Bulletin*, 24, 546–57.

Sheldon, K. M., & Elliot, A. J. (1999). Goal striving, need satisfaction, and longitudinal well-being: The self-concordance model. *Journal of Personality and Social Psychology*, 76(3), 482–97.

Sheldon, K. M., & Houser-Marko, L. (2001). Self-concordance, goal-attainment, and the pursuit of happiness: Can there be an upward spiral? *Journal of Personality and Social Psychology*, 80, 152–65.

Sheldon, K. M., & Kasser, T. (1998). Pursuing personal goals: Skills enable progress but not all progress is beneficial. *Personality and Social Psychology Bulletin*, 24, 546–57.

Sheldon, K. M., & Schuler, J. (2011). Needing, wanting, and having: Integrating motive disposition theory and self-determination theory. *Journal of Personality and Social Psychology*, 101, 1106–23.

Sheldon, K. M., Kasser, T., Smith, K., & Share, T. (2002). Personal goals and psychological growth: Testing an intervention to enhance goal-attainment and personality integration. *Journal of Personality*, 70, 5–31.

Sheldon, K. M., Prentice, M., & Osin, E. (2019). Rightly crossing the Rubicon: Evaluating goal self-concordance prior to selection helps people choose more intrinsic goals. *Journal of Research in Personality*, 79, 119–29.

Sifakis, N. (2007). The education of teachers of English as a lingua franca: A transformative perspective. *International Journal of Applied Linguistics*, 17(3), 355–75.

Silverstein, M. (1979). Language structure and linguistic ideology. In P. R. Clyne, W. F. Hanks, & C. L. Hofbauer (Eds.), *The elements: A parasession on linguistic units and levels* (pp. 193–248). Chicago, IL: Chicago Linguistic Society.

Skinner, E. A., & Belmont, M. J. (1993). Motivation in the classroom: Reciprocal effects of teacher behavior and student engagement across the school year. *Journal of Educational Psychology*, 85(4), 571–81.

Skinner, E. A., & Pitzer, J. R. (2012). Developmental dynamics of engagement, coping, and everyday resilience. In S.L. Christenson, A. L. Reschly, & C. Wylie (Eds.), *Handbook of research on student engagement* (pp. 21–44). New York: Springer.

Skinner, E. A., Furrer, C. J., Marchand, G., & Kindermann, T. A. (2008). Engagement and disaffection in the classroom: Part of a larger motivational dynamic? *Journal of Educational Psychology*, 100(4), 765–81.

Skinner, E. A., Kindermann, T. A., Connell, J. P., & Wellborn, J. G. (2009). Engagement and disaffection as organizational constructs in the dynamics of motivational development. In K.R. Wentzel, & A. Wigfield (Eds.), *Handbook of motivation at school* (pp. 223–45). New York: Routledge.

Skutnabb-Kangas, T. (2000). *Linguistic genocide in education or worldwide diversity and human rights?* Mahwah: NJ: Lawrence Erlbaum Associates.

Skutnabb-Kangas, T., Phillipson, R., Panda, M., & Mohanty, A. (2009). Multilingual education concepts, goals, needs and expense: English for all or achieving justice? In T. Skutnabb-Kangas, R. Phillipson, A. Mohanty & M. Panda (Ed.), *Social justice through multilingual education* (pp. 320–44). Bristol, Blue Ridge Summit: Multilingual Matters.

Sowden, C. (2012). ELF on a mushroom: The overnight growth in English as a Lingua Franca. *ELT Journal*, 66, 89–96.

Sprenger, M. (2013). *Teaching the critical vocabulary of the common core*. Alexandria, VA: ASCD.

Stallard, P. (2002). *Think good - feel good: A cognitive behavioural therapy workbook for children and young people*. UK: John Wiley & Sons, Ltd.

Steinmetz, H., Schmidt, P., Tina-Booh, A., Wieczorek, S., & Schwartz, S. H. (2009). Testing measurement invariance using multigroup CFA: Differences between educational groups in human values measurement. *Quality & Quantity*, 43(4), 599–616.

Stevick, E. (1980). *Teaching languages: A way and ways*. Rowley, MA: Newbury House.

Stewart, N. A. J., & Lonsdale, A. J. (2016). It's better together: The psychological benefits of singing in a choir. *Psychology of Music*, 44(6), 1240–54.

Stone, M. H., & Drescher, K. A. (2004). *Adler speaks: The lectures of Alfred Adler*. New York, NY: iUniverse.

Storbeck, J., & Clore, G. L. (2007). On the interdependence of cognition and emotion. *Cognition and Emotion*, 21(6), 1212–37.

Sulis, G. (2020). *An exploration of fluctuations in motivation and engagement in second language (L2) learning within the lesson and across the academic year*. Unpublished doctoral dissertation. United Kingdom: Lancaster University.

Sundqvist, P. (2015). About a boy: A gamer and L2 English speaker coming into being by use of self-access. *Studies in Self-Access Learning Journal*, 6(4), 352–64.

Sunstein, C. R. (2016). *The ethics of influence: Government in the age of behavioral science*. New York: Cambridge University Press.

Sutherland, S. (1996). *International dictionary of psychology* (2nd ed.). New York: Continuum.

Svalberg, A. M. L. (2009). Engagement with language: Interrogating a construct. *Language Awareness*, 18, 242–58.

Svalberg, A. M. L. (2017). Researching language engagement: Current trends and future directions. *Language Awareness*, 27(1–2), 21–39.

Taguchi, T., Magid, M., & Papi, M. (2009). The L2 motivational self-system amongst Chinese, Japanese, and Iranian learners of English: A comparative study. In Z. Dörnyei, & E. Ushioda (Eds.), *Motivation, language identity and the L2 self* (pp. 66–97). Clevedon: Multilingual Matters.

Taylor, G., Jungert, T., Mageau, G. A., Schattke, K., Dedic, H., Rosenfield, S., & Koestner, R. (2014). A self-determination theory approach to predicting school achievement over time: The unique role of intrinsic motivation. *Contemporary Educational Psychology*, 39(4), 342–58.

Taylor, K. (2006). Brain function and adult learning: Implications in practice. In S. Johnson, & K. Taylor (Eds.), *The Neuroscience of adult learning* (pp. 71–85). New Directions for Ault and Continuing Education, No. 110. San Francisco: Jossey-Bass.

Taylor, S. E., Pham, L. B., Rivkin, I. D., & Armor, D. A. (1998). Harnessing the imagination. Mental simulation, self-regulation, and coping. *American Psychologist*, 53, 429–39.

Teimouri, Y. (2017). L2 selves, emotions, and motivated behaviors. *Studies in Second Language Acquisition*, 39(4), 681–709.

Thaler, R. H., & Sunstein, C. R. (2008). *Nudge: Improving decisions about health, wealth, and happiness*. New Haven, CT: Yale University Press.

The Douglas Fir Group. (2016). A transdisciplinary framework for SLA in a multilingual world. *The Modern Language Journal*, 100(S1), 19–47.

Thompson, A. S. (2017a). Don't tell me what to do! The anti-ought-to self and language learning motivation. *System*, 67, 38–49.

Thompson, A. S. (2017b). Language learning motivation in the United States: An examination of language choice and multilingualism. *The Modern Language Journal*, 101(3), 483–500.

Thompson, A. S. (2021). LOTEs in U.S. universities: Benefits, trends, motivations, and opportunities. In U. Lanvers, A. S. Thompson, & M. East (Eds.), *Language learning in Anglophone countries: Challenges, practices, ways forward* (pp. 181–204). Basingstoke, UK: Palgrave MacMillan.

Thornbury, S. (2005). *How to teach speaking.* New York: Longman.

Thorsen, C., Henry, A., & Cliffordson, C. (2020). The case of a missing person? The current L2 self and the L2 Motivational Self System. *International Journal of Bilingual Education and Bilingualism, 23,* 584–600.

Thurlow, C., & Jaworski, A. (2017). Introducing elite discourse: The rhetorics of status, privilege, and power. *Social Semiotics, 27*(3), 243–54.

Tokuhama-Espinosa, T. (2018). *Neuromyths: Debunking false ideas about the brain.* New York: W. W. Norton & Company.

Totterdell, P. (2000). Catching moods and hitting runs: Mood linkage and subjective performance in professional sport teams. *Journal of Applied Psychology, 85*(6), 848–59.

Totterdell, P., Kellett, S., Teuchmann, K., & Briner, R. B. (1998). Evidence of mood linkage in work groups. *Journal of Personality and Social Psychology, 74*(6), 1504–15.

Tremblay, P. F., & Gardner, R. C. (1995). Expanding the motivation construct in language learning. *The Modern Language Journal, 79*(4), 505–18.

Trowler, V. (2010). *Student engagement literature review.* York: Higher Education Academy.

Ur, P. (2010). English as a lingua franca: A teacher's perspective. *Cadernos de Letras (UFRJ), 27*(1), 85–92.

Urciuoli, B. (2011). Discussion essay: Semiotic properties of racializing discourses. *Journal of Linguistic Anthropology, 21*(1), E113–E122.

Ushioda, E. (2001). Language learning at university: Exploring the role of motivational thinking. In Z. Dörnyei, & R. Schmidt (Eds.), *Motivation and second language acquisition* (pp. 93–125). Honolulu, HI: Second Language Teaching & Curriculum Center, University of Hawai'i at Manoa.

Ushioda, E. (2003). Motivation as a socially mediated process. In D. Little, J. Ridley, & E. Ushioda (Eds.), *Learner autonomy in the foreign language classroom: Teacher, learner, curriculum and assessment* (pp. 90–102). Dublin, Ireland: Authentik.

Ushioda, E. (2009). A person-in-context relational view of emergent motivation, self and identity. In Z. Dörnyei, & E. Ushioda (Eds.), *Motivation, language identity and the L2 self* (pp. 215–28). Bristol: Multilingual Matters.

Ushioda, E. (2011). Language learning motivation, self and identity: Current theoretical perspectives. *Computer Assisted Language Learning, 24*(3), 199–210.

Ushioda, E. (2012). Motivation. In A. Burns, & J. C. Richards (Eds.), *The Cambridge guide to pedagogy and practice in second language teaching* (pp. 77–85). Cambridge, UK: Cambridge University Press.

Ushioda, E. (2014). Motivational perspectives on the self in SLA: A developmental view. In S. Mercer, & M. Williams (Eds.), *Multiple perspectives on the self in SLA* (pp. 127–41). Bristol, UK: Multilingual Matters.

Ushioda, E. (2016). Language learning motivation through a small lens: A research agenda. *Language Teaching, 49*(4), 564–77.

Ushioda, E. (2020a). *Language learning motivation: An ethical agenda for research.* Oxford, UK: Oxford University Press.

Ushioda, E. (2020b). Researching L2 motivation: Past, present and future. In M. Lamb, K. Csizér, A. Henry, & S. Ryan (Eds.), *Palgrave Macmillan handbook of motivation for language learning* (pp. 661–82). Basingstoke: Palgrave Macmillan.

Ushioda, E., & Dörnyei, Z. (2017). Beyond global English: Motivation to learn languages in a multicultural world: Introduction to the special issue. *The Modern Language Journal*, 101(3), 451–4.

Valsiner, J. (2001). Process structure of semiotic mediation in human development. *Human Development*, 44(2–3), 84–97.

Valsiner, J., Molenaar, P. C. M., Lyra, M. C. D. P., & Chaudhary, N. (Eds.) (2009). *Dynamic process methodology in the social and developmental sciences*. New York, NY: Springer.

Van Lier, L. (1996). *Interaction in the language curriculum: Awareness, autonomy and authenticity*. New York, NY: Longman.

Vandenberg, R. J., & Lance, C. E. (2000). A review and synthesis of the measurement invariance literature: Suggestions, practices, and recommendations for organizational research. *Organizational Research Methods*, 3(1), 4–70.

Vansteenkiste, M., Lens, W., & Deci, E. L. (2006). Intrinsic versus extrinsic goal contents in self-determination theory: Another look at the quality of academic motivation. *Educational Psychologist*, 41(1), 19–31.

Vansteenkiste, M., Simons, J., Lens, W., Soenens, B., Matos, L., & Lacante, M. (2004). Less is sometimes more: Goal content matters. *Journal of educational psychology*, 96(4), 755–764.

Vasalampi, K., Salmela-Aro, K., & Nurmi, J. E. (2009). Adolescents' self-concordance, school engagement, and burnout predict their educational trajectories. *European Psychologist*, 14(4), 332–41.

Veresov, N. (2017). The concept of perezhivanie in cultural-historical theory: Content and contexts. In M. Fleer, F. González Rey, & N. Veresov (Eds.), *Perezhivanie, Emotions and Subjectivity* (pp. 47–70). Singapore: Springer.

Veresov, N., & Fleer, M. (2016). Perezhivanie as a theoretical concept for researching young children's development. *Mind, culture, and activity*, 23(4), 325–35.

Verspoor, M. (2015). Initial conditions. In Z. Dörnyei, P. D. MacIntyre, & A. Henry (Eds.), *Motivational dynamics and language learning* (pp. 38–46). Bristol: Multilingual Matters.

Verspoor, M., De Bot, K., & Lowie, W. (Eds.) (2011). *A dynamic approach to second language development: Methods and techniques*. Amsterdam, The Netherlands: John Benjamins.

Vygotsky, L. S. (1987). *The collected works of L. S. Vygotsky. Volume 1: Problems of general psychology, including the volume thinking and speech.* (R. W. Rieber, & A. S. Carton, Eds.). New York: Plenum.

Vygotsky, L. S. (1993). *The collected works of LS Vygotsky. Volume 2: The fundamentals of defectology.* New York: Plenum.

Vygotsky, L. S. (1994). The problem of the environment. In J. Van Der Veer, & J. Valsiner (Eds.), *The Vygotsky reader* (pp. 338–54). Oxford: Blackwell.

Vygotsky, L. S. (1997). *The collected works of L. S. Vygotsky. Volume 3: Problems of the theory and history of psychology* (R.W. Rieber, & J. Wollock, Eds.). New York: Plenum.

Vygotsky, L. S. (1998). *The collected works of L. S. Vygotsky. Volume 5: Child psychology* (R.W. Rieber, Ed.). New York: Plenum.

Wang, I. K.-H., & Mercer, S. (2021). Conceptualizing willingness to engage in L2 learning beyond the classroom. In P. Hiver, A. H. Al-Hoorie, & S. Mercer (Eds.), *Student engagement in the language classroom* (pp. 260–279). Bristol: Multilingual Matters.

Wang, T., & Liu, Y. (2020). Dynamic L3 selves: A longitudinal study of five university L3 learners' motivational trajectories in China. *Language Learning Journal*, 48(2), 201–12.

Waterman, A. S. (1993). Two conceptions of happiness: Contrasts of personal expressiveness (eudaimonia) and hedonic enjoyment. *Journal of Personality and Social Psychology*, 64(4), 678–91.

Waterman, A. S., Schwartz, S. J., & Conti, R. (2008). The implications of two conceptions of happiness (hedonic enjoyment and eudaimonia) for the understanding of intrinsic motivation. *Journal of Happiness Studies*, 9(1), 41–79.

Wehlage, G. G. (1989). Dropping out: Can schools be expected to prevent it. In L. Weis, E. Farrar, & H. Petrie (Eds.), *Dropouts from school* (pp. 1–19). Albany: State University of New York Press.

Weinstein, N., Przybylski, A. K., & Ryan, R. M. (2012). The index of autonomous functioning: Development of a scale of human autonomy. *Journal of Research in Personality*, 46(4), 397–413.

Wenger, E. (1998). *Communities of practice: Learning, meaning, and identity.* Cambridge, UK: Cambridge University Press.

White, C. J. (2018). Emotional turn in applied linguistics and TESOL: Significance, challenges and prospects. In J. de Dios Martínez Agudo (Ed.), *Emotions in second language teaching: Theory, research and teacher education* (pp. 19–34). Berlin: Springer.

Widdowson, H. G. (1994). The ownership of English. *TESOL Quarterly*, 28(2), 377–89.

Wierzbicka, A. (2004). Preface: Bilingual lives, bilingual experience. *Journal of Multilingual and Multicultural Development*, 25(2–3), 94–104.

Wild, T. C., Enzle, M. E., & Hawkins, W. L. (1992). Effects of perceived extrinsic versus intrinsic teacher motivation on student reactions to skill acquisition. *Personality and Social Psychology Bulletin*, 18, 245–51.

Wild, T. C., Enzle, M. E., Nix, G., & Deci, E. L. (1997). Perceiving others as intrinsically or extrinsically motivated: Effects on expectancy formation and task engagement. *Personality and Social Psychology Bulletin*, 23, 837–48.

Williams, L. (2009). Navigating and interpreting hypertext in French: New literacies and new challenges. In L. B. Abraham, & L. Williams (Eds.), *Electronic discourse in language learning and language teaching* (pp. 43–64). Philadelphia: John Benjamins Publishing Company.

Williams, M., & Burden, R. L. (1997). *Psychology for language teachers.* Cambridge: Cambridge University Press.

Willis, D., & Willis, J. R. (2007). *Doing task-based teaching.* Oxford: Oxford University Press.

Willis, J. (2010). The current impact of neuroscience. In David A. Sousa (Ed.), *Mind, brain, & education: Neuroscience implications for the classroom* (pp. 53–4). Bloomington, IN: Solution Tree Press.

Wittleder, S., Kappes, A., Krott, N. R., Jay, M., & Oettingen, G. (2020). Mental contrasting spurs energy by changing implicit evaluations of obstacles. *Motivation Science*, 6(2), 133–55.

Wodak, R., KhosraviNik, M., & Mral, B. (Eds.) (2013). *Right-wing populism in Europe. Politics and Discourse*. London: Bloomsbury.

WorldAtlas.com. (n.d.). *The 10 biggest cities in West Virginia*. Retrieved May 22, 2020, from https://www.worldatlas.com/articles/the-10-biggest-cities-in-west-virginia.html

Yashima, T. (2002). Willingness to communicate in a second language: The Japanese EFL context. *The Modern Language Journal*, 86, 54–66.

Ybarra, O., Burnstein, E., Winkielman, P., Keller, M. C., Manis, M., Chan, E., & Rodriguez, J. (2008). Mental exercising through simple socializing: Social interaction promotes general cognitive functioning. *Personality and Social Psychology Bulletin*, 34, 248–59.

You, C. J., & Dörnyei, Z. (2016). Language learning motivation in China: Results of a large-scale stratified survey. *Applied Linguistics*, 37(4), 495–519.

Zarrinabadi, N., & Tavakoli, M. (2017). Exploring motivational surges among Iranian EFL teacher trainees: Directed motivational currents in focus. *TESOL Quarterly*, 51(1), 155–66.

Zeichner, K. (2012). The turn once again toward practice-based teacher education. *Journal of Teacher Education*, 63, 376–82.

Zheng, C., Liang, J.-C., Li, M., & Tsai, C.-C. (2018). The relationship between English language learners' motivation and online self-regulation: A structural equation modelling approach. *System*, 76, 144–57.

Zheng, Y. (2013). An inquiry into Chinese learners' English-learning motivational self-images: ENL learner or ELF user? *Journal of English as a Lingua Franca*, 2(2), 341–64.

Zimmerman, B. J. (1989). Models of self-regulated learning and academic achievement. In B. J. Zimmerman, & D. H. Schunk (Eds.), *Self-regulated learning and academic achievement: Theory, research, and practice* (pp. 1–25). New York, NY: Springer-Verlag.

INDEX